ADVANCED PRAISE FOR PAY NO MIND

"Fallon Rowe offers a vivid, if startling view into a chapter of life rarely shared with such detail and intensity. Pay No Mind is a brutally honest look at how passion and obsession can decay into the horror of pathological abuse. Its pages not only detail the trauma one woman has endured, they reveal the tragic patterns of what it's like for anyone to fall prey to another's sickness and manipulation. This courageous memoir is a powerful reminder that we are not alone, and that we have the power to move on – no matter how stuck we may feel. It will encourage readers to take a shrewd look at their own relationships and inspire them to do anything possible to avoid what Rowe has suffered."

—Chris Weidner

"Far more than just another climbing book, this is a raw and unflinching look at the mental and emotional terrain that parallels the physical world we all experience in our adventures. It can be uncomfortable at times, but that's the type of writing we need more of in this industry."

—Tom Randall

"Pay No Mind is a powerful and honest account of how a passionate climbing life became entwined with a deeply manipulative relationship. Fallon does an exceptional job showing the gradual ways someone can be pulled into abuse, painting her decision making with nuance and clarity that really resonated with me. As a climber, I also appreciated her vivid descriptions of the places she visited from Southern Utah to Patagonia. Coincidentally, it seems our paths may have possibly crossed during some of her adventures. That added a layer of meaning to the story, reminding me how little we may know about what someone is going through, even when they're right in front of us. This book stayed with me long after I put it down."

—Brette Harrington

"In *Pay No Mind,* Fallon Rowe confronts subjects that mountain literature has only rarely addressed in the past: the dangers of intimate partner violence and sexual assault. With awe-inspiring courage, she describes how the journey to escape an abusive relationship can be more hazardous and arduous than any alpine climb. And with raw, powerful stories, she evokes what it means to regain freedom in the hills and in the rest of life."

—Katie Ives, author of *Imaginary Peaks: The Riesenstein Hoax and Other Mountain Dreams*

PAY NO MIND

Pay No Mind: A Memoir of Climbing, Abuse, and Survival is published under Catharsis, a sectionalized division under Di Angelo Publications, Inc.

Catharsis is an imprint of Di Angelo Publications.
Copyright 2025.
All rights reserved.
Printed in the United States of America.

Di Angelo Publications
Los Angeles, California

Library of Congress
Pay No Mind: A Memoir of Climbing, Abuse, and Survival
ISBN: 978-1-962603-37-9
Paperback

Words: Fallon Rowe
Cover Design: Elisha Zepeda
Interior Design: Kimberly James
Editors: John Long, Willy Rowberry

Downloadable via www.dapbooks.shop and other e-book retailers

No part of this publication may be reproduced, distributed, or transmitted in any form or by any means without the prior written permission of the publisher, except in the case of brief quotations embodied in critical reviews and certain other noncommercial uses permitted by copyright law. For permission requests, contact info@diangelopublications.com.

For educational, business, and bulk orders, contact sales@diangelopublications.com.

1. Biography & Autobiography --- Women
2. Sports & Recreation --- Rock Climbing
3. Family & Relationships --- Abuse --- Domestic Partner Abuse

PAY NO MIND
A MEMOIR OF CLIMBING, ABUSE, AND SURVIVAL

FALLON ROWE
FOREWORD BY JOHN LONG

For Jen and Sarah, for never giving up on me

CONTENTS

DISCLAIMER & CONTENT WARNING — 11

FOREWORD — 13

PART 1: PREPARATION — 17

CHAPTER 1: PIPE DREAM — 19

CHAPTER 2: STATUS QUO — 27

CHAPTER 3: UP IN SMOKE — 36

CHAPTER 4: THUMB PUMP — 46

CHAPTER 5: RAVENS, RED WINE, AND RED BULL — 55

CHAPTER 6: OVERDRIVE — 62

CHAPTER 7: OVERSTOKER KID — 78

CHAPTER 8: HEAVY AND TOXIC — 90

PART 2: PATAGONIA — 103

CHAPTER 9: SAY IT — 105

CHAPTER 10: VENOM — 122

CHAPTER 11: PAMPAS FOR PORRO — 139

CHAPTER 12: WITHDRAWALS — 153

CHAPTER 13: MAKE ME A BIRD	168
CHAPTER 14: QUICKSAND	184
CHAPTER 15: SANGRE	195
CHAPTER 16: VALENTINE	209

PART 3: THE WEST — 217

CHAPTER 17: KNIFE AND HAMMER	219
CHAPTER 18: PSYCH WARD	234
CHAPTER 19: NEXT TO A CORPSE	248
CHAPTER 20: SHATTERED	264
CHAPTER 21: MEMENTO MORI	281
CHAPTER 22: SLOW CRAWL	296
CHAPTER 23: "I'LL KILL YOU"	308
EPILOGUE	329
AFTERWORD	335

ACKNOWLEDGMENTS	343
ABOUT THE AUTHOR	347
ABOUT THE PUBLISHER	349

DISCLAIMER & CONTENT WARNING

The stories in this book are true. Every effort has been made by the author to recollect events and dialogue to match the essence of what happened, but do not consider it an exact word-for-word transcript. Certain names, and some locations, have been changed to protect the privacy of those depicted.

This book contains difficult content, including but not limited to: abuse, suicide, mental illness, self-harm, addiction, substance abuse, domestic violence, sexism, rape, sexual assault, and strong language. Many readers may find the content disturbing or triggering. Take care when reading.

FOREWORD

Imagine a nineteen-year-old girl who grew up in climbing gyms and reading about bold mountaineers scaling high walls in the wild places of the world. She imagines questing to those places and scaling those walls, if only in her dreams. She meets the guy: a force of nature and another climber. Older. More world-wise. More resources. Obsessed with extravagant goals and the conviction he can make them happen—though not alone. And so far, not with his other partners. Long story. But the girl, she's so skilled. So much potential. And if they teamed up, he swears to God she can make his dreams her own and they can fly, sky-high, and do everything. From here to Patagonia, "the end of the world." It's intoxicating, how anyone can believe in her with such passion and certainty. They are immediately a thing—everything is right now with the guy. It's all so goddamn hot. Coming of age with a crush, questing up the big rocks, shimmering on the horizon. She doesn't feel ready. She feels scared and unsure and has little money and no safety net. But the guy promises they'll figure it out. They pick up speed, flouting obstacles, some deadly—and author Fallon Rowe can tell you the rest. Just know, going in, that for what must have felt like ages, she wore "the guy" and the havoc he wrought like a pair of cement shoes, as she stumbled toward the light.

Most of us encounter events and circumstances we cannot easily resolve. When these events involve an abuser, and the abuse is more than we can bear, some part of us shatters, triggering beastly, involuntary states like traumatic shock and existential meltdown that can fossilize our lives. The lived experience, and the nuclear, trembling dread at the core, is the dark night of every victim's soul, and can take a lifetime to transform. Every trauma epic is in some way unique and in other ways universal. Jarringly invasive. Brutal and perilous and charged with such shame and apprehensive fear that stories drawn from this deep well read like thrillers from hell. And like a train wreck, we cannot look away.

Until recently, the world of outdoor sports, where *Pay No Mind* resides, gave little to no press to abusers within its ranks. As if the adventure world was above it all. Then a celebrated climber went down on a rape charge and the feds gave him life in prison. Stories and articles, books, podcasts, and videos on abusers and abuse, in our very own ranks, trickled across the internet. We eased into it, first taking up self-abuse in the form of eating disorders, another dirty little secret of the climbing world. The rest followed in a rush.

Countless of us have survived trauma, and reading such memoirs confirms we are not crazy or alone with our panic and rage, and the terror of losing our center when the neighbor's car backfires. What we seek is evidence of an escape hatch. A way out of feeling all spooked and torn open and waiting for the sky to fall. And the promise that freedom is possible because trauma can feel like a permanent curse. A claw that never lets go. When that happens, the motto, "hurt people, hurt people," often comes to pass, whereby the abused become abusers. Perhaps not criminally, but the untreated can easily devolve into undignified rogues who sow pain, chaos, and deceit. But transformation is possible, even for the worst of us.

When we are unable to change our circumstance or our past, we are challenged to change ourselves. The paradoxical fact is that recovery starts with attending to our brokenness, without seeking to hide it, or fade it, or even fix it. Such unconditional self-acceptance, of reality just as it is, rarely develops without mentoring and a safety zone. Once those are found and explored with discipline, we can rattle our way back to wholeness because our capacity for truth, courage, and renewal, is stronger, even, than trauma. Recovery might be the greatest adventure of them all. Not easy. What they say in some non-duality camps: When you get to hell—and you *will*—keep going.

Few of us don't have a friend or relative who carries a bellyful of trauma. No one is unscathed, and in that regard, *Pay No Mind* is one way to better understand both ourselves and others. Miracles do happen. Fallon Rowe made one for herself. That's why we read her book.

—*John Long, May 2025*

PART 1

PREPARATION

(i)
i am dying
i have known this since
death kissed me on the nose
so soft
like a lover leaving too early
in the morning
when there's just a hint of dawn
outside among the dew
footsteps in the frosted grass
— what size shoe does
death wear? —
i didn't catch that when he
last paid me a visit

the first time death kissed me
i was under fluorescent lights
breathed in the scent
of gasoline
god, it's perfect, isn't it?
gasoline
and freshly lit tobacco
god, it's perfect, isn't it?

middle of the night
middle of nowhere
we danced between the pumps
scuffed up the pavement
a dreamer with death in her mind
death in her taped up heart
dizzy dizzy
kissed me on the lips
a sweet beginning
i nudged death
right into the moon

CHAPTER 1

PIPE DREAM

Early December 2016

"Fitz Roy? You've gotta be fucking kidding me," I said, rolling my eyes. I'd only known Dan for a few weeks, and he was already trying to convince me to join him on an alpine climbing expedition. Ludicrous. I was nineteen, flat broke, and drowning in my geology research and classes while running a collegiate climbing team. Plus, I didn't have enough experience to climb in Patagonia—one of the most notorious, remote mountain ranges on the planet.

Dan's American Spirit burned toward the filter. Smoking had always disgusted me, but I secretly cherished the sweet smell that reminded me of childhood summers hiking in the Idaho wilderness with my stepdad and his tobacco pipe. Dan cranked the truck window down so the cigarette smoke could join the Utah wind.

"Seriously, Fallon. I think we have a real chance this year. I'm way more prepared than when I tried last season."

"Yeah, you may be prepared, but I sure as hell am not."

I winced while ripping off the sandy tape gloves wrapped around my hands, tugging the raw skin underneath. Dried blood crusted my chalky knuckles, a remnant of the day's exciting, but frustrating, climbing efforts on 'The Headache' in Zion National Park. I was still learning how to jam my hands properly in the vertical sandstone cracks, and in the freezing weather, I'd cut myself on sharp sections in the rock. My consuming drive to become a proficient crack climber eclipsed all of my competition climbing goals. Dan was my mentor, my partner, my ticket to success.

"You know Patagonia is a mess with the weather, but you're the best climbing partner I've ever had. C'mon, at least think about it," Dan said.

Best in what way? I wondered. I certainly wasn't the most competent partner he could ask to come with him on this trip. My glaring inadequacy made me feel young and small.

The imposing orange and white cliffs of Zion receded in the rearview mirror. We raced through the desert toward the sunset over the Pine Valley Mountains, en route to nearby St. George to crash at his parents' vacation home. I'd fallen in love with this part of the desert. It provided a welcome respite from the winter gloom and copious snow where I lived up north at Utah State University in Logan.

"I'm registered for spring semester though, and I'm almost out of money. I don't have a passport. I don't know if that's a realistic idea, hun," I said, shooting him down. Excuses easily sprang to mind. I thought back to the last time I'd checked the banking app on my phone; on a good day, I had about one hundred dollars total in my account. Affording a trip to South America was not within my current budget.

"The Way We Get By" by Spoon played through the cassette tape audio adapter attached to his cracked iPhone. Dan paused our discussion about Argentina to sing along. I rubbed the aching muscles in my forearms and thumbs. This crack climbing apprenticeship was kicking my ass. Everything hurt, but I was pleased to be making incremental progress.

He refocused, and launched into an elaborate sales pitch. "Imagine, Fallon. Endless granite cracks on huge spires!" He mimed the action of hand jams while driving with his knee. "Beautiful fucking glaciers! El Chaltén! Ah, God, it's so good. We could leave next month. You already know some Spanish, yeah?" I nodded. "Oh, and we could check out Cochamó, it's supposed to be like the Yosemite of South America. Granite big walls waiting to be explored and climbed."

His enthusiasm was bright enough to overpower the darkness of my doubts. Despite my stoic rationality, I had to admit to myself that what he was describing sounded amazing. Picturing myself climbing on wild granite spires slicing the sky over an endless icy landscape sent a shiver through me. Something tugged me from within. It welled up with a vengeance—undeniable and overwhelming. I shifted in the vinyl seat of the truck as the unsettling feeling washed over me. The discontent with my endless responsibilities, the longing for adventure, and the desire for something new all screamed at me. Images from the climbing magazines I cherished so much flashed through my brain. I tried to ignore the feeling.

To Dan, it was abundantly clear that the summit of Fitz Roy and big wall ascents were well within our reach. After all, he'd tried before, so what was keeping him from trying again? He'd been to South America multiple times, finding success on peaks like Aconcagua and Alpamayo. I'd summitted Mount Rainier, Mount Hood, and Gannett Peak as part of my journey of climbing 49 of the 50 state highpoints in high school, but those weren't nearly as serious as Patagonian peaks. I wasn't ready for a mountain as epic as Fitz Roy.

I'd failed on mountains before, for the whole spectrum of reasons: weather, glacial conditions, lack of fitness, and unpreparedness. Any peak that had eluded me became a central focus until I could return and succeed, so Dan's burning desire to summit Fitz Roy was relatable. Despite our recent climbing momentum, I had reservations about committing to a trip of that caliber with a brand new boyfriend. I barely knew the guy, and he might as well have been proposing a trip to the moon.

My head swam with the possibilities, exploring logistics, finances, and likely roadblocks. The scientific side of me reasoned against the trip: lack of funds, college commitments, no passport, and limited (read: zero) big wall or ice climbing experience. I'd never been out of the United States. I dreamed of being the kind of climber that could confidently embark on a serious expedition, but I clearly wasn't there yet.

When I voiced my doubts, Dan reassured me that I had all the essential skills I needed. I figured he knew better than I did, and I desperately wanted to travel, so I reluctantly trusted his judgment. Dan was manic and determined, a fierce combination that made me susceptible to his whims. Truthfully, I didn't mind being sucked into his grand ideas—it was exhilarating. That's why I'd broken up with Alex, my previous boyfriend of four years, within two days of getting to know Dan. I couldn't help but willingly attach myself to someone so full of energy and thrilling possibility.

He handed me his plastic bag full of weed, and I automatically started rubbing a nugget between my thumb and forefinger, letting the small pieces form a green pile in my other palm. This familiar chore was expected of me as the co-pilot. I grabbed his glass pipe, ornate and multicolored, plugged up with blackened resin, and skillfully pressed the bowl and my hand together in a swift motion, depositing the bud into it. Dan grabbed it from me with a slight grin, and he smoked it while driving with his knee again.

The demands on my time and energy were enormous with my university life. My plate wasn't just full; it was overflowing. I could feel the cracks spreading through the proverbial plate, the weight crushing it. Suddenly, Argentina didn't seem so out of reach. College and stress felt impossible as the alternative. My life felt like it was crumbling, and this was a chance to morph it into something new.

I glanced over at Dan. He was happily smoking and confidently singing along to the music as usual. He'd left his window cracked, and his dark brown hair ruffled in the breeze. Out of the corner of his eye, he spotted me and gave me a mischievous smile. I put my hand just above his knee, rubbing his toned thigh. He interlaced his fingers with mine. They were just as rough and covered in calluses as my hands, except for his tape gloves were still hanging on to his dry skin.

"Fallonnnn . . ." he said, dragging out my name as a plea.

I raised my eyebrows at him. "What?"

"Please. We've gotta escape the snow and bullshit in Salt Lake. It's miserable. Let's just go to Argentina. It'll be summer there. And we can finally have endless climbing!"

Jesus, he really won't drop it. He had a point: Salt Lake City was uninviting, shrouded by the inevitable gray inversion that descends on the valley every winter. Falling out of love with Alex, into a pit of stress and unhappiness because of school, had made me vulnerable. Dan pulled me out of the hole I'd dug myself into, and it felt like he had thrown me a lifeline.

"God, I don't know. I told you, I can't bail on spring semester.

And I don't have any money, remember?" His lack of solutions was annoying. *Is he even listening to me?* He had to at least acknowledge how far-fetched the trip sounded.

"It's 'cause you haven't gotten bit by the money bug," he explained.

"What the fuck's that supposed to mean?"

"Money comes. Money comes, if you want it bad enough. You just gotta work some shitty jobs and do whatever it takes. We'll make it down there if you want it bad enough. But you're gonna have to get to it. Fast." He bobbed his head up and down knowingly. I had no idea how to get bit by the money bug. If I did, I'd probably have more than a measly hundred bucks to my name.

"When would we leave, anyway?"

"Well. It's December. The season has already started down there. So . . . As early in January as we can."

Fuck, I thought. *I have a month to make thousands of dollars. What in the world could I possibly do as a college student to make that kind of money, while also taking my final exams, and packing and training for an expedition? There's no way.*

"I could try to find more jobs in Logan, I guess," I said, searching for a way to appease him. "Start 'em during finals week and then have money saved up by the time we leave. I don't know how I'd pay for the flight right now, though."

"Don't you have a credit card?"

"Yeah . . . And it's empty."

His open bottle of Malbec fell over on the floor between us. I lurched for it, returning it to an upright position before too much spilled onto his Converse.

"Well, then we'll get one way tickets. Climb until we're done and maybe come back eventually." He shrugged. "I hate the States right now anyway. Fucking Trump. Let's just move down there." He took a long drag off his pipe. I breathed in the weed smoke as it swirled in the cabin before the open window stole it.

The current political atmosphere made my blood boil. On the night of Trump's election, I'd spent the night drunk on tequila and crying uncontrollably on the kitchen floor with my roommates, Ashleigh and Taylor. I'd made empty threats to leave the country if Trump was seriously taking office. Here was a real chance. But could I actually move to another country? It seemed unreasonable.

The extent of my thoughts about world travel had been childhood fantasies, my three sisters and I spinning the globe with our eyes shut, letting a finger brush along the surface, and then randomly stopping to see where we'd landed. We'd run over to my dad's old Britannica encyclopedia set, look up the country, and read about all of these exotic, unreachable places. I was captivated by Iceland, New Zealand, Japan, Ecuador, hungry to learn as much as I could—but knowing deep down I'd never be able to afford that kind of travel.

"Let me see what I can work out with USU, and my scholarship, and money for the trip. My family won't like it." They already disapproved of Dan for pulling me away from my classes and work. None of my sisters had ever taken time off from their degrees, and my dad made it clear that school always came first. When I mentioned this, Dan scoffed.

"Fuck 'em." He spit out the window, and reached over to mess up my hair. I laughed and slid over closer to him on the seat, leaning into his side as he wrapped his arm around me, his right hand playing with one of my curls. I set my head on his shoulder and breathed into his touch. I closed my eyes and tried to picture Patagonia. It seemed unlikely that a trip would actually happen, but it was thrilling to imagine it anyway. I'd never let myself dream that big before.

CHAPTER 2

STATUS QUO

Three Weeks Earlier, November 2016

My 4:00 a.m. alarm jolted me awake, and I rushed to shut it off before it could disturb my best friend, Ashleigh. I squinted in the dark, relieved to see she was still fast asleep on her side of the bed. We'd gotten the mattress for free from another student, and decided it would be cheaper and simpler to just share the bed in our room. It felt no different than sleeping next to each other in a tent on our weekend geology field trips. Our rent was less than two hundred dollars a month each, a great deal for a dirtbag college kid like me.

I groggily got dressed, inhaled a bowl of cereal, popped a caffeine pill, and slung both backpacks over my shoulder—one for school and one for climbing gear. Opening the front door, I braced myself for the blast of bitterly cold wind from Logan Canyon. I trudged uphill in the dark, the spire of Old Main looming above me, my mind racing with the day's coming agenda. As the coach for the Utah State University climbing team, I had to be the first one to the gym in the morning to get ready for practice. The bright fluorescent lights of the rec center blinded me as I stumbled inside, still waiting for the caffeine to kick in as I went over the practice plan in my head. The guys dragged themselves in one after another, all cursing that this was the only time slot the gym could offer us for our team practices.

I looked over my assembled team with pride: nearly twenty ragtag climber dudes. There had been a couple other girls originally, but they dropped out of school to become ski bums. Being the only girl was a familiar experience for me in a male-dominated sport, and I thought myself no different than my teammates. There was no reason I shouldn't be equally as strong, skilled, and capable as the guys, so I held myself to the same standard, if not higher, to earn their respect and continually hone my climbing ability.

As the founder, president, coach, and one of the members, it felt like a one-woman show running the team while also training to compete. I'd poured my heart into getting this program started; competing in climbing had been my primary focus since I was six years old. It was my junior year, and I'd finally gotten climbing approved as an official club sport at the university so I could continue my competitive career at the collegiate level.

Plus, it helped in the constant effort of convincing my dad that climbing was a "legit" endeavor. He'd tolerated my climbing, but would've preferred if I'd chosen a sport that offered athletic scholarships. During his brief forays to watch me in the climbing comp scene back in the '00s, the hacky-sack-playing, slacklining, dreadlocked stoners and dirtbags living on the fringes of society hadn't exactly been his crowd as a baby boomer, conservative cop from the East Coast. It's a miracle he'd let me travel and compete with my team at all when I was a kid.

I ran the team through our typical practice routine, feeling the energy start to pulse through me as I climbed at my limit so early in the morning. Instinctively flowing through the sequences provided a motion-based meditation that gifted me effortless joy and confidence unlike anything else. In my element, I felt most like myself. The first light of dawn coming over the Bear River Mountains filtered in the massive window next to the climbing wall as we all went our separate ways for our classes.

I got a good morning text from Alex, and responded the same thing I did every day, with the usual lovey emojis. It felt stale, like an obligation, after four years of dating, but I didn't have time to ruminate. I kept up what I thought I should be doing to be a good girlfriend, but with him living eight hours away to attend college in Colorado, I felt us drifting apart more every day. It was the only serious relationship I'd ever been in. Everyone expected us to get married. We'd lived together in Boulder during the summer, and our incompatibilities had risen to the surface and stared me in the face. Alex and I could never agree on money due to our vastly different upbringings, and he'd lost his stoke for climbing. Holding him at arm's length was all too easy with the long distance. It was safe and comfortable to maintain the status quo.

I sat through my lectures in geomorphology and vertebrate paleontology, and completed homework between classes, my headphones blasting artists like The Black Keys and Gorillaz. Sneaking glances out the windows at the limestone cliffs above campus surrounded by brilliant fall colors, I wished I was out climbing instead of cooped up inside. I needed to focus. I had to get all A's to keep both my academic scholarship and my father's approval. Doing well in school was a necessity, and anything less than perfection was not an option. I felt the pressure weighing on me, but I knew I could handle it to continue the golden record I'd kept up thus far. Plus, I wanted to earn more geology scholarships for my upcoming senior year. Long term thinking would keep me on track.

After class, I walked to the geology lab basement to process samples for research and meet up with Ashleigh to discuss our geochronology project. We'd been collaborating on undergrad research together, characterizing sedimentary units and dating them with uranium-lead radioactive decay. She was presenting our research at an upcoming conference, and we were preparing rocks for various geochemical tests for another professor. Working in the lab was one of my favorite things in the world; I felt like a real scientist, and I got to hang out with my best friend.

In the afternoon, I ran outside to join my friends at the Secular Student Alliance and help man their booth at an on-campus event. Fostering a secular presence on a Utah campus felt crucial to me as an atheist kid who'd grown up in a Mormon-majority town in Idaho. I talked to curious students who passed by, showing them the resources our club offered, before I had to head down to the main climbing gym in town to routeset (install the holds on the climbing wall while choreographing the movement it would require to ascend). I was exhausted, but I needed the money, and I loved working at the climbing gym. Creating climbs for others to enjoy and challenge themselves on was deeply rewarding for me.

I wolfed down my typical meal of plain white rice while chatting with Ashleigh and our other roommate, Taylor, a geology grad student. We sat together at our kitchen table and worked on our homework while joking around and discussing our weekend plans. As an ambassador for the College of Science, I had an event to attend one night, and the next day I was going to a climbing competition down in Lehi, a couple hours away.

I was barely keeping up with my breakneck schedule, but somehow it was working out. Despite always feeling tired, I was following through on all of my commitments. I had a hard time saying no. It was overwhelming, but I had convinced myself that I was managing just fine. My philosophy was that life is short and I needed to make the most of it. Yet . . . it was getting harder to deny that everything was spiraling out of control. My planner was a visual, chaotic reflection of my mind, and my to-do list grew longer every day. As much as I loved geology and my other clubs and activities, all I really wanted to do was climb. I told myself to be patient, and that I'd be able to climb once I finished my degree. I couldn't make myself quit any of my jobs or clubs. I desperately needed money, and I was convinced that I needed to be the best because that's what everyone expected of me.

My three older sisters, all well-educated and great athletes in their respective sports, left big shoes to fill. Some of the pressure was external, but much of it was internal, wanting to live up to the family standard and my own potential. Growing up, I couldn't avoid feeling inadequate, ugly, and unsettled compared to my sisters as I watched them strut confidently across the stage of a beauty pageant or ace all of their exams. When I was little, I felt like I'd never be as smart, stunning, or capable as my sisters, and I wondered why I was the odd one out with my constant behavior problems and mysterious chronic health issues. I remember staring in the mirror in middle school and concentrating with all my might to try to imagine myself as an adult: could I grow up to be pretty and brilliant like them? As a kid, the only time I tasted confidence was when I was excelling in climbing, so I clung to that. That was my domain, my safe place, the one thing that allowed me to shine. I spent the rest of my childhood time in the shadows.

That weekend, the College of Science outreach event passed by without incident, another check in a box on the to-do list of unending responsibilities. Finally, I could go enjoy myself down at the climbing comp in Lehi. I hopped in my old Suzuki and raced down south to the gym. I'd never been to this location before: it was a sprawling bouldering gym with all the latest training equipment and newest, best holds on the market. While checking out the boulder problems for the competition, I bumped into professional climbers I'd always idolized, and tried to play it cool as I fangirled over them. In the comp, I had an average performance, but savored the new-to-me terrain, holds, and routesetting movement. Climbing at a new gym was a massive treat.

After the main portion of the comp, the pros went head-to-head in the finals round. The gym bustled with activity, the spectators all shoulder to shoulder, straining for the best view. They dimmed the lights and put spotlights on the wall as the pros came out one by one to try the wildly difficult boulder problems, the crowd cheering them on as chalk dust filled the air and music thumped through the speakers.

I felt a tap on my arm and turned to find someone who looked vaguely familiar. He leaned in to tell me who he was and it clicked into place: Dan, from Facebook, who I'd messaged with recently to discuss climbing together near Salt Lake City. He'd been posting some climbing videos that had piqued my interest, especially of his trad climbing, which I was trying to advance in after learning that summer in Boulder. I figured he'd be a good partner to climb with to work on my trad climbing skills—where you place your own gear into the rock to protect against falls, rather than sport climbing where the bolts have already been drilled into the rock as protection points. Trad climbing is more serious, and takes far more instruction and practice to master safely. I was a newbie at it, but with my strong background in sport climbing, I was eager for capable partners so I could progress in the discipline.

The crowd was roaring, so we had to lean in to hear each other. Dan and I managed to have a brief conversation to introduce ourselves, and make plans to go climbing together soon. Dan seemed anxious about the big crowd around us but sounded nonchalant when talking about climbing. His eyes locked onto mine, and I felt uncomfortable receiving such intense attention from a stranger. Our exchange was short-lived, but I left that night feeling energized and looking forward to getting out with him.

I texted Alex about how fun the comp had been, and how I wished he'd been able to come with me. Alex and I grew up together on the same climbing team in Boise, Idaho. Our shared love of the sport was something that had held us together for years, but with his waning interest in climbing, I felt a divide growing between us. It had reached a breaking point that previous spring, when I'd broken up with him for a couple days. It had felt so wrong to be apart that we'd quickly gotten back together, the only hiccup in our four years as a couple, vowing to never drive each other away again.

That summer in Colorado, I practically had to drag him out of the house to go practice trad climbing with me. We still bonded over our mutual love of science, but it didn't feel like enough. Coming back to Utah alone for the fall semester had felt refreshing. I valued him and his steady, reliable friendship, but I felt guilty for not reciprocating his love and excitement about our relationship.

The overwhelm of full-time college, research, clubs, working, training, competing, and managing a long-distance relationship was wearing me down, and I felt a restlessness that I couldn't repress. Every time I climbed, my heart soared, and I was addicted to that feeling. Here was something where I felt totally in control, like I had all of the answers, like my body knew how to perform every sequence, like my motion was perfectly in sync with the rock. I've always had an insatiable craving for adventure, travel, and challenge—I must get it from my dad, a hunter, outdoorsman, and jack of all trades who traveled the world as a military pilot for most of his career.

In my classes, I found myself daydreaming about climbing in the amazing places I saw in the magazines I'd obsessed over for my entire life. At climbing comp raffles in the early '00s to mid '10s, I'd often win free subscriptions to magazines like *Rock & Ice, Climbing, Urban Climber, National Geographic,* and *Outside*. Every day after school, I'd eagerly check the mailbox for the latest issues, and I read them cover to cover every time.

Their pages contained my earliest climbing culture curriculum, and I devoured their stories. This was mostly pre-YouTube and pre-social media, so besides watching *Masters of Stone* VHS tapes at the YMCA with my team, the magazines were my only window into the current world of rock climbing. And boy, was I transfixed by that universe.

These mags transported me to the crags I dreamt of constantly, inspired me with the adventurous tales of pros I admired, and taught me about the latest gear, fashions, and techniques. Whenever I saw a really spectacular photo, I'd add it to the collage on my wall. And I kept every issue—there are still hundreds of magazines in a bin in my dad's shed. As a kid, I fantasized about getting to go on expeditions, receiving free gear to review, and writing or shooting for climbing magazines.

When I caught myself daydreaming in class, I'd just sigh and snap back to attention, reminding myself of my goals in school like

I was appeasing a little devil and angel on each shoulder. I couldn't quite sort out if climbing and school were respectively the devil and angel, or vice versa. Either way, the internal tug-of-war jarred me.

CHAPTER 3

UP IN SMOKE

November 2016

The next weekend, I rolled up to Little Cottonwood Canyon, with its pristine granite routes right above Salt Lake City, and had no problem spotting Dan: beat up Converse, black Prana climbing pants, and a chalk-covered black Patagonia hat, with a cigarette hanging out of his lips like he'd been born with it there. He was pulling climbing gear out of the bed of his truck. Internally, I scoffed at the cigarette, but kept my mouth shut. I told myself that if I wanted to climb with men and master trad climbing, then I needed to grow up and get over it.

"What's up? You psyched to climb?" he greeted me, smiling.

"Yes! So stoked. I've never climbed here before," I said, gesturing to the canyon, trying not to make it too obvious as I admired his forearm muscles rippling as he moved his climbing rope onto his pack. He was fresh off a summer of climbing in the sun, tanned and buff, and at five eleven, about an inch taller than me.

"No way! I climb here all the time. It's the best—you're gonna love it."

We shouldered our packs and hiked over to the cliff, a smooth gray panel of crystalline rock rising out of the trees.

"Sweet! Yeah, I've heard good things. All I have up in Logan is the sport climbing, which is good, but we don't have any trad climbing, so I'm excited this is working out today. All I wanna do is climb. It's so nice to get a break from school," I said, ever the chatterbox, the Saturday morning sun refreshing me as I picked my way through the boulders.

"Oh yeah, I bet. I know how it is. I'm taking a break right now from the U," he said, and picked up on the next question before I asked it. "Studying English. I love writing." His dark brown hair crowned his rugged face, the shadow of facial hair darkening his features, his hazel green eyes bright and inviting.

"No way! I love writing. I wanted to study English or journalism or something, but my dad said I should do something in STEM because of the job prospects. Well, I didn't actually want to go to college at all, but the military didn't work out, and ya know, rocks . . . so geology. I ended up loving it, so it's working out pretty well," I rambled. "But I still love writing. I'd love to read some of your stuff sometime."

He smirked. "Yeah dude, we can make that happen," he said. He looked so sure of himself, settled in his strength and attitude. I internally cringed at my inability to shut up or play it cool. I needed this guy to like me so I could climb more, and I needed to not make a fool of myself. *Get it together, Fallon.*

As we racked up for the climb, I worried about the first pitch. The opening slab section looked difficult, but I didn't want to show too much hesitation. He flaked out the rope and kept talking to try to put me at ease. "So . . . Do you have any siblings?"

Oh man, we're really doing the awkward get-to-know-your-new-climbing-partner thing. Here we go.

"Yep, youngest of four girls. Megan, Bryn, and Shannon. We all live in different states now. My poor father raised us on his own," I said. "I'm the only climber though. Two of my sisters did beauty pageants, actually."

"You didn't do the pageants too?" His eyes met mine in an assessing stare that made my breath catch. *Damn, he has nice eyes.*

I laughed at the idea. "No, definitely not. I'm not cut out for that." I shook my head. "What about you? Do you have siblings?"

"Yeah, a bunch of them. Mormon family and all, you know how it goes," he said. "I'm not Mormon anymore. Obviously." He held my gaze while lighting a cigarette, adjusting his hat and pushing his hair out of the way. *Why is smoking suddenly hot? What is wrong with me? Jesus.*

"For sure. Oh, Utah," I sighed, racking cams on to my harness. "I'm just here for college, and the climbing of course." I patted the granite and looked up at the beginning of the climb with a grin to hide my urge to wince. For some reason, I had horrible new stomach cramps and was experiencing severe abdominal pain. I didn't know what was wrong, but tried to downplay it since it was my first time climbing with him. At this point, I'd been climbing for thirteen years, but as a relatively new trad leader, I was nervous for our day of climbing.

"You'll do great. Seems like you're quite the climber." Dan looked me up and down while putting me on belay. "And I've done this route a million times," he said confidently, and I couldn't help but believe him.

He's five years older than me. Does he actually like me? No. No way. I'm just a nerdy kid. And he's so cool. Don't go there. He's probably just being friendly. Think about Alex. My mind spun as I started up the climb. I danced up the slippery granite, familiarized myself with its features and textures, and cautiously evaluated my gear placements.

Dan led a harder second pitch; following it was my first time ever climbing a true crack. His ease with placing gear and jamming the crack made me envious. During the previous summer, I'd cut my teeth in Boulder Canyon and Eldorado Canyon in Colorado, and then I had summitted the Grand Teton without a guide. My experience was limited, but I had just enough to scrape by. I still second guessed every piece of protection I placed in the rock, so I was grateful to climb with someone who could help me advance. The gear placements here were thankfully far more straightforward than the rock I was accustomed to.

My stomach pain became harder to ignore and I felt like I would vomit or faint, so after climbing, Dan insisted I didn't drive home to Logan—I could stay in a spare room at his parent's house in Lehi, only a half hour south. He explained that it would be more comfortable than his cramped rental in Salt Lake City. Reluctantly, I agreed to tag along until I felt better. We left my car at a coffee shop, jumped in his pickup, and rallied to his childhood home. I was floored by the house when we pulled up in the driveway. He'd mentioned that his dad had been a successful CEO, but holy-fucking-shit-this-was-a-mansion.

I'd grown up in a lower middle class, modest household, so seeing this kind of extravagant wealth was shocking. I'd never set foot in a house this large.

Dan made dinner in the sprawling kitchen and offered me red wine, but it only hurt my stomach even more. I lay on the living room couch in pain, taking it all in as the clock ticked closer to bedtime. He busied himself in the kitchen and we chatted across the space as I held my abdomen, as if that would ease the sharp pain distracting me from our conversation. I didn't want to seem like a wimp.

"You know, society fucking sucks at taking care of its artists," he lamented while stirring the veggies on the stove. "How are we supposed to create, to survive, to make it artistically? I mean, it's just impossible now. This place isn't set up for people like me."

"Hmm, I guess I've never really thought about it." I was at a loss for an answer. "What do you think would make it better?"

"I don't know, man, but this isn't it. There have to be better ways to care for artists, to give us the freedom we need to do our thing. Our current system is so fucked. We have to make some major changes so people can pursue their art." He sipped from his wine glass while checking on the rice. We discussed the recent presidential election, education, love, religion, climbing, and our childhoods while eating the meal he'd cooked. It was delicious, but with my stomach pain, all I could manage were small, infrequent bites.

I'd never met someone quite like Dan; such intensity, bursting with passion and conviction. I'd never heard anyone talk like him before. He burned brightly, and I couldn't look away. I felt a magnetic pull toward him and his ideas.

He admitted to being a former cocaine addict and having slept with a prostitute when he lost his virginity as a freshly minted ex-Mormon. As shocking as it was coming from him in this lavish, perfectly maintained family home, I found this information intriguing rather than scary. The delivery was so casual, and who was I to judge his backstory? Maybe I naively craved something different after being bored with my relationship with Alex for so long.

Maybe it was just too familiar. When I was in the fourth grade, my mother had told me that one of her boyfriends had traveled to Thailand, and had a heart attack while fucking a hooker—but I needed to be careful not to tell her other boyfriend about it. There's a reason my dad raised all of us girls.

Dan and I stayed up late, our conversation traversing endless topics like we would never run out of things to discuss. His undivided attention and pointed questions made me feel special and seen, like he genuinely cared about my life, my stories, and my opinions. An undeniable connection buzzed between us.

Eventually, sleep couldn't be delayed any longer. He showed me a spare bedroom decorated with pictures of Mormon Jesus and Joseph Smith. In Idaho, I grew up in a community that was almost entirely Latter-day Saints (LDS, colloquially referred to as Mormons), so I was familiar with the faith. My childhood best friend was LDS, and her family took me in when I needed help, feeding me, letting me sleep over, and even bringing me with them on trips. I went with them to church sometimes, and attended their Family Home Evenings and Mutual activities. Although I never converted, her mom lovingly took me in as one of her own, and their house was my favorite safe place whenever I needed an escape.

In high school, I was one of the only outspoken atheists in a sea of cookie-cutter Mormon peers. In class discussions, my teachers looked to me to give a unique perspective, anything to interrupt the echo chamber of all the indoctrinated kids with the exact same worldview and bubble. For a few years, militant atheism captured my attention; I wrote about my extreme views for a radical newsletter, and my dad cautioned me to tone down my online presence so I didn't ruin any chances of future employment. As an out of place teenager, I found solace in my strong urge to rebel, to advertise that I didn't subscribe to the dominant culture. The strict dress code and LDS seminary building attached to my high school were constant reminders that I was not *one of them*.

By college, I had become more tolerant. Most of my friends now were either active in the church, or were ex-Mormons. I had read *The Book of Mormon* with Sarah, one of my devout college roommates, and now she was one of my best friends. Although I didn't believe in the church, I figured I might as well better understand the community I'd been immersed in for most of my life. Dan resented the church since he'd left, and he hated that he had to deal with it since his family was still active. He'd spent much of the evening complaining about LDS doctrine.

As I lay alone in the upstairs room, I wondered what Dan was doing downstairs. *Is he going to come up here? I should really just go to sleep. What are we going to do in the morning? Should I tell Alex I'm staying here? Does Dan like me? No, don't even go there, he's just being nice.* I fell asleep with too many thoughts bouncing around from our long, stimulating conversation.

The next morning, since I had nothing planned, we climbed up American Fork Canyon on mellow limestone sport routes. A freezing November morning thawed out to a pleasant, crisp day among the pines and steep dark gray cliffs. When I was climbing at the crag with Dan, I looked out over the canyon, back towards the city, up to the sun, down at the air below my carefully-placed feet, and happiness flooded me. Truly joyful in a way I hadn't experienced in months, I gained a sense of freedom and clarity. *This* was what life was all about; not laboring over assignments and running around between jobs.

During the two days Dan and I spent climbing together, he analyzed my relationship with Alex. I'd been feeling antsy about it and figured he'd have good advice since he was five years older, more experienced, and had a fresh perspective.

"So this guy loves you unconditionally, but you're clearly over it. That's fucked up. Not fair to him. He doesn't deserve that." He shook his head.

"I love him, Dan. I can't just leave after almost four years. When I lived with him this summer, I even wore a ring."

"You were engaged?" His eyes flared with a mix of surprise and disappointment.

"No, not really. It was a promise ring of sorts, I guess. Alex has been everything to me for so long. I can't just leave him. It would destroy him. He loves me so much."

"Yet, here you are complaining about your relationship," he said.

"Well, yeah. This summer I could barely drag him out of the house to climb. I think he's depressed or something. I don't really feel the connection we used to have. I don't think I'm attracted to him anymore, and without climbing, it feels so . . . empty. But maybe he'll get his psych back, and we can go back to normal." I looked up at Dan, unsure of myself.

"Bullshit. I see right through you, dude. You clearly don't want him anymore."

Holy shit, he called me out. It sent a rush through me. "I mean, yeah, things have been better. I don't even like texting him lately. It feels like a *chore*. And I dread our phone calls," I admitted shamefully, playing with my climbing harness and avoiding eye contact.

"Why are you holding on to it so strongly then?"

"I don't know. I feel bad. I've been so committed to him, and we've always talked about our future together, and he's been so unconditionally loving and good to me. He's smart and kind and supportive. I feel like an asshole for not giving that back to him."

"Dude, you've gotta break up with him. It's so fucked up to drag him along like this. It's not fair to yourself either. You know it, too. What do *you* want, Fallon? Stop being a coward and tell him how you feel." He put a gentle hand on my shoulder, and I couldn't ignore his gaze any longer. I saw the truth in his eyes, the hazel reflecting my own like a matching set. He was right, and we both knew it. He was telling me things I already knew, but had been too stubborn and immature to acknowledge.

Staying with Alex had been the comfortable thing to do, but it was unfair to us both to live in a lie. People had repeatedly told me that relationships with high school sweethearts often fail, but I'd wanted to be the exception to the rule. I was simultaneously appalled at Dan, enamored with Dan, and incredulous at his ability to have such an intimate knowledge of my emotional state after knowing me for such a short time.

We finished climbing, said goodbye with a hug, and I drove home to Logan as if in a trance. There was a moment of clarity as the finality of the decision to break up with Alex occurred to me. It was the day after his birthday and, even through the phone, he could sense something was wrong. We'd been together long enough that we could pick up on the smallest change in each other's tone or energy. I sat in my apartment's kitchen with my leg propped up on a wooden chair, staring at the refrigerator. I felt passive and robotic as I held the phone up to my ear, as if it wasn't really me breaking up with him.

Alex sobbed into the phone. He demanded answers, expressed his confusion, and couldn't contain his heartbreak. Almost dreamlike, and shockingly emotionless, I slammed the final nail in the coffin, burying the past four years of our relationship, and over a decade of friendship. Surprisingly little convincing was required for me to make the decision; Dan was just the catalyst, the one who'd pulled back the curtain to reveal the harsh truth.

Although a sense of guilt crept in, I had made the right choice in breaking up with Alex. I had only stayed with him because it was the path of security and stability. Continuing the relationship would have been a disservice to him since my heart wasn't in it. Ending it had been a long time coming, and it was especially timely since I had undeniably strong feelings for Dan already.

My boredom and restlessness felt cured by Dan's mere presence. He exuded excitement and opportunity. His no-fucks-given attitude was irresistible, and I felt little hesitation confiding in him with even the most personal details—about my deepest insecurities, childhood struggles, and my dreams for the future. I found it refreshing when he called me out. I enjoyed the challenge and lack of sugar coating. Here was someone who was really *alive,* who didn't hold back, who didn't care what society thought of him. I admired his authenticity and drive.

Back in Logan, I attended classes and dealt with the fallout from the breakup with Alex. He kept commenting "I love you" on our old Facebook photos together, and I had to delete all of his comments, each one breaking my heart despite being firm in my decision.

I was sitting in class, taking notes, and trying to process being newly single, when I got a text from Dan: "Hey, wanna join me in St. George this weekend? Climbing on Zion splitter cracks!" A smile spread across my face as I accepted the invite, my heart thundering. Here was my chance—the escape I'd been craving. The desert was calling me.

CHAPTER 4

THUMB PUMP

November 2016

My bags landed with a heavy thud in the bed of Dan's pickup on Friday afternoon in Salt Lake City. We barrelled south down I-15, music blasting, snippets of our conversation picking right back up where they'd left off the previous weekend. His lips moved to one side in a half grin, and he bobbed his head up and down really slowly while talking to me, like his words needed a beat to keep flowing.

Dan handed me the aux cord and told me to play a song that I knew by heart and could belt out. I protested, but he insisted. I glanced out the window, thinking, the sun glowing red over the Oquirrh Mountains. I hardly knew Dan, and this request felt ultra-vulnerable. *Don't embarrass yourself.* I was no singer like him, and I'd never sung in front of someone else. I frantically scrolled Spotify, trying to remember which songs I had memorized. Maybe a song by Creedence Clearwater Revival? The White Stripes? I had a couple of false starts, unsure of myself.

"You've gotta really mean it, Fallon. Like, c'mon, belt it out." He was serious. I was so nervous I could barely read the song titles as I skimmed through song options, shifting in the leather seat.

Eventually I settled on "Ramblin' Man" by The Allman Brothers, and I mustered every cell in my being to try to belt out the song. I've never been a good singer, but he assured me it'd be fine as long as I tried, so that's what I did. I felt like an amateur kid at a middle school talent show being judged by my peers, craving his approval.

We laughed together at my lack of ability and he graciously commended my effort. I felt embarrassed, but I was grateful it was over. For the rest of the ride, I sang along more softly to songs that we both loved, letting him take the lead.

When night fell on the high desert bordered by pine-coated peaks, he asked me to scoot over on the bench seat next to him. The moment my left thigh touched his right leg, it was electricity like never before. The tension between us was unfamiliar, and I could hardly grasp how I felt. It was never like this with Alex. I sweated, overthinking everything. We sat there like that with our legs barely touching, and nothing more. I tried to stare straight ahead, but I could feel his eyes on me instead of the road.

We pulled off at a Chevron to get gas, shocked by the nighttime November cold. My jacket was buried in my duffel bag in the bed of the truck, so he offered me an extra coat—a gray puffy. It fit me marvelously, and I gladly accepted it, nuzzling into the warmth of the down.

We leaned close together against the side of the truck, our breath visible in the freezing air. He unabashedly took me in, willing me closer. He grabbed my waist and we kissed for the first time under the fluorescent lights of the gas station. I felt dizzy with the touch, the first new man I'd felt in years. Winter was setting in, and I kicked my feet to stay warm after pulling away. Huge, goofy grins spread across both our faces. I felt like a silly high schooler again. I ran into the gas station to grab drinks, and then we returned to our seats side by side in the truck, satisfied with our new arrangement.

The remainder of the drive to St. George continued on in this way, totally torturous for the both of us, wanting more, making small advances. His fingers roamed freely, and I was unable to focus on anything but his touch. Despite the late hour, we were wide awake. I was high on the attention he was giving me, in love with the idea that someone new found me attractive.

Upon arrival at his parents' desert home, tucked away in a fancy neighborhood below red rock cliffs, I had the exact same moment of shock but to an even greater extent this time—this was some real top 1% shit. We loaded our bags into the master bedroom of the house. High ceilings towered over furniture and decor with sticker prices that would probably send me into cardiac arrest. Perfect glass surrounded a central courtyard, and a piano sat next to the spotless kitchen. I tried to play it cool, but my brain told me I didn't belong in this tax bracket, and I felt extremely out of place.

He told me that some climbing friends would be arriving later that night, but for the time being, we had the house to ourselves. He put on music through an installed speaker system hooked up to a giant television, and we settled into the opulent sitting room.

He softly grabbed my hand, and asked me to lie down on one of the couches. I reclined on the couch as instructed, and he held my hand and stared at me. He was studying me, his expression welcoming and filled with desire. His lips found mine, soft and searching, and he took off my shirt. He stopped in his tracks for a moment and sat on the rug next to the couch, staring. I thought he might cry. *This guy can't be serious.* His fingers very carefully traced my figure, exploring, and he complimented me on my lace bra.

I was confused, having never seen a man behave like this, but welcomed the affection. We walked together to the master bedroom, with a giant chandelier and a luxurious king-sized bed covered in fluffy blankets and pillows. I'd only been with my high school boyfriend before, and this kind of sex was an entirely new experience, greedy and lustful. The novelty of the situation, and the satisfaction of being desired, consumed me far more than the actual act. Afterward, he studied my body for a long time like he was starving and I was a feast. His attraction to me was so foreign that it was hard for me to fathom.

We got our clothes back on just in time for the arrival of the other three friends joining our trip. Introductions were made, wine was flowing, and pipes and cigarettes were passed around. I was surprised that he didn't care about the smoke inside the house. As a vehement anti-smoker, I had never smoked anything. Hating weed had been ingrained in my brain from an early age by my cop father, who was always warning us about the dangers of drugs and complaining about the deadbeat stoner criminals he had to deal with on a daily basis. I politely declined when offered the pipe, unsure of how to use it and not wanting to make a fool of myself.

I was hyper-aware of Dan's attention, undressing me with his gaze from across the room, the tension between us still taut, our earlier foray a promise of future exploration. The evening turned to the wee hours of the morning as we exchanged climbing stories, and we all went to sleep, plenty of bedrooms for all of us with leftover rooms still remaining.

The next morning, we drove to Zion National Park to climb as a group. I'd only been to Zion once before to hike, and was itching at the chance to attempt my first sandstone splitter crack climbs. The massive brush-stroked walls rose impressively on both sides of the canyon, and I admired the cross stratification while sharing my geology knowledge. My stomach pain was a constant annoyance, and I still had no idea what was causing it. I tried to ignore it so I didn't sound like a whiner.

Dan taught me how to wrap my hands in tape gloves for crack climbing as we sat on a boulder at the base of the climbs. I fumbled with the angles and the tightness of the tape, knowing it would take a lot of practice to get it right. I toproped the first pitch of 'Cherry Crack' after Dan's smooth lead, struggling my way up even though it got an easy grade of only 5.9, a grade I "should" have been able to cruise. Jamming my hands in the smooth opening of the rock wasn't working for me like everyone else. *What am I doing wrong? I suck.* The group convinced me to try to lead 'Squeeze Play,' but I failed and lowered to the ground in defeat. I couldn't yet master the jamming required—I wasn't making my thumb fat enough when I folded my hand.

I was used to proving myself around men, so frustration reared its ugly head. On my competitive youth team of mostly boys, I was always trying to keep up. In high school, my climbing team at the local gym Urban Ascent trained like fiends for hours on end. I did 100 pull-ups every day, convinced that it would help my upper body get as muscular as my male peers. Bryn—my gymnast sister—and I would complete a cheesy workout video called Ab Ripper X multiple times a week, and I spent hours outside of climbing practice at a regular gym doing cardio and lifting weights.

I was ravenous every day after school—the pantry was emptied out constantly by the black hole that was my stomach, and no matter how much I ate, it was never sufficient to keep up with the overtraining. I'd flex in the mirror and never be satisfied. Why couldn't

I get as jacked as the boys I climbed with? In my head, I was one of them, and there was no excuse to be weaker. I just needed to try harder.

I felt even more pressure to perform around all the strong dudes on the USU team, to prove myself worthy of being their leader. I couldn't have fear while climbing and I couldn't show any weakness, or else I'd risk losing credibility to the team. Falling short in climbing drove me nuts, but I had to remind myself that although I'd been climbing for many years, crack climbing was a whole new animal for me.

Dan easily finished the lead for me, and I spent the rest of the day toproping other cracks, trying to perfect my technique and fight the inevitable thumb pump, ankle aches, and sliding sand grains. The views were beautiful, with the near-dormant Virgin River trickling below the famous Angel's Landing ridgeline. At the time, it was the most picturesque place I'd ever climbed.

The following day, Dan and I hiked to a different area of Zion and climbed 'Smashmouth,' a classic route that ascends a few hundred feet up a highly-rated 5.11 finger crack. Apprehension stuck in my throat as I looked up at the four-pitch climb. I had only climbed a handful of multi-pitch trad routes, and I had never been on a 5.11 trad climb. I followed the first pitch and got a small confidence boost.

Dan gave me a quick kiss at the belay station as we switched leads. *Man, this is perfect.* I found myself rising to the challenge of the second pitch, an easier section of the climb with a few bolts at the beginning, which gave me a sense of security to quest up into the trad section. I wanted to make Dan proud, to have him see me as a competent partner. He whooped and shouted encouragement from below.

I was proud of my send of the pitch, and Dan fought his way up, leading the remainder of the route. I learned how to fingerlock on the fly, experimenting as I tested out this new kind of movement. We topped out the climb, and the exhilarating position—perched high on a sandstone buttress overlooking Zion—felt special. Dan congratulated me; climbing 5.11 in Zion was no joke, especially for a teenage girl who had no clue how to crack climb. At the time, it was by far the hardest trad route I'd ever tried. His grin reached his eyes, and his genuine approval bolstered me. This was exactly what I'd needed. It was like I'd walked into some sort of ideal dream life practically overnight.

Riding on our stoke, Dan smoked some weed when we got to the base, and I decided to give it a try. Why the hell not? I knew lots of people who smoked weed and were totally normal, and it seemed less harmful than tobacco. At first, it just made me a bit silly. I hiked more tentatively and felt dizzy and off balance.

The sun set abruptly, and suddenly I was confused as to my whereabouts. I felt like I had just finished rappelling the route, and now I was bushwhacking in the desert in total blackness. We lost the trail since it was our first time there, but we knew the general direction to hike. Prickly brambles assaulted our skin, and we slid down loose gullies of rock and sand, navigating difficult terrain. We were lost, but could see the road down below. I kept losing track of time. Minutes would completely go missing and then I would snap to attention, alarmed.

I cursed myself. If I wasn't high, I surely wouldn't have found myself in this situation. I should have listened to Dad and avoided weed. We eventually popped out at the road, but we were many switchbacks downhill from where we'd parked.

As cars sped past, Dan instructed me, "Try to look cute. Smile real big and stick your thumb out." He flashed a smile, his arm extended with thumb up. "Be confident. They're more likely to pick us up if they see a cute girl." He winked at me.

We tried this tactic for a while, but no one took the bait. Dan left his pack with me and started jogging up the road. I sat there, my head swimming, feeling out of control and disoriented as I sat against our climbing packs in the dirt. The weed made me paranoid that I would be a target as a solo woman with lots of expensive climbing gear. On his run, a family reluctantly picked Dan up and dropped him off at his truck, and in fifteen minutes he was back to me. He drove us to St. George in the dark, his typical American Spirit smoke whirling in the desert breeze as he reached over and squeezed my hand. I slouched into my exhaustion.

Rain the next day. Sandstone breaks when it's wet, so we couldn't climb. All but one of Dan's friends said their farewells and left. The three of us that remained hiked around Snow Canyon, just above Dan's house. Jagged black basalt cut cross-stratified sandstone in the form of petrified dunes. The canyon floor is graced by juniper, creosote, and prickly pear, and sometimes, if you're lucky, you'll see desert tortoises. We leisurely strolled up and down washes, looking for minerals and creatures, Dan and I stealing touches and glances every chance we got. He called me gorgeous constantly, and I was intoxicated by the attention as I wandered around wearing his puffy jacket.

I'd never climbed in Snow Canyon, so Dan pointed out some of the climbing areas, promising to take me someday when the rock was dry. Zion would tower over these cliffs, but they were still worthy: sheer sandy faces with swaths of iron-oxide desert varnish forming black patina splatters on the surface.

The rain was relentless, so we drove back north to the Wasatch. On the way, we made a stop in the Kolob section of Zion to see if the rock was dry. After a peaceful hike back into Namaste Wall, we discovered it was wet and cold. We admired the streaked overhanging climbing and vowed to return someday when it was dry.

My eyes were wide with all of the new sights; familiarizing myself with new climbing areas was just the kind of exploration I'd been longing for. We drove home, our fingers interlaced between us on the truck bench seat. Our hands were nearly the same size, but his fingers and knuckles were thicker than mine, carrying the scars of years of crack climbing. By his side, I felt a dreamy future unfolding before me. We were now officially in a relationship after less than two weeks of knowing each other.

CHAPTER 5

RAVENS, RED WINE, AND RED BULL

November 2016

Dan and I began climbing with a frenzied drive on the weekends: bolting down to the desert and climbing until everything we owned was full of sand and stained with blood and wine. For me, the weeks were still packed with classes, exams, research, team practices, and work. Friday would arrive and I'd jet out of my last class, speed down to Salt Lake City, and meet up with Dan for a forty-eight-hour adventure bender. I'd collapse in my desk Monday morning after yet another exhausting but satisfying weekend, thinking I could keep up my double life.

Thanksgiving Break was upon us. Though I'd originally planned to go home to Boise to see family, Dan had convinced me to come with him to Moab to climb. I'd always been the black sheep of my family, the only climber and the most rebellious sister. My family and I were typically on relatively good terms, but their disappointed and harsh reaction to my choice not to come home for the holiday only solidified my decision to run off to the desert. My sisters called me selfish, asking how I could go climbing instead of seeing family, especially since my dad was undergoing cancer treatment. All I could think about was taking advantage of my new opportunities to pursue trad climbing. Like a typical teenager, I figured they just couldn't possibly understand.

On the morning of Thanksgiving, I drove south through the disgusting gloom of Salt Lake City until I arrived at Dan's house in Lehi. He was smoking weed outside, and offered me some. After what had happened to me in Zion, I was curious if I'd be able to handle it better this time. He encouraged me and promised it would be fine. I took two deep inhales, coughed uncontrollably, and drank juice in an attempt to calm my throat. Within a few minutes, I knew something was seriously wrong. At first it felt like it had the previous time in Zion, but this was much more potent.

I rapidly felt as if I'd fallen into a deep, black pit of despair, with the weight of the world crushing me into an infinitely small ball of nothingness. I was under the impression that if I let myself fall asleep, I'd surely die. I knew it; it was inarguable. I sat on the couch and cried and cried. The feeling of being incredibly tiny, with so much pressing on me from every direction, made me feel like I couldn't breathe, like my head was exploding. This was the end. *Oh fuck, what have I done?*

For what felt like hours, I sank down into the black hole, and for a few seconds at a time, I'd be just coherent enough to talk to a very concerned Dan, who held my hand and stayed by my side. I told him how I felt. He said I just needed to wait it out. In the brief moments where I'd emerge from the stupor, I was unsure whether it would be the last time—*I'm out, I'm free!*—or if I'd descend into blackness and fear once more. Every time, without fail, I'd apologize profusely to Dan, over and over, and ask how long it had been since the ordeal had begun. Minutes felt like hours and I couldn't tell the difference. I wanted it to end. Now.

After agonizing hours like this, I came back up for air, relieved but wary. I thought surely this isn't the end of this torture; I'll soon be consumed once more. Finally, I was safe. Dan and I agreed that I should never smoke weed again. I couldn't decide if I was more horrified or embarrassed by the experience.

We loaded up the truck and went south to Moab, passing familiar geologic units that made me feel at home. I'd studied these rocks on class field trips; I knew the stories they told, knew how to read the history in their ancient layers. In the middle of the night, we pulled up to his secret camping spot on Potash Road, walking through an ominous underground tunnel to reach the semi-hidden site on the other side in a small desert basin.

Dan downed Xanax and Seroquel with swigs of red wine, his typical nightly cocktail. He cooked an outstanding Thanksgiving meal over the campfire, the light from the flames dancing on the sandstone boulders around us, the only other light coming from the moon and stars overhead. I shivered in a thin dress—Dan loved it when I wore dresses—while sitting on a camp chair, feeling at peace, and thankful for my opportunities, for warm food, for this man, for everything.

The morning greeted us with frost, but quickly warmed up under the Utah sun. We cuddled against each other in our sleeping bags, our rosy-cheeked faces the only visible skin on our bodies. Dan popped an Adderall and we packed up camp. We climbed at Wall Street, and I put up a couple of sport climbs, along with an easy trad route. Cragging with Dan felt like a dream. He made me feel strong and commented on my sport climbing ability. I beamed and pushed myself even harder. Despite my young age, I'd been climbing longer than him and was eager to show off my skills so he'd keep climbing with me. At sunset, we drove up Long Canyon to peer at potential first ascents. We were treated to stunning lighting over the La Sals, Arches National Park, and the surrounding labyrinth of desert as night fell.

We drove back to Moab, then up the Colorado River, and turned off toward the La Sals. It was well after dark, which was becoming a theme for us, and we camped illegally on private land in Castle Valley. I was concerned we'd get caught, but Dan shrugged and seemed unbothered. We whipped up a meal over the campfire; he half-melted a plastic bottle of olive oil just as I burned a pot of rice. We scrounged the rest of the food together, ate with numb fingers, and cuddled under the romantic array of stars.

At first light, we threw everything in the bed of the truck and boogied out of there to avoid getting caught at our illegal spot. It was my first time seeing Castle Valley. Our sights were set on 'Fine Jade,' a famous multi-pitch desert tower climb with a coveted 5.11 finger crack. I gazed up at Castleton Tower, the Rectory, and the other red sandstone spires piercing the clear sky and could hardly believe I'd be standing on the top later that day. I'd come a long way from the grungy YMCA climbing wall of my youth, buzzing with the possibilities of my new opportunities.

After a long hike up the unconsolidated talus cone, I was thankful that there was a line to get on the route—I felt perfectly at home lying at the base on a rock in the sun, taking it all in. It was easy to forget about the homework I was procrastinating thanks to this incredible landscape.

We grinned our way up the climb, and celebrated together at the belay stations. I dug deep on the cruxes, still trying to figure out how to crack climb, battling for every foot of progress. I led one pitch, feeling gripped but determined to show him I was worthy. At one of the anchors, we howled like wolves, embracing as we hung next to each other in our harnesses, totally surrounded by open air. We laughed together, fully savoring the exposure and movement. Dan's pure joy was contagious. Dan couldn't finish the last pitch, which ended with a bolted section to the summit. I dispatched the pitch first try and we topped out during the golden hour.

Ravens circled around us, waving their dark, inky wings in welcome to this upper desert realm. Growing up, my family had a German Shepherd named Raven; between her eyes, there was a black marking in her fur in the perfect shape of a raven. On long hikes in the Idaho backcountry when I was a kid, she'd run far ahead, scouting, and she would always run back periodically to check on me. Sometimes it felt like all ravens had a piece of her, swooping by to make sure I was okay.

I'd spent the earliest part of my childhood in Alaska since my father was a Coast Guard pilot in the '90s. We had an Alaskan children's book that my sisters and I often read, which told a story about raven symbolism in Indigenous cultures, such as the Tlingit—they view the raven as the bringer of sunlight. Ravens had always lit me up since then, making me smile and reminding me of where I came from. I lived for sunshine.

We enjoyed our stay on the summit, but Dan was eager to get down before dark. I was elated, basking in the joy of my first desert tower climb. The daydreams fueled by my classroom boredom had come to life, and I was ecstatic. Castleton Tower cast a long shadow on the slopes below, and snow on the high peaks of the La Sals provided a dramatic contrast.

We rappelled in the glowing red light of sunset. At the last rap station, Dan went down first to the ground. I was alone and found myself in a situation I'd never encountered before. My gym climber background wasn't going to help me now. There was an arête with a set of bolts on each side. The rappel ropes were running through the left set, around the corner, and I was tethered into the right side.

I loaded my ATC and tried to transition on to the left set of anchors to rappel, but discovered that my tether wasn't long enough, so I was suspended between the two anchors. I couldn't transfer my weight onto the rappel ropes, but I couldn't take my weight off the tether on the right anchor either. *Fuck. What should I do?*

My inexperience was showing, and I started to freak out. I yelled down to Dan, mortified, which only worsened things. I knew I had to come up with a solution on my own, but I felt stuck. The wall was nearly sheer and blank, but I used the nearest holds to carefully pull myself up to unweight and unclip my tether, and delicately swung around the corner onto the rappel ropes, relieved. It was such a minor thing, but it made me realize how much I had left to learn to become a proficient climber outside of the gym.

When I got back to the ground, Dan was visibly annoyed as he shoved gear into his backpack. He chastised me between inhales on his cigarette in the fading light.

"What the fuck was that? It's so simple, I don't get why you couldn't figure it out. Next time, don't freak out. Jesus." He rolled his eyes, and my heart sank. I told myself that this wasn't anything personal. It was simply a climbing partner thing, and he had a right to be frustrated by my show of incompetence—but his annoyance still stung.

Although I hadn't been in any danger, I was shaken from my

panic. I had a strong track record of good decision making in the mountains, and I was confused as to why I'd lost it this time around. I apologized and promised not to screw up again. I was ashamed that I had let something so inconsequential freak me out. *Did I mess everything up with Dan already?* I made sure to be extra hardworking and nice to try to win him over again. I didn't want him to ditch me to climb with his other friends who were more experienced.

At dusk, we could just barely make out the trailhead far below. We tried to memorize it so that we wouldn't get lost on the trail, a faint line down the giant rock pile. We slid down the steep talus cone surrounded only by the small orbs illuminated by our headlamps, ready to get back to town for burgers and hit the road back home.

CHAPTER 6

OVERDRIVE

December 2016

Thoughts about a possible Patagonia trip dominated my mind. December was flying by and I felt rushed. I scrambled to complete final projects, take my geology exams, and prepare for an expedition far beyond my scope of experience. I picked up another job at a shitty call center. Among the chaos of school and working multiple jobs, Dan and I kept up our exhausting routine of climbing in Moab or Zion every weekend, ticking off routes in the bitter cold. It was the busiest time of my life.

"This is perfect preparation for Patagonia," he'd shout to me from the belay, "because when we get there, it'll all be heavy loads and fucking wind! Gotta be able to climb in the cold!"

I nodded along, trying to keep up with him. Since our initial conversation about it, I hadn't explicitly agreed to the trip, but we were moving forward with preparations regardless. I was progressing beyond my beginner trad skills, and I went into overdrive to play catch up. Since I had a strong background from sport climbing my entire life, it sped up the process. I finally learned how to jam efficiently, led cracks at my limit in below-freezing weather, and took whippers on gear to prove myself to him.

I continually relied on caffeine pills to get through coaching the climbing team in the mornings before long days of class and work. We got our first set of team shirts in the mail. When I opened up the package and put mine on, pride coursed through me. This was something I had created. I had built this team from scratch, and now, the shirts symbolized that we were official. After working so hard on this team for months, I felt a pang of sadness knowing that I would be leaving them while I was in Patagonia. Something felt wrong about abandoning the team mid-season, but I didn't have much time to dwell on it.

On the weekends, I downed Red Bull, coffee, and gummy worms to keep the stoke going on long drives—my attempt to match Dan's manic level of motivation. I reveled in my new crack prowess, enjoying the novelty of it all. After a few years living in Utah, I was getting properly acquainted with desert climbing. I saw the state unfolding before my eyes, full of opportunity and, most importantly, sandstone.

I shivered my way through frigid belays in the shade, my gangly frame wanting for insulation, poised hundreds of feet in the air on multi-pitch climbs in Zion. Dan pushed me out of my comfort zone to lead harder and harder trad routes, determined to morph me into his "rope gun." He always talked me up way above my ability. Tourists gawked at us from the highway below. When we rode the National Park shuttle with all of our gear, we got lots of questions. Families would give us curious looks as Dan and I were crushed by giant backpacks in our cramped shuttle seats, pointing out routes to each other. His mania manifested in stoke: a runaway train of psych for climbing. Always more, more, more.

I became accustomed to confusing approaches, frozen hands and toes, and plugging cams in sandy cracks. I was desperate to rise to the occasion, feeling like no amount of climbing could possibly prepare me for the horrors I'd heard about Patagonian climbing. The process was enjoyable though; I was rewarded with magnificent light shows over orange monoliths at sunset, challenging routes that revealed to me a strength I had never before tapped into, and an unfaltering motivation to prove to myself, and the world, that I was more than a sport climber. My relationship with Dan revealed a new side of me, something within that I had never brought out to play until now, and our love felt like a deliverance. We were in sync, obsessive, and burning hot.

The intense schedule took a toll on my body, and the unbearable stomach pain was ever present. I wrote it off as a symptom of my many food allergies, foolishly believing that I'd just been accidentally eating some allergen. After weeks of increasing pain and an inability to eat, I did some research into other possible causes. The culprit became glaringly obvious: ibuprofen. Along with copious amounts of caffeine and alcohol, I'd been popping tons of ibuprofen to combat my inevitable aches and minor injuries from climbing. Its daily overuse had caught up to me, and now I had stomach ulcers.

I had traded one kind of pain for another.

I immediately stopped my regimen of ibuprofen and quit drinking, which was hard since Dan downed a bottle of red wine per day. I monitored my diet and tried my best to heal my body before we left for South America. Thankfully, my vigilance was ultimately successful, and I avoided ibuprofen altogether for a few months.

The day after we climbed 'The Headache' in Zion and Dan had first brought up his Patagonia idea, we drove down to Red Rock to climb. Las Vegas sprawled before us with its usual level of tackiness and sin, and we flipped off Trump Tower as we drove by. *Fuck Trump.* We were still disoriented after the shocking election, and I felt a deep resentment toward him, along with confusion at how so many supported him. I knew things were only going to get worse, and I dreaded the future of the country. *God Bless America. Save these idiots from themselves.*

Glad to be out of the city, we drove to the trailhead for Oak Creek Canyon, hiked and scrambled up brushy, boulder-filled drainages for hours, and searched for a climb called 'Levitation 29.' The 4th and 5th class cliffs of rock were complicated, and I was uncomfortable being unroped on the high, sandy slab. I got sketched out on steep, exposed slickrock hundreds of feet up the final approach, and Dan begrudgingly belayed me across a section. After hours of exploring, we found ourselves high up in the canyon, with only rock climbing above, but unable to find any established routes.

He spied a nearby dihedral crack that seemed possible, but dirty and unclimbed. He opted for a potential first ascent, and quested upward into the unknown, with just the gear on his harness. Grunting, swearing, and trundling loose rocks, he made slow upward progress. He found a reasonable spot to end the pitch after some spicy, runout climbing, and left a couple pieces of pro as an anchor.

"Alright, babe. She's all ready for you. Not my best work, but at least we can say we climbed something."

I delicately toproped the pitch to avoid setting off loose rock or ripping out gear. It was very forgettable climbing—not a worthy consolation prize. I wished we'd been able to find 'Levitation 29' like we'd intended. What a waste of effort and time.

The noise of engines, unmistakable, took us off guard. We

looked away from the cliff to see small planes doing amazing tricks between the canyons and spires. They dove, turned, and played in the evening light, silhouetted against the dappled sandstone. I took a video of the planes maneuvering wildly all around us.

"Holy shit! That's so beautiful! Christ. I wish I could fly!" Dan whooped. He always talked about BASE jumping and flying, desperate for that free, airy feeling. Whenever we watched *Valley Uprising*, his eyes got really big during the BASE jumping section of the film. He idolized them, and talked frequently of his desire to fly.

We hiked down, making some rappels over tricky sections, and eventually scrambled out in the dark. At one point, I slid down a slab into a pool of water, lucky not to have sprained an ankle. The bushwhacking got so bad that I felt at times as if I was entirely suspended in the bushes, floating in a web of vegetation.

We got lost at the mouth of the canyon, wandering among cholla, unable to find the trailhead or the car in the darkness. We could see a familiar road in the distance with passing headlights, so we hiked to it, and then Dan dropped his pack and ran to his truck. My first day in Red Rock had yielded essentially no climbing, and all I had to show for it was epicing on the hike. We left disappointed and hungry for more climbing. That night back at his parents' desert house, I had to finish writing a massive geomorphology paper, busting it out before the deadline as I fought the urge to fall asleep. I pretended not to care much about school anymore, but I still put in enough effort to earn good grades despite my shifting focus.

Dan cooked me dinner and danced in the kitchen while I worked diligently on my paper, giving me a smooch on the cheek when he set a steaming plate down next to my laptop. When I was finally done, I snuggled next to him on the couch, letting my heavy head rest on his chest. He held me and stroked my hair, telling me stories. In moments like this, he'd tell me about his time playing competitive tennis, aid routes he'd climbed in Yosemite, leaving Mormonism and nearly dying from cocaine, backpacking the Cordillera Huayhuash in Peru, and free soloing on Lone Peak high above his childhood home. I felt like he'd been everywhere and tried everything.

During our December climbing bender, one cragging day specifically stood out. We started out by working on 'Crimson King,' a 5.11 pitch that was mostly a finger crack. Dan tried it, took some falls, and then asked if I wanted to lead it. I was uncertain, not feeling like I would be strong enough or able to handle the placements that weren't as straightforward as a typical splitter. He left some of the gear in for me to try to "pinkpoint" the first half of the climb and then lead the rest, and I ended up whipping all over the route. It was one of the first times I had really tried hard and taken multiple lead falls on gear, which was exhilarating and essential for my progress.

Dan set up his camera to get footage of me on the route. He reviewed the clips and told me, "Fallon! I'm gonna make you famous. People are gonna eat this up. Beautiful girl taking whips on a trad route in Zion. Man . . . I gotta get shots for this film. It'll start with all this preparation. We'll have it right before clips of us on Fitz Roy." He held up his hands in a rectangle shape, like he was framing the shot he could already see in his mind. All of the climbing only contributed to his mania, energizing him, making him feel like we were unstoppable.

I raised my eyebrows, thinking it would be unlikely to make me famous. I thought to myself that an appropriate title for the footage would be, "Inexperienced Girl Pathetically Falls All Over a Moderate Route," but Dan was caught up in his delusions of grandeur, convinced of my success. It was endearing. (I ended up returning years later and easily succeeded on the climb in a full circle moment.)

We decided to finish up on the ultra-aesthetic classic climb called 'Inner Chi.' The route ascends a unique finger crack splitting a dihedral in brilliant orange stone. I attempted the lead first, filled with nerves. Dan reassured me that my sport climbing background would come in handy, and that I "could just layback if needed."

I started up the climb, plugging in a few finger-sized cams and making better progress than expected up the crack. I pulled a strenuous move, and a sharp, familiar pain struck my finger: a tweaked tendon. I fell onto the rope, and Dan lowered me to the ground. I felt defeated, worried that this finger tweak may be a hindrance if it was still hurting when we got to Patagonia.

"I hope you didn't just fuck everything up, Fallon." He was pissed. "Give me the cams."

I handed him the rack of cams, and marveled at the sunset while he put on his climbing shoes. He smoked a cigarette and popped an Ambien to calm his nerves while we watched ravens gracefully flying in the twilight. The peaceful scene was soon interrupted by the fact that we hadn't brought headlamps. We'd intended on a full day of cragging that didn't extend into nighttime.

He started up the climb, soon surpassing my highpoint. Eventually, he fell, burnt out from the long day of climbing and the physical nature of the route. He tried to work out the moves, and my concern mounted as darkness enveloped us bit by bit. I patiently belayed him, shouting encouragement from the ground. Dan climbed a few feet, plugged in a cam, and then swore as he had to take again, blindly reaching for jams or holds.

He decided to aid up the rest of the route since he was so drained and could barely see. This proved to be harder than he'd imagined due to his minimal rack of cams, and the increasing difficulty of the route. Encountering the final crux, he finagled in a tiny cam, placed his foot in a jerry-rigged sling as an aider, stepped up into it, and then—*pop!*—the cam blew. *He's so close to the top. It can't be that hard. Why doesn't he just do the move?* I pondered during the long belay.

"Fuck! I don't have the right gear for this!" he yelled down.

All the while, a mouse tried to chew on the flaked rope at my feet. Without a headlamp, I could only hear its fidgeting and scuttling in the dirt, and barely make out its form attacking the rope. I kicked dirt at it, shouted at it, and tried my best to protect the rope from the pest. The last thing I needed while Dan struggled up the crack was for the rope to be chewed on by a damn mouse.

"Any progress?" I shouted up to him in the dark, catching a glimpse of the stars before returning my attention to the mouse.

"Yeah, I'm gonna aid this section a little differently so I can hopefully finish this fucking thing." He moaned and cursed, swinging around chaotically while trying to reach the chains in the blackness. *What is he doing up there? Dude, get it done. I wish my finger didn't hurt so I could just finish it myself.*

After what seemed like ages, he called off belay, rappelled through the anchor, and cleaned his gear. To the best of my ability without a light to assist me, I packed up gear at the base of the route, shoving tape and water bottles into our backpacks. Back on the ground, he pulled the rope and helped me pack up. We looked around and didn't see any remaining gear, so we hiked back to the car, dodging cactus and ankle-rolling loose rocks.

On the long, snowy drive back north, we zipped up I-15, blowing through highway towns, only stopping for gas. Dan always insisted on driving, a cigarette or pipe in one hand and a Red Bull in the other. Our favorite climbing podcast, the *Enormocast*, was our preferred way to break up the monotony of the drive—engaging interviews with pro climbers, fun banter, and captivating storytelling. Dan attentively listened to every episode. We arrived at his parents' house in Lehi in the middle of the night, and crashed in the basement, totally beat.

The evil sound of my 4:00 a.m. alarm woke me from a deep sleep. I rubbed my eyes with scraped hands and quietly gathered my belongings. As I fought off sleepiness, I dreaded the two-hour drive back to Logan for my Monday morning classes.

I was almost done packing up my stuff when I realized I couldn't find most of the rack of climbing gear. Any semblance of drowsiness vanished in an instant. *Oh shit, oh shit.* I found our harnesses, shoes, a few slings, and a couple cams, but the majority of the rack of cams was nowhere to be found. I ran out to the truck in my bare feet, praying I'd find the gear under the seat. No such luck. Just crushed cans of Red Bull and forgotten rolls of climbing tape.

I sprinted back inside, waking up Dan. "Hey, did you put the rack somewhere?"

He scowled at me. "Nope. Did you look in the packs?"

"Yeah, I can't find it anywhere. The packs, the truck, the house. I don't know where all the cams are. No gear sling either," I said.

He was fully awake now. "Fuck, dude!"

He joined me in the search, and then a terrible thought dawned on us. We'd hung up the gear sling with all the other cams on a dead tree at the base of 'Inner Chi' the night before. It must still be hanging there. Dan started freaking out.

"All of my fucking money is in those cams! Now they're gone, and I'll have nothing! I can't restart the process of getting all that gear again! Shit!"

The wildness in his eyes was a deep-seated fear amplified by his drug use. He slumped down against the wall, and wrapped his arms around his ribs, hyperventilating.

"Hey hey hey. It's going to be alright. I doubt there's someone climbing there on a Monday morning in December." I tried to talk some optimism and reason into him.

Dan's dad, Mark, heard the commotion in the basement and joined us. I explained the situation while Dan looked increasingly upset. Mark offered the idea to call the Zion rangers to see if they could get the gear and hold on to it until we could pick it up.

"No, Dad, they're all fucking corrupt! They'll probably hike out there, steal it, and then tell us that it was already gone when they got there! Fucking rangers!" He shook his head frantically. "We can't tell them where the gear is. No!"

I gave Mark a desperate look, trying to find a solution. It was a four-hour drive to get back to Zion.

"Maybe you could drive back there today to see if it's still there. I mean, if it is, then it's gotta be worth it, right?" I offered. In the back of my head, I was thinking about how badly I needed to leave in order to make my Monday morning geology class.

"Fallon! You don't understand. I bet someone already got the gear. What if I drive down there and it's gone?! I'll kill myself! That's my whole life in those cams! Fuck!"

Dan bashed his head into the wall repeatedly. I felt a mixture of surprise and concern as he kept slamming his head. I'd never seen someone do this before. *Oh god, that's so not helpful. Holy shit.* Dan had warned me that he had bipolar disorder, but I didn't realize he'd self-harm like this. I sat down next to him against the wall, trying to restrain him from hitting his head.

I tried on my most comforting tone. "Dan, calm down. We're going to figure this out, okay?" He punched himself in the temple again and again, finally balling up on the floor, screaming. My anxiety about missing class was eclipsed by concern about his breakdown. *Shit, what should I do?* I watched in horror as he hit himself and let out demented shrieks.

"I don't wanna drive down there alone. It's so far and we just did the drive last night! Fuck! I can't live my life without those cams. Someone must've stolen our shit!" His voice sounded strained, and completely different than anything I'd heard from him before. *Is this really Dan? This is so fucking weird.*

I thought for a moment, weighing my options. I'd been skipping class more and more lately. What was another day? If it meant this much to him . . .

Dan slammed his head into a door now, and I struggled against his strong arms to prevent his violence, not wanting to get caught in the crossfire. Mark wandered back upstairs, seemingly accustomed to his son's alarming psychosis. I guess this didn't fit into their Mormon need for the mirage of a perfect family. Turning away from the darkness was easier than engaging with it. Or maybe he just knew intervening was useless and didn't want to bother. Regardless, I needed to think of something to make this better, and fast.

"Alright, if you don't trust the rangers, and you won't drive alone, then that means we have to go get the gear together. We have to at least try." I was pleading now. Anything to get him to stop.

"You'd go with me? Skip class?" He sounded hopeful for a second in his rage, his eyes lighting up ever so slightly.

I nodded, gently coercing him to calm down. "Yep. Let's get our shit together." I felt pride at having found a solution to get him to stop screaming and hurting himself. Maybe I was cut out for this relationship after all.

We jumped into the truck, and ripped back down all the way to Zion. We both were lost in our thoughts on the drive, considering the outcomes. I hoped with all my heart that the cams were still there. I feared Dan's prophesied suicidal episode if the cams were gone. He took a Xanax to try to relax in anticipation of the worst case scenario.

A heavy feeling hung over the both of us as we approached the park, finally winding our way up the switchbacks and parking below the tunnel. I consoled him as he was still on the verge of majorly losing his shit once again, his eyes sullen, his posture defeated, his leg bouncing up and down. *God, I hope the cams are still there.*

It felt like I was trying to diffuse a bomb without an instruction manual.

A classic southern Utah winter morning—arctic, blue, sharp, sensation turned up to full blast—absorbed us as we exited the truck at the trailhead. We carried nothing with us as we walked the familiar trail (a nice change from our first time getting lost hiking out on it in the dark). I felt as if I was holding my breath as we got closer to the climb, finding it difficult to appreciate the beauty of Zion's stunning views.

The gear sling was hanging on the dead tree, still adorned with all of our cams. Visible astonishment washed over Dan. I grinned ear to ear.

"See, hun? I told you there was a good chance we'd find it!"

He grumbled something back through his weed pipe, exhaling smoke into the frosty air and avoiding eye contact. He shoved his free hand into his jacket pocket, silent. I was overcome with relief, more about his mental state than about successfully retrieving our gear. I'd passed my first test in avoiding a full-on bipolar crisis. Still, he didn't seem as relieved or excited as I would have expected, which threw me off. I thought he'd be jumping for joy, but instead he was brooding as we stood there among the angular boulders.

Since we'd driven all the way back, I'd already missed class. We decided to make the most of the additional trip and at least climb something before heading back north again. Dan chose 'Touchstone,' a popular big wall aid route, as our objective. We wouldn't have time to climb the whole thing, of course, but he wanted to project the first pitch that supposedly went free at the difficult grade of 5.13.

We drove down to the base of the wall. Dan spent a couple hours desperately throwing for small crimps, unsuccessful on his free attempt. It turns out he was in the wrong place—the free variation has a different start—so he was up against the impossible face of the bolt ladder. Perched on the belay ledge during his fruitless attempt, I gazed around at Angel's Landing with its endless conga line of tourists on its high ridge, the imposing Great White Throne, and the other walls rising around me. The crystal clear Virgin River lazily snaked its way through the canyon down below. *How did I end up here?*

As a kid, I never thought I'd be able to trad climb because of the prohibitively expensive gear. I envied the adults in the climbing gym who told stories about trad climbing in far off places, feeling a heavy jealousy that I'd never be rich enough to experience that kind of climbing or adventure. I had to rent old shoes from the YMCA each year in order to train and compete with my first youth climbing team. I remember using such careful footwork when I finally got my own pair for the first time, trying to preserve the precious toe rubber. Now, here I was trad climbing in a place I'd never even let myself dream about—my childhood self would have been stunned.

I shook my head, stomped my feet to warm them, and felt dizzied by the heights above me as I peered up from the belay. Dan gave up on freeing the blank section, and aided the rest of the pitch so we could retreat.

We repeated the stretch of boring interstate for the third time in less than 24 hours, returning north to Lehi.

"Ya know, Fallon, I'm glad we're going to Patagonia together. You dealt with me really well this morning, and I wouldn't have come back to get the gear without you. That shows a lot." He nodded up and down while driving, which I now knew was one of his tics. I thought maybe he used it to convince himself that he was correct: *yes, yes, that must be right.* I smiled, knowing that I'd pleased him, but I felt uneasy about his violent behavior.

"No problem." I sank into my thoughts, concerned that he'd have a breakdown if anything went wrong again. I pictured him slamming his head into the wall over and over, and I shuddered. Traveling internationally with someone prone to psychosis and self-harm sounded challenging, but I hid these concerns. I convinced myself that Patagonia would be worth it regardless—here was my chance to advance my climbing with someone familiar with the area, to see a remote part of the world like I'd always dreamt about, to break out of the monotony that had plagued me for so long. His behavior wasn't enough to deter me. After all, he was usually so fun, energetic, and loving. It wouldn't be fair to judge him for something he couldn't control.

I went back to Logan late that night, and attended my classes the rest of the week. I missed Dan's 25th birthday because I had to take a final exam, and I had another job interview in a last-ditch attempt to make more money before the trip.

After we'd solidified plans for Patagonia, I'd filed for a leave of absence from the university. I received an email saying it had been approved, and that they would defer my full-ride academic scholarship until my return. I had mixed feelings about it, but was grateful I wouldn't lose my scholarship altogether.

My dad worked hard to raise us to value education. Growing up, he knew we wouldn't be able to afford college, so scholarships were our only ticket to a better life. My sisters and I spent much of our free time blowing through educational workbooks, quizzing each other with BrainQuest cards, and devouring books. We were all 4.0 students and were involved in clubs and sports. Anything less than an A was unacceptable, and that expectation weighed on me, knowing that mistakes were not an option. My future depended on perfection. During my brief visits to my mom as a kid, the sentiment was the same: she would scold me for using the erasers on her mechanical pencils, telling me that I should just not make mistakes in the first place. The pressure to achieve academic perfection came from multiple fronts.

We didn't see my dad often since he worked long hours as a cop; he wanted us to be independent and capable on our own. My sisters and I enjoyed summer days in Idaho unsupervised, exploring the irrigation canal in our backyard, riding our bikes for miles around town, watching movies, climbing trees, playing foursquare, arguing over our desktop Sims and Oregon Trail games, walking the dog, practicing scooter tricks, and fighting each other constantly. As the youngest, I spent a lot of my time alone, and would bike to my best friend's house whenever I got hungry or was sick of the fighting. We sisters had a strong bond to each other despite our frequent conflicts, knowing that all we really had was each other.

When I got to high school, my dad said I only had to follow three rules: get a 4.0, don't get pregnant, and don't die. Anything else was basically fair game. The social freedom gained by my academic performance was a reward I constantly enjoyed—I stayed out late with friends and was up to all kinds of shenanigans (like reckless "buildering" in downtown Boise), but as long as I had perfect grades, my dad didn't care much. Education was what mattered. He pushed us so hard in school as an act of love; success was the only outcome he'd entertain for his girls. I dreaded telling my dad that I would be skipping a semester, even though I knew in my heart I would go back to finish my degree.

I called Dan to tell him the news about my leave of absence, and he told me that all I had to do now was make as much money as possible before we flew out in a few weeks.

"Oh, and review your Spanish and glacier rescue skills. Fitz Roy! Oh my God! We're coming for the bastard!"

Patagonia was becoming a reality.

CHAPTER 7

OVERSTOKER KID

December 2016

"You bitch! I bet you're sleeping with her! You're such a slut. This is over. You cunt!" Dan screamed through the phone.

I slumped in my parked car, hands on the steering wheel. Confused. Sobbing. Out the windshield, the red siding on my apartment building and the nasty gray slush on the sidewalk provided no comfort for this surprise attack.

"Dan, what the *hell* are you talking about? Ashleigh and I are just friends. Just because we share a room doesn't mean we're hooking up. I promise."

This didn't seem like Dan at all. He'd never previously mentioned a problem with my living situation, and he'd never yelled at me before. *Where is this coming from?*

"I don't trust you. I can't believe you're such a whore. Jesus, Fallon. Whatever." His tone was perplexing—at once, he sounded enraged, disgusted, and apathetic. He hung up on me.

I was appalled that he'd called me such terrible things, and accused me of something I hadn't done. Alex had never done something like that to me. I'd never been treated so poorly by a partner. I didn't think it was possible that someone who loved me could immediately shift to hating me so passionately. I couldn't fathom what had put the idea in his head that I was cheating on him with my roommate.

Dan and I had only been together about a month, and this was a total shock. Recently, we'd said "I love you" for the first time. I shuffled into my apartment crying, overcome by the total devastation unique to the teen brain. I dared not tell Ashleigh and Taylor because I'd just told them how great things were with Dan. They'd been surprised when I'd told them about our Patagonia plans, but I'd assured them that he was a good guy and that we'd be perfectly safe. We were such close friends, yet I couldn't bear to tell them of my doubts.

My reservations proved unsuccessful when they could tell something was upsetting me. I didn't mention that he'd accused me of sleeping with Ashleigh, but I did admit that he broke up with me completely out of the blue. I figured that was the end of it; a break up meant it was all over. They supported and comforted me. I distracted myself with homework for the evening, full of emotion, the feeling of betrayal lodged solidly in my throat as I fought back tears. I told myself that I just needed to get through this semester.

In my mind, people didn't break up with such venom in their words and then get back together. The end was final. Our relationship, and Patagonia, would be entirely canceled. *Thank God we hadn't bought the plane tickets yet,* I thought, trying to stay positive.

The next day, Dan called me back with a new attitude. He said that he regretted yelling at me, and that he trusted that I hadn't been sleeping with my roommate. I was equally surprised by this turn around, and questioned what made him change his mind. I didn't know what to make of our conversation. He now spoke like he assumed we were back together, just like that. This was an odd concept to me. How could I reconcile that he had called me a cunt, a whore, a cheating liar? I was rightfully still upset about the insults he'd tossed at me so carelessly, so I explained my feelings. Why should I take back a man who insulted me and thought so lowly of me?

He told me that he didn't actually think I was a bitch, and he wrote it off that he hadn't taken an Ambien to calm down when his brain assumed the worst of me. He'd been drunk, and attributed the entire interaction to his bipolar disorder, absolving himself of blame. The matter-of-fact nature of his calm explanation made the delivery very convincing.

Gears turned in my head. Our relationship, and climbing partnership, was important to me. His ability to make my life interesting and exciting allowed me to overlook his flaws. I accepted him back, thinking this was just a rare slip up, and feeling like I was being gracious and understanding of his mental illness.

I wasn't familiar with bipolar disorder, so I did some research so I could better handle Dan's behavior. I spent hours poring over the Internet, and I read the book *An Unquiet Mind*, which details the life of a person with the illness. I grappled with understanding his condition. I figured that I could handle his challenges better than anyone if I did enough research. I treated it like any other project: with enough effort and learning, why shouldn't I be capable of understanding him? I figured his other qualities more than made up for the difficulty of his moods. I loved the climbing, the fast-paced road trips, the boldness, the music, the thrill of what we had going. Despite all my research, I naively couldn't see that I was addicted to his mania; that realization occurred to me years later.

On our weekend climbing trips to the desert, he'd play guitar for me across the campfire, a satisfied smirk spread across his face, and it was hard not to feel smitten with him. Out there, it was easy to forget about everything that was going wrong. We had each other, and climbing, and a shared mission. If we just moved fast enough, maybe we could outrun any problems.

At one point, Dan told me, "If you can deal with my bipolar, then I'll put up with all your food allergies." It seemed like we'd reached an agreement to deal with our respective health issues, as if that provided a fair balance in our relationship. He found my food allergies to be deeply annoying and inconvenient, and made me feel ashamed of the situation, which convinced me that our deal was an equal trade.

I learned by trial and error what worked to please him and calm him down, and what fueled the fire of his moods as our Argentina trip rapidly approached. As I learned more, he hid less and less of his psychosis. The day where he'd first lost it and we drove back to Zion to retrieve the gear was just the beginning of an unpredictable string of strange behaviors. Maybe he figured I was better equipped to respond to it now, so he could freely show me his struggles.

He cycled up and down constantly. He'd be morose, chain smoking, glaring at me, giving me the silent treatment one morning, and then do a 180 to be psyched, smiling, fist bumping me after climbing later in the day. The emotional whiplash was jarring, but I tried not to take it personally, reminding myself that it was his brain fucking with him. It wasn't in his control, and as a fan of Stoic philosophy, I was all about focusing on what's in your control. I reassured myself that the good times were more than worth the hard times. It wasn't really *him* acting that way, but his illness.

I'd frequently press him for advice about reacting to his psychotic breaks and mood swings. "How should I respond when you start to freak out? What do you want me to do if you're hurting yourself? What things should I say if you're suicidal again?" I asked him, desperate for solutions.

His responses to these questions felt unhelpful and vague, as if he expected me to inherently know what to do in crisis situations with him. I tried to prepare for his moods the best I could manage, knowing that it would be even more crucial in Patagonia.

I struggled with his lack of specificity, hungry for solid steps and phrases I could employ to help calm him down. I needed the right tools, and I couldn't find them. His tools were Ambien, Xanax, Seroquel, wine, weed, nicotine, Benadryl, Adderall, caffeine, and whatever else he could get his hands on—usually taken all at once in a wild cocktail of stimulants and depressants. He veiled his substance abuse by calling it "self-medication," and when asked about it, he would say, "At least it's not the coke anymore. That shit almost killed me. And lithium . . . Hell no. Never again."

I figured it was his body, and he got to choose what to do with it. The words of Marcus Aurelius echoed in my mind: "Be tolerant with others, and strict with yourself." This radical freedom I granted others in my life made me feel like I was being the bigger person, but I couldn't see at the time that the Stoic quote comes with a caveat—be tolerant with others, but not at the expense of your own well-being. I loved him, and I wanted to do whatever it took to help him be healthy and happy.

One night, we used my credit card to buy our one-way flights to Argentina. When the nagging feeling that it was the wrong choice bubbled up, I pushed it back down, trusting that Dan knew what he was doing; the trip was going to be fine. I was committed now, and I wasn't going to back out. Fear couldn't rule me. I had to believe that everything would work out because the chance of success was so enticing. I wanted to go to Patagonia. I wanted to explore places like

I saw in the magazines. I wanted to travel, to become the woman and climber I knew I could be. Dan made that possible, so I willingly hitched my path to his, no matter the cost.

I endured shifts at the call center with hate in my heart, and relished shifts at the climbing wall and geology lab. My weekend warrior identity outpaced my school work, my jobs, my research, my social life. Dan texted and called me frequently to check in and see what I was doing. It bothered him to have me an hour and a half drive away most of the time, and he often couldn't make it from weekend to weekend without seeing me. Sometimes on weeknights, we'd meet up at different climbing gyms to train together since it was too dark and cold to even think about cragging outside.

His behavior was notably different in public settings: he wouldn't show any of the psychosis, but he would avoid people, wary and lurking, observing the gym carefully. Excuses flowed out of him in endless supply for his poor performance on gym routes—never attributing his lackluster ability to deficits of strength or technique, but rather blaming external factors like the routesetter, hold choice, or noise in the gym. With my background in comp climbing, I felt right at home floating up the plastic routes. He sulked when I sent routes harder than he could climb, which confused me. *What's his deal?* I reminded him that he wanted me to be his rope gun, after all. My strength could only benefit our climbing partnership.

I ordered an expedited passport, which put an additional dent in my ever-dwindling finances. At the university office, I got my photo taken with a straight face, looking like a carbon copy of my father, just with the addition of eyeliner and long hair.

"Miss Rowe? Sign here," the employee said, sliding me the final paperwork.

"It's actually pronounced Rowe, like 'wow.' It's weird, I know."

He looked up at me. "What?"

"Forget it. It doesn't matter." I signed and left, crossing my fingers that the passport would arrive in time.

At Dan's urging, I also paid for rushed shipping on sized-up crack climbing shoes that I could wear with socks, imagining the icy cracks of Fitz Roy freezing my poor toes. I ate white rice for most meals, my stomach still healing from the ulcers, and my bank account dismally low.

As the semester drew to a close, I rolled up to the geology department Christmas party, feeling mostly at ease after a few years of excelling in the program. I'd started slipping this semester, and I could tell some of my professors and peers were puzzled by it.

Kyle, a non-traditional student in his early forties who bragged about how many women he'd knocked up, and that he'd gotten away with taking tequila shots off the geology museum's giant halite (salt) sample, approached me at the party. He'd tried to climb with me before and I'd always found a way to decline. I often observed him being belligerent at the university bouldering wall. I wasn't thrilled when he came up to me. His breath stank of beer.

"Dude. I heard you're going to Patagonia to try to climb. Who the hell do you think you are?" he drawled.

My jaw dropped and I furrowed my eyebrows, taken aback. I

started to defend myself and my climbing resume to him, but he wouldn't let me finish.

"You're going to die down there, man. I mean, I've done 5.12 finger cracks in the desert"—he gestured finger locks in the air— "and I'm way stronger than you, but you don't see *me* going to Patagonia. You're gonna get destroyed. You're just an overstoker kid."

Tears welled up. Kyle didn't know jack shit about my climbing or my ability. Dan had assured me that I'd do great, that I'd had enough experience both in the mountains and with rock climbing to survive there. Why was Kyle so intent on shooting me down? And why had he felt it appropriate to approach me and make fun of me at this party? I hardly knew the guy; most of our interactions were him bothering the other undergrads in the communal geology study room. Plus, he was more than twice my age. Was I really such a threat to his toxic, masculine climber ego?

He drunkenly rambled on about how I wasn't worthy of Patagonia or Fitz Roy or trad climbing. The urge to punch him almost got the best of me. I felt small and young, but I knew I'd been able to climb some hard routes with Dan. I grasped at whatever I could, trying to defend my experience, skill, strength, and determination. I asked him why he hadn't gone to Patagonia then, if he was so amazing at climbing. He wasn't self-aware enough to see through his own insecurity.

His attack threw me off so much that I couldn't argue in a productive manner. I was used to being the target of my three older sisters, but this was different. His words cut through my skin, which I'd thought was thick, and I began to doubt myself. Maybe I wasn't ready, or cut out for alpinism, or even trad climbing for that matter. The self-questioning was torturous.

I made a getaway, and cried to Ashleigh and Taylor. My efforts to enjoy the rest of the party were only partially successful, laughing at my wasted professor whose ass was hanging out of her Christmas-themed onesie outfit. She certainly knew how to party, and constantly blurred the lines of professor-student boundaries. When Ashleigh and I had gone with her to Arizona on a geochronology research trip the previous year, she'd bought us wine even though we were underage, talking with us about our love lives while we all sat on a bed together in the hotel as if we were peers. She was drunk constantly, even at department functions or on geology field trips. The other faculty didn't seem surprised.

In the back of my head, I wondered if this would be the last time I saw all of these folks. *What if I die in Patagonia?* My mind raced. I desperately wanted to forget Kyle's words, but I dwelled on them.

When we finally left, I was stewing. Was Kyle right? Was I totally screwed? Probably. But then again, who was he to tell me what I could and couldn't do? I decided to draw on the interaction as motivation, and let it fuel me. *Fuck him. I'll show him what I can do. I can prove him wrong. I can prove everyone who doubts me wrong.* I got up extra early the next morning to train at the climbing gym.

Dan drove for Lyft in Salt Lake City to make some extra cash before the trip. He'd jack himself up on caffeine and Adderall and drive as much as he could, especially late at night. I continued working, juggling my jobs at the climbing gym, call center, and geology lab. In between shifts, I called my family to finally tell them about the Patagonia trip, and to plan out my visit for Christmas.

My dad, who was receiving treatment for prostate cancer, was upset. He was convinced that I'd never return to college to finish my degree. "You know, Fallon, most kids don't go back to school once they leave. You don't wanna end up like these Dutch Brothers barista girls who dropped out."

I tried to reassure him that I loved geology, and was too committed to give up on my degree this far in. I promised him I'd return to school after my leave of absence.

"South America can be dangerous. I don't know, Fallon, there's some sketchy people down there," he said. I rolled my eyes and promised him I'd be careful. *He's being so dramatic.*

I reminded him that he spent much of his young adulthood traveling the world, flying for the military, and visiting all kinds of crazy countries. He didn't budge.

My whole family was alarmed by my choice to go to Patagonia, and couldn't understand the finances of the plan. I told them I'd been saving up from all my jobs, instead of the truth—I'd put the flight on my credit card. Every time I got a meager paycheck, it disappeared instantly to bills or last minute essentials like gear for the trip. Dan kept repeating "money comes," nodding knowingly without offering a solution when I voiced my concern.

I managed to pass all my classes with mostly satisfactory grades—good enough to ensure my scholarship would continue after my leave of absence, which is all I needed. I'd hardly attended the last half of the term, but I'd pulled it off anyway. Vertebrate Paleontology, my first graduate-level class, had kicked my ass, but I'd managed a B. It turns out I wasn't very good at memorizing the differences between dozens of species of Devonian fish. Go figure. Thankfully the B grade wouldn't impact my undergrad GPA.

Climbing in the sub-freezing temperatures of Utah's December was ideal training for the trip. On a snowy day, we ventured up American Fork Canyon in search of dry rock, and ended up trudging through the forest. Dan had to wear me down to get me to complete an icy river crossing on slick logs, and then we hiked up to a cave with a few established routes. I belayed him on something chossy, dodging bits of falling limestone, taking in the view of the wintry pines.

My hair fell in perfect curls and I wore long earrings, just how Dan liked. He encouraged me to dress girly every day and wear full makeup, even when we were out climbing, and I was all too eager to please him. There must have been some subconscious insecurity telling me that getting dolled up would make me a more worthy partner, and his attraction was positively addicting. We made a fire down the hill from the cave, trying to warm our frozen, wet fingers and toes. I asked myself if it was really worth being out there since we could hardly climb in those conditions. Dan bitched about the cold, yet seemed content to be there regardless as I lay in his lap next to the fire, massaging his pumped forearms.

One night at his parents' desert home, after watching *Valley Uprising* for what felt like the hundredth time, we felt stoked to keep pushing ourselves. We had such an intense connection and created so much synergy that when we joined together, whether intimately or with a common goal in climbing, it was like we set the world on fire. There was an urgency to everything we were doing. Dan lived with intention and vision and couldn't fathom putting anything off. The time is now. We had to live immediately, as the Stoics put it.

The next morning, we hiked out to an obscure basalt crag near St. George, where we tested ourselves on thin cracks with numb hands and feet, taking whippers all day in puffy coats. Our visible breath fogged around us as we braced ourselves against the wind. I shivered, which shook the cams dangling from my harness, and wondered if Patagonia would be even colder. Dan had a huge smile on his face when he reviewed the drone video he'd taken of me whipping on a trad route. He was fixated on making a film that would start with our preparation and all the desert climbing we'd been doing lately, and then transition to epic alpine climbing in Patagonia. I indulged his idea, wanting to support his creativity, and curious to see if he'd be able to pull it off.

We almost got lost hiking out of the steep canyon at dusk, but located the car after splitting up and searching across the empty mesa. Wandering around in the dark, chilled to the bone after a long climbing session, was exhausting. The car vents blasted precious heat and we huddled together, united in our goals, satisfied to be trying hard and growing together as climbers.

On the slog back to the Wasatch on I-15, Dan thought he saw a cop on the side of the road, so he threw his weed pipe out the window, shattering the glass on the side of the highway.

"Can't risk the cops finding anything in the truck." He winked at me, and turned up "Fuck Tha Police" by N.W.A. as we sped through a snowstorm, surrounded by the barren landscape of central Utah. He loved that album so much that I'd memorized it through pure exposure and repetition. We rapped along to the lyrics we both knew by heart as he played with the hem of my dress.

"Can you keep a secret?"

I glanced over at him. "Sure." I had no idea what to expect.

"I blew up a cop car a few years ago." His hands flew up to mimic the explosion as he beamed with pride.

CHAPTER 8

HEAVY AND TOXIC

December 2016 – January 2017

I read through my Wilderness First Responder (WFR) manual religiously, studying it harder than any materials from my fall semester classes. With Patagonia just a few weeks away, I tried to anticipate everything that could go wrong. I pictured one of us bleeding out after a fall or hypothermic after an avalanche, and broke down the scenarios in my head, outlining the necessary steps to fix any potential injury. My imagination ran wild, and the first aid reading material fueled it. I decided I needed to take the class seriously so I could be a capable partner in the mountains. I'd read that there were no rescues available in Patagonia. Self-sufficiency was a must.

My expedited passport arrived in the mail just in time. Flipping through the blank pages filled me with possibility and visions of distant places. I wondered how many stamps would fill its pages someday. I was in disbelief that all of the pieces were falling into place to pull off the trip with Dan.

I stayed in Boise for Christmas, and my family was surprisingly pleasant—especially compared to our conversations before my visit. I wondered why their attitude had shifted. I figured that once they'd realized I was going through with the Patagonia trip, they'd decided to support me after all since they couldn't change my mind. Regardless of the cause, we only had a few days together. My dad had just proposed to his girlfriend a few days before, a welcome event to take some of the focus off of me. I'd be getting a stepmother sixteen years after he and my mom had divorced. I was happy for him to have healthy love. My mother had cheated on him and left when I was a toddler. He deserved a second chance with someone better.

Politics became the main point of contention and drama since the recent presidential election had rattled the country. Some of my family supported Trump, which was hard for me to swallow, but we set aside politics the best we could for the duration of my stay. In the back of our heads, I think we were all wondering if this was the last time we'd ever see each other.

I wandered into the bedroom I'd shared with my sister Shannon when we were kids. Back then, our bunk bed had divided the room, making a tiny corridor for each of us, our stuff piled high on our desks and shelves in the cramped space. It felt wide open now that my dad had converted it into an office. My old hangboards for finger training were still mounted above either side of the doorframe, the only remnant of my years there. In this little room where I'd grown up, I told my dad what I wanted done with my body if I died, and I was grateful that he took me seriously. It felt more like an act of pragmatism than melodrama.

I drove down to Salt Lake City for New Year's Eve, and spent the evening working on the online portion of my WFR course from Dan's bedroom: modest, basic, utilitarian, devoid of color. It seemed like he spent most of his time in Lehi and St. George at his parents' houses anyway, where he could scrounge for free food and supplies. This room was more of a stopover, like a private liminal space he could inhabit when his main freeloading resources were worn out or when he needed some distance from his Mormon family.

New Year's Eve was one of Lyft's busiest days of the year, so Dan spent it out on the town, driving drunk partiers home from the bars. At exactly midnight, he came home to kiss me under the Christmas lights, a sweet, heartwarming gesture before he jetted back out the door to keep driving. His bed was shoved in the corner of the room and bare save for a single quilt he'd taken from his parents. A few pieces of mountaineering art hung on the walls, and tea candles flickered on his dresser. The gentle scent of weed lingered as I drifted off to sleep.

I awoke on the first morning of 2017 alone in bed, and stepped out of the bedroom to find Dan upset. He wanted to talk to me outside so his roommates wouldn't hear. *Great way to ring in the new year. What's this all about?* I threw on my coat and sat next to him on his back steps while he smoked a cigarette. Our visible breath and the smoke mixed in the frozen air. I buried my hands in my pockets and crossed my legs.

"I can't believe you didn't spend my birthday or Christmas with me. You're so selfish," he complained.

"Babe, I was busy on your birthday, and you told me it was fine for me to go home to see family for Christmas. I'm sorry." I kicked at some ice on the concrete, my nerves mounting as I anticipated a blow up. My muscles became tense, my chest tight.

He flicked the ash off the end and spit. "Yeah, well, I guess I should be used to being fucking disappointed." He stared straight ahead, avoiding eye contact, his leg bouncing up and down. His

Prana pants had burn holes all over the fabric.

I grabbed his free hand. "Dan, if I'd known it would hurt you, I wouldn't have gone. It's just that I didn't go home for Thanksgiving since I spent it with you, and we're leaving soon, so I wanted to see them one last time. I'm really sorry. Please, let's just get past this." *Please, don't lose your shit on me*, I wanted to say.

"Whatever. You shoulda known. You only think about yourself. I need to get used to it. I mean, girls have always done this to me. I guess I couldn't have expected anything different from you."

I sighed and didn't know what to say. How do you respond to that? How was I supposed to have read his mind and known he'd wanted me to stay when he didn't tell me prior? Anxiety about pleasing him and wanting to keep the peace prevented my inner urge to tell him to fuck off, and that if he needed something, then he should've told me first instead of complaining about it now. I felt like I was bending over backwards for him all the time, and it still wasn't enough. I chalked it up to my youth and inexperience; if I'd been more mature, I would've anticipated his needs and been a better partner to him. My apologies didn't seem to land.

He pulled his hand away from mine and changed the subject to the success of the previous night and his anticipation for Fitz Roy and Cochamó. Once I felt things were resolved enough for him to avoid spiraling more, I kissed his cheek, packed up my things, and drove home to Logan. The gray inversion of the Wasatch hung over me, heavy and toxic. I realized that deep down, I wanted out of this trip, but I felt like I had no choice. We'd already bought flights. I'd already told everyone we were going. I didn't want to find out what Dan's reaction would be if I decided to back out now. Bailing wasn't an option. When you commit to a climbing trip, you follow through so you don't leave the other person hanging. It would be too late for Dan to find a different partner for the trip on such short notice.

I didn't have much time to worry about it because I spent early January totally engrossed in my WFR course. Ten-hour days full of learning and testing exhausted me. I tried to memorize all the content. It was a fantastic training, despite the sub-zero temperatures during our outdoor practice scenarios—a low of -21 degrees F on the coldest day of the course. At the end of the class, I felt a confidence boost for going out in the backcountry. I had the medical knowledge I needed to save a life, whatever may happen in the wilderness. It was empowering.

Ashleigh and Taylor returned to classes and I felt like the odd one out. Having been a student all my life, it felt bizarre to not be taking the spring semester classes I'd previously signed up for and then bailed on. As soon as the WFR course ended, I was back in the basement geology lab, working hard: operating the rock crusher, epoxying rocks, labeling samples, and cutting pieces for thin sections. Time passed at its own speed in the basement since there was no light—not like there was much daylight outside in the dead of winter, anyway. After shifts at the lab, I'd usually go straight to the climbing gym or call center to continue working. *Hello, this is Fallon calling on behalf of Acura in Houston. Do you have a few moments to take a brief customer service survey?* I watched the number in my checking account creep upwards, but not nearly fast enough.

I decided to apply for another credit card. I'd hardly be able to afford basic necessities when we got down to Argentina, let alone a flight home. Since my first credit card was full from the flight there, I needed another one. A few days before we flew out, I got an email that it had been shipped.

I reviewed my Spanish whenever I got a free chance. Dan and I didn't have much time to climb, and I was worried about our fitness heading into the trip. I knew we both needed to be in tip-top shape for the long approaches and hard climbing in inclement weather. Work had hindered my training, and Dan was more interested in wine, his acoustic guitar, and smoking weed than climbing in the single digit temps of the Wasatch.

I couldn't wait to escape the northern Utah winter and the lingering inversion of disgusting air. I needed a fresh start and an adventure to get away from my messy life here. Alex crossed my mind occasionally, and Dan had forbidden contact between us. I knew not talking to an ex was an important boundary, but I felt like I'd never gotten to resolve things with him after ending everything so abruptly. Guilt weighed on me.

Life with Alex had been stagnant though, so I focused on how thrilling life was with Dan—travel, music, big goals, climbing—and convinced myself that those things were the reward for dealing with his moods. He would oscillate between adoring me as his beautiful climbing goddess, and resenting me as a nuisance who was out to make his life harder. I never knew which I would get, minute to minute, hour to hour, day to day. I'd watch him sulking and try to piece together his blend of emotions, energy, and substances.

Finally, time was up. The big day arrived, whether I was ready or not. I rolled into Salt Lake City with everything I'd need for the trip, and I felt a huge sense of trepidation wrapped up in excitement. It was January 14. Dan and I groaned as we lifted our heavy bags into the bed of his truck, each of them resounding with a large thud, straining against their zippers. The drive to St. George was spent reviewing trip reports, route descriptions, weather forecasts, and flight schedules. Money was tight for me, which wasn't a great omen before the trip, so Dan paid for all the gas. He stomped his Chucks in the slush while shifting back and forth, waiting for his truck to fill up.

At his parents' vacant desert home, we resumed our usual routine for a couple days: grocery shopping at Smith's down the road, cooking nice dinners, and listening to Father John Misty. I felt our connection deepen, the bond and stability between us strengthening as we worked together in the kitchen, cuddled while watching climbing videos, and excitedly flipped through the Patagonia guidebook together. One night, we watched *101 Dalmatians,* and he took to calling himself Pongo and me Perdy (or sometimes Perdita) like the dogs in the movie. It was half romantic, half weird (fully weird, in hindsight). He'd bark at me playfully and give me puppy dog eyes.

Dan stayed up later than I did, smoking California weed his Mormon dad had muled for him and singing while playing guitar or piano in the living room, sometimes stopping to write something down when inspiration struck him. He was a real tortured artist type. I hated how much I adored that.

In the last couple days of preparation, we went up to Snow Canyon to practice hauling, fixing a line, and ascending the rope. Dan said we needed to get our systems dialed so we could operate efficiently even when cold and tired. It felt like cramming before a test, but the stakes were infinitely higher than earning a grade.

The next day, we went up to Zion and climbed 'Kung Fu Fighter,' our final climb to train for Patagonia. Tricky cracks and cold weather were starting to feel normal, which was relieving. The sun set over Mount Spry in Zion, golden hour warming the light on the rock as I swung my arms in the shade to force blood to my numb hands.

That night back at the house, we dumped out our bags and reorganized all of our gear, meticulously going through packing lists and discussing what we actually needed for the trip. The floor was strewn with harnesses, shoes, crampons, ice axes, backpacks, socks, cams, jackets, gloves, energy chews, headlamps, helmets, and miscellaneous items for alpine climbing. After we were done with Fitz Roy, we planned to head to Cochamó, a granite big wall climbing destination in Chile, so we brought a quadruple rack of cams and a portaledge, which greatly increased our amount of gear. We had a substantial amount of climbing and camping equipment, clothing, a drone, and multiple cameras. I raised my eyebrows as the pile grew next to the piano.

Next, Dan said he needed help with another problem: how to bring weed down to Argentina. I swallowed hard, nervous about the repercussions of getting caught, picturing us in handcuffs in a South American prison. My upbringing in a police household had rightfully made me cautious of serious offenses. I pleaded with him not to bring any, but it was futile. I didn't have a choice—I could help him do a good job hiding it in his luggage, or I could increase the risk of being discovered by not helping him.

He was firm that he absolutely needed weed on the trip, or he'd lose his shit. "It's my meds, Fallon. Fuck lithium. Weed is natural and calms me down. I can't live without it."

Arguing with him was useless, since I knew it would end with veiled threats, and him getting what he wanted anyway. Better to cut out the drama and yield to him.

This was certainly the most illegal thing he'd ever asked me to do. I typically took a laissez-faire attitude with Dan; if he wanted to do something that broke the law or that I otherwise didn't approve of, I might say something, but I almost always just let him do his own thing. He could make his own choices, as long as it didn't affect me. This time, it had big potential to fuck up my life. I helped him, but made him agree that it would all be in his luggage, not mine. I didn't smoke weed—my terrible experiences both in Zion and on Thanksgiving were too horrible to consider trying it again—and I wanted no part of it.

The first order of business was preparing our materials. He'd determined that not having all his eggs in one basket would be best, so we divided the hidden weed up into multiple vessels. I watched him carefully, worried about messing up, wanting to make each hiding place perfect.

First, we made small slits in yerba maté tea bags, emptied them out, and refilled them with bud. Then, we carefully resealed them and returned them to the bigger bag full of actual maté tea bags. He figured any drug dogs would be duped since the smell of the real maté would veil any weed smell. I figured that was a load of shit, but it was his scheme, not mine.

Next, we took a package of his favorite little tea candles, and removed the wax from a few of them. We wrapped nuggets of bud in plastic wrap, and then melted the candle wax, letting it reform around the bud in the small metal tins. The end product was plastic-wrapped bud completely encased in the wax, the top of each candle still appearing flat and flush with the edges, a perfect wick sticking up. The candles looked innocent and untampered with. We intermixed the weed candles with the regular candles, and re-wrapped the entire package so it looked new from the store.

Then we took more plastic wrapped bud and deposited pieces below hunks of twist-up deodorant. Again, Dan predicted that the smell of the deodorant and the thick plastic sides of the stick would hide any smell.

The last hiding place he decided on was books. We had a few novels and guidebooks for the trip. Dan had the idea to sprinkle bits of bud between the pages, fluttering the pages of each book as he peppered green crumbs into the binding. I watched topos of Cerro Torre and photos of alpine granite cracks quickly come and go as he thumbed the pages like a deck of cards. Then, he plastic wrapped each book and put a fake price tag on the outside so it looked like he'd purchased each one used and individually wrapped.

After a few hours of this, we observed our handiwork and took turns sniffing each item. We couldn't smell anything, and Dan was pleased with the result. We finished packing and stood in the hallway over our giant bulging bags, wondering how in the hell we'd carry it all through the many airports and up into the mountains.

On the morning of January 17, we rode a shuttle down to Las Vegas, and then spent an hour at the airport weighing our bags and shuffling gear around. Per airline regulations, each bag could weigh a maximum of 50 pounds, so we had to keep moving things from one bag to another to even them out. When all was said and done, we had six 50 pound checked bags, and then two carry-ons each: one smaller backpack as a personal item, and one medium sized duffel for the overhead bin.

It was an almost unmanageable pile of luggage, and we struggled to carry everything. I was dragging a giant piece of luggage, and I had multiple backpacks on: one on the front, one on the back, and one on each arm. I felt exhausted already. Other travelers at the airport eyed our shitshow, rolling their eyes at the amount of stuff. I wanted to scream at them that we were going on a climbing expedition, that I didn't normally pack this much, and that they should mind their own goddamn business. We ditched the checked bags—the gear, and all the weed, was out of our hands now. I tried not to look guilty or suspicious, but I was incredibly nervous as we strolled to our gate.

Now was the time for bravery, the time for climbing, the time to test myself. If I could get through this, maybe I could get through anything. The plane took off; we were destined first for Houston, then Santiago, then Argentina. There was no turning back now.

PART 2

PATAGONIA

(ii)
the second time death kissed me
i lay under new lights
writhing with pain
from a new beast
i ached for the mountains
of last week
for the fresh air not in my lungs
for the dirt not in my hair
for the glacier not under my boots

because now, this was the closest
i'd ever been with death
he was late to the occasion
i yelled at him
"death what took you so fucking long"

he must've been tied up
but i had begged
been begging for hours
yearning for him more with
every needle
every nurse

every ounce of fluid lost

yes, yes, i know

yes, yes, let's go

make this end

groaning on the bed

"death, hurry up you bastard!"

begging went unheard

he arrived too late

a peck on the cheek

and he vanished

CHAPTER 9

SAY IT

January 17 – 21, 2017

"Are you serious right now? What the fuck, dude! How did you not get caught?" My jaw was practically on the floor as the unmistakable smell of cigarette smoke emanated off of Dan.

"Be quiet." Dan looked around at the other passengers on the plane, seeing if anyone noticed the smell.

"Why the *hell* would you do that? Do you wanna go to prison?" I was incredulous. I couldn't risk drawing attention to us, but I wanted to smack him for his stupidity.

"I couldn't stand the nicotine withdrawals, man. I had to. I'd just quickly light one, puff, then flush it down the toilet. I did that a few times so the smoke alarms wouldn't go off."

As if the weed in his checked luggage didn't give me enough anxiety, now I was worried he'd get arrested for smoking on the plane. *What an idiot. How could he jeopardize us like that?* I was livid, but there was nothing I could do about it.

"Why the fuck didn't you just buy nicotine patches or gum or something if you knew this was gonna happen?" I said under my breath. "You should have thought about that. This flight is so long."

Dan didn't have a good reason. Once it seemed like he had actually gotten away with it, he grinned, pleased with his sneakiness like a kid who'd broken into a stash of candy. I shook my head and prayed we'd make it to Argentina with no further mishaps.

I had no such luck. In the airport in Santiago, I felt groggy and stiff—our first time walking since Houston. I stumbled my way through ordering some food in Spanish at a restaurant, my former confidence in my skills evaporating as soon as it actually mattered. In the airport bathroom, I was surprised to see that used toilet paper was thrown away here rather than flushed. Dan came out of the men's bathroom reeking of smoke again.

"Oh my god. Do they not have a designated smoking area here? Why would you risk that *again*?!" I asked him, exasperated.

"I was desperate, okay? Don't worry about it. You're too nervous all the time."

"Christ." I rubbed my temples. "Also, how gross is it that they don't flush the used toilet paper here?"

"Oh, yeah. It's like that everywhere down here. You'll get used to it." He shrugged.

When we landed at the airport in Buenos Aires, all of our bags had to go through various scanners and security checks before we could access them. We anxiously watched the luggage creep along the conveyor belts, grateful when we had claimed all of our bags.

Dan opened up the long, skinny portaledge bag which had been stuffed full of other gear when balancing the bag weights.

"I coulda sworn we had more cams in this bag. Look at these straps. They seem looser than when we tied them up in Vegas. Dirty motherfuckers probably stole some of our shit."

I doubted it and shrugged, taken off guard by his racist assumption. We wouldn't know for sure until we got to a place where we could organize everything. For now, we needed to figure out how to get to our hostel, where we'd stay during our long layover until our flight the next morning to El Calafate. We found the airport exit, and I emerged into the summer afternoon of Buenos Aires, hot, sticky, and bustling. The scene was nothing less than pure chaos, with hundreds of people on the move, transferring luggage, and shouting to bus drivers. The heat and humidity shocked my system; just yesterday I'd been immersed in the Utah winter. I peeled off layers and collapsed on a large duffel bag, exhausted from the flights.

Dan had planned to take a bus into the city, but when that didn't work out, he ran back into the airport to get us a taxi. I sat on the concrete outside with all of our shit, the lone guard for our thousands of dollars' worth of gear.

Finally, Dan re-emerged and our taxi pulled up. We looked at each other and laughed. The car was comically small; fitting everything inside required a Tetris strategy. The trunk filled up quickly, as did the back and front seats. The driver helped us with the mountain of gear, and we squeezed in where we could, sitting on top of and underneath backpacks and duffels. The climbing gear weighed us down even more than the humidity.

The taxi driver was a patient man, accustomed to interacting with foreigners. He spoke English and answered some of our questions, clueing us into the unique pronunciation of certain Spanish words in the area. I was alarmed at the lawlessness of all the drivers; no one followed traffic rules or speed limits here. It was every man for himself. We got closer to *el centro*, the downtown of the city, and I took note of all the unfamiliar plants, architecture, and billboards.

He exchanged money for us—$1 USD for 16 pesos at the time—and warned us about the cash shortage, encouraging us to hold onto our cash whenever we could, and take advantage of opportunities to use our cards instead. Once we got to Patagonia, most vendors would only accept cash, and there were limits on how much we could withdraw at ATMs.

The driver deposited us on a narrow street below our lodging, the Parla Hostel. An old metal grated elevator creaked upwards to a tiny room, overflowing with a bunk bed, dresser, and bookshelf surrounded by our bags. It was cramped, but sufficient for the short layover. I peeled off my sweat-soaked clothes and opted for a moisture-wicking dress in an attempt to survive the heat.

Relieved to have a safe place to ditch our gear, we ventured back into the hostel lobby, where young locals who worked the front desk handed Dan a glass bottle of Quilmes, the beer of choice in Argentina, and one of the locals offered me a joint. I politely declined, and Dan eagerly claimed it. We chatted with them in a mixture of English and Spanish. Our flight was at 4:00 a.m. the next morning, so we only had that evening to explore the city. Cameras in tow, Dan and I set out with no plan; our only goal was to see the city and experience whatever it threw at us.

It was January 18, my 20th birthday, and I could hardly wrap my head around the fact that I got to celebrate it in Buenos Aires. Just a couple months ago, I hadn't known Dan, hadn't even had a passport, and now I was wandering around South America. Life comes at you fast. The streets throbbed with people, the typical city mix from all walks of life, and small *quioscos* graced every corner, advertising beer, cigarettes, and candy. The prices seemed astronomical until I reminded myself to divide by sixteen.

Our first stop was at The Palace of the Argentine National Congress, an imposing structure with a tall, bronze-plated dome on top, before we kept up our walking tour, our curiosity serving as the sole guide. Taxis darted by with no regard for speed limits or signs, and we raced to cross busy streets.

Rectangular visions of concrete jungle mixed with quaint Argentinian art, of marvelous buildings towering over dingy street vendors, captivated me. We let the blocks funnel us along as the evening light faded. We found a small restaurant that miraculously offered gluten free pizza. I sipped wine—an Argentinian Malbec—legally for the first time thanks to the lower drinking age, and we toasted to our adventure and my birthday as the sun set on the bustling city. *If this is how my twenties are going to be*, I thought, *then I'm in for an exciting decade.*

Walking back to our hostel in the dark with our cameras visible was riskier than we would have liked. Dan picked up a rock to carry, and I hid my pocket knife in my hand. His paranoia rubbed off on me. We stayed on high alert, Dan suspicious of every person we passed as we walked a couple miles through the dark city.

Back at the hostel, we sat side by side on the curb. It was late, quiet, and no one was out in this neighborhood. Dan smoked a cigarette. I sighed in the night air and set my chin on my knees, still in disbelief that I was really here. Everything seemed romanticized. Everywhere I looked, I was struck by the contrast of ornate facades and art with the dilapidated storefronts.

"Well, Perdy, I hope you enjoyed your birthday. In a couple days we'll finally be in Patagonia, and you're gonna lose it. Fitz Roy is fucking beautiful! The granite is so good."

With his arm around me, we talked for hours: the places we wanted to travel, the climbs we fantasized about, and our goals for the future. Love and possibility filled the world, and my previous doubts about the trip shrank. The gentle sounds of the city faded into the background as we fueled each other's dreams. We stayed up all night in our private universe on that sidewalk, our bubble undisturbed, our laughter echoing, our kisses unsupervised, not bothering to use the hostel room we'd rented before dawn broke and our perfect soiree came to a forced end. I felt loved and hopeful, the kickoff to my twenties giving me momentum. Dan seemed to levitate as if he was free of any struggles, totally in his happy place in the infancy of the trip, where the possibilities are still endless and one sees their life unfolding like the untroubled beginning of a storybook.

Up we went on the old grated elevator to grab our bags from the room, and then quickly back down again to catch a new taxi. We had to transfer to a different airport than the one we'd arrived at. This time, our driver only spoke Spanish, and we rushed along each *calle* downtown until we were on the outskirts of the city again. This airport was much smaller, as was the plane for the domestic flight to El Calafate.

We were sleep deprived, yet I couldn't doze at all in my cramped seat. When we landed, my hip was extremely sore and stiff. I have a genetic connective tissue disorder called hypermobile Ehlers-Danlos Syndrome (hEDS) that makes my collagen structurally faulty, and causes instability and pain throughout all of my joints and tendons. Sitting in one place for long periods of time is often excruciating and difficult. I limped through the airport with my share of the bags, wincing in pain. I was so tired from the days of travel, I wanted to cry. I felt dehydrated from all the flying, and my body was out of whack.

We emerged to much cooler weather, grateful to be farther south. We stuffed our luggage into a taxi, and took off for El Calafate. The landscape was dramatically different now—far less tropical, more mountainous, with giant freshwater lakes glittering at the edge of the ice cap. Dan pointed in the direction of Fitz Roy, but I couldn't see the mountains quite yet.

We went directly to Don Pepe, a hostel Dan had stayed at on a previous trip. He still remembered the owner, who was gracious to us during our stay. The hostel had a welcoming greenhouse attached to it, and we enjoyed the garden, swinging on a bench among the greenery. I closed my eyes and felt the air blowing past as I swung forward and back, a calming movement after all of the hustle and bustle of the airports.

I got an email about my new credit card from my roommate Ashleigh, who'd agreed to handle my mail and other issues while I was away. I responded to her quickly, and she texted me the card number and information. I saved it, thankful to have it as a backup. Without the physical card, I wouldn't be able to use the account day to day, but at least when it came time for the trip to end, I'd be able to purchase a flight home.

Dan and I walked to dinner in town along cobblestone streets. We passed a local bookstore, and I bought two maps of the Fitz Roy area, my eyes eating up the terrain, analyzing every map name in Spanish. The paper was thick and water resistant, and the massif spread out before me from a bird's eye view. The layout of the range, its glaciers, its proximity to the ice cap, and its rivers all intrigued me. Fitz Roy is the crown jewel and highest point of the range, with a line of other unbelievably steep peaks rising skyward on either side of it. Dan pointed out some of the landmarks and trails we'd encounter during our gear carries and climbing.

The following morning, we lugged all of our bags down a hill and across the main road to a plaza dedicated to veterans and graced with a commemorative statue. We sat there for hours, Dan absent-mindedly smoking cigarettes while I read a book, waiting for the nearby Hertz rental car office to open. Finally, in the early afternoon, Dan drove away with a Chevrolet Classic, a small, silver sedan with just enough room for the two of us plus the bags. Dan stopped to buy an aux adapter so we could play our own music, and then blasted our favorite songs with the windows down as we embarked on the highway toward El Chaltén, our final destination.

Dan hadn't been able to bring a pipe with him, so he carefully bent a Red Bull can and smoked weed out of it while driving. He made sure to demonstrate so that I could craft new makeshift pipes for him out of cans in the future. The drive took a few hours, and we first passed Lago Argentina, and then Lago Viedma, each massive and shimmering blue. Dan barrelled down the empty highway past rural outposts.

We sang along to "Ooh La La" by Faces as loud as we wanted, beaming, delighted to have our own means of transport and to be free of the cramped planes and taxis. I was amazed that we were the only vehicle on the highway.

I geeked out over geologic folds on barren hills visible from the road, the strata arcing elegantly in sweeping bands hundreds of feet high. I put my hand out the window and traced the layers like a conductor of sedimentary structure. Dan, uninterested in my geologic observations, pointed out where we would be able to see Fitz Roy and Cerro Torre on a clear day, but the mountains were shrouded in clouds.

We arrived in El Chaltén, a small touristy town that sits at the base of the mountains, attracting mostly trekkers and climbers. It was January 20, a bit on the later side of the season, but there were still many climbers in town eager for breaks in the weather to bag their objectives. It was also the day of Trump's first presidential inauguration.

"Fuck, I can't believe he actually took office."

"I know. It's so ridiculous. I'm glad we're not there. It's nice to be far away from all of that nonsense." I looked around. It didn't get much further away than *this*. I felt like I had reached the end of the earth.

"I doubt it'll last for long though. I bet someone will"—Dan used his hand like a gun and held it up to his temple—"take care of him before too long. He's just too evil."

Our first hostel had a robin's egg blue exterior and a stone path through a vibrant garden leading back to our room, where we slept like the dead as it drizzled rain outside.

The next morning, I woke up with intense pain from a UTI, so I stayed at the hostel. Dan left with the car so he could get to the trailhead to complete the first gear carry up to what would become our basecamp at Piedra Negra, a rocky spot on the northern side of the range. Our intended route was a long rock climb called "*Maté, Porro y Todo lo Demás*" (which means "Maté, Weed, and Everything Else"—a fitting name for the contents of our packs). The route ascends the North Pillar (*Pilar Goretta*), and after that, one can opt to continue up to the summit of Fitz Roy (*El Chaltén*). Dan wanted to get an early start on lugging our gear up there, and grumbled that he'd have to do this carry alone. Exhausted from travel and the infection, I went back to sleep.

When I woke up, I walked over to the medical clinic in town. I stepped out of the hostel and was immediately staring straight at Fitz Roy for the first time. My heart surged. I could only see the top few thousand feet of pure rock piercing the sky right next to the summit of Poincenot, a fine mist forming a hazy vision. It was so unexpected, so striking, so steep. I stared at it in awe. It was even more impressive than all of the times I'd seen it in climbing films; the sheer scale of the mountain is hard to overstate. At once, I was afraid, but I also longed to be up there, remembering my previous outings in alpine environments. The peaks beckoned to me and I imagined the rush of climbing on the exposed shoulder of a spire thousands of feet above.

I got antibiotics for my UTI after a quick conversation with a local doctor in the tiny medical clinic. I'd gotten too dehydrated on the long flights and hadn't peed often enough, but thankfully the antibiotics would easily clear up the infection.

I went back to the hostel to rest, but got antsy, so I walked around town, getting familiar with the main roads and shops. El Chaltén was nestled in a valley among smaller foothills at the base of the big mountains; it had a surprisingly low elevation, which explained the extreme relief of the Fitz Roy massif shooting straight up into the sky above town. Most of the buildings were fairly modest, and it was easy to tell the brightly colored, modern-looking tourist trap gift shops meant for rich Western trekkers apart from the mom-and-pop joints that mostly served the locals. As I walked, I noticed this divide in the people milling about as well: it was an even split of Argentinian locals and foreign adventurers. The main streets in town were paved, but most of the side roads were dirt. There was no shortage of cafes, restaurants, and hostels to cater to the travelers. Other amenities were limited since the resident population was quite small.

I started to feel a bit better, and decided to go for a mellow hike to get my legs moving after all the days of travel; I needed some exercise. Dan had told me if I felt up to it that I should check out a hike that began near our hostel and went up to Laguna Torre, the stunning lake below Cerro Torre, an iconic and dangerous peak. I put together a small daypack, left him a note on the counter, and started up the trail in the afternoon.

I moseyed along, taking photos of everything along the way. Cerro Torre was still encased in clouds, but the other dramatic mountains all around were magnificent. I wore borrowed mountaineering boots that I still needed to adjust to, and they felt awfully heavy for this mild trail. In less than two hours, I arrived at Laguna Torre in howling winds. My hair flew every which way as I snapped photos of the ice bobbing up and down in the frigid water. The wind barraged my camera too harshly to get decent videos. I could only laugh as I struggled to stand upright. *So this is the infamous Patagonia wind! Holy shit!*

Waves crashed with white foam, smashing ice blocks together. The sun tried valiantly to break through the storm for brief moments, but then the black clouds engulfed it once again. I could barely see the base of Cerro Torre, but I knew it was giant and looming right in front of me. I stared at the wall of clouds, willing myself to be able to see through them to capture a glimpse of it, but was unsuccessful.

I walked back down the trail, happy to have completed the hike to the lake, arriving back to El Chaltén by dinner time. As soon as I was back in view of the town, I saw Dan's rental car recklessly flying down the dirt road toward the trailhead. I assumed he was going to pick me up so we could go get dinner, but as I approached the car, I noticed something was wrong.

"I cannot fucking believe you! You're such a whore! Who the fuck were you hiking with?" Dan screamed at me as soon as I opened the passenger door.

"Dan, whoa whoa whoa. I was alone. I started to feel a little better so I went for an easy hike like you'd told me. I didn't talk to anyone. I don't know what you're talking about!"

"You lying bitch," he fumed. "I know you were with some Israeli bastard! I leave you for one day and of course you'd go meet another man."

"Why do you think that? I am so confused. I have no clue what you mean. I literally just went for a small hike alone because it seemed like the right thing to do to try to get some training in." In my head, I was wondering about the Israeli part. Was there something I had missed? Where did that come from?

Dan drove hectically, careening around corners that sent gravel scattering into the air. I didn't know where he was going, but it wasn't in the direction of the hostel.

"You locked me out! You knew I wouldn't be gone that long, and you fucking left. I couldn't get back in. If you felt good enough to hike, you should've helped me with the gear carry! You're a horrible partner!" He was hysterical and screaming. I was taken off guard. I cried, feeling very out of control of the situation. I worried someone would hear him as we haphazardly drove what seemed like every road in the tiny town.

"Dan, I was in so much pain from the UTI when you left this morning for the gear carry. I didn't know I'd start to feel better later in the day. I didn't expect it. I've never been up the trail for the gear carries, so of course I didn't know how long you'd be gone. How was I supposed to know how far of a drive and hike it is? Plus, you told me to do this hike if I was feeling up to it!"

"Tell me who you were with today! I know you were probably fucking some guy up there!" he demanded.

"It's literally my first day here! How in the world would I have met someone? And you seriously don't trust me? What the fuck!" I yelled back, exasperated.

I couldn't reason with him. I was so upset by his assumptions and targeted questions, and I had no clue where this was coming from. I cried in the front seat, leaning as far into the passenger door as I could to create space between us. He kept yelling at me and punching the steering wheel and his thigh. *What am I going to do? It's the first day and he's already having a psychotic break. What happens now?*

He drifted a dirt corner, screeched to a halt, and slammed the car into park out front of the hostel. He stormed inside. I sat in the car for a few minutes, staring out the window, silently crying. I couldn't bring myself to do anything. I was frozen. I felt so sad that he thought I'd fucked up, and that nothing I said was changing his mind or bringing him back to reason. There was nothing I could say to make him stop screaming, so I just had to hope that he would calm down eventually. It seemed like all of my responses were always the wrong thing to say, and would inflame him even more.

I grabbed my daypack and went inside, hoping to avoid him. He immediately came up to me, face to face, and I started shaking. An intense dread washed over me.

"I can't believe I ever trusted you! I should have known better. Women always do this to me. You fucking cunt!"

"I promise, nothing happened! I literally went for a hike. I can show you the photos and videos and you'll see that I was alone." *Why does he think I was hiking with another dude? I'm so lost.*

"I fucking hate you! You left me to do that gear carry alone and locked me out so you could go flirt with other guys! It makes me wanna die!"

He was making no sense at all, so fixated on this false story he'd made up out of nowhere. He cried, yelled, and punched himself in the head. The blows were hard and repeated. It was as if his thoughts were causing him so much emotional pain that he wanted to knock his own brain out—show it who was boss.

"Dan, stop hurting yourself! It's not helping anything!" I pleaded with him.

"No! This is what I do, Fallon. I hurt myself so I don't have to hurt other people. You're fucking lucky I hit myself instead of you. This is how it works."

"That makes no fucking sense! You don't have to hit anyone else or yourself, Dan." *This is useless. He's not listening.*

I was so overwhelmed by this unexpected, undeserved confrontation that I decided to get in the shower. After all, I'd just gone on a hike, and I thought it would help him calm down to have me out of sight for a while. I wanted a break from this hell.

Before I got in the shower, he cornered me. I was backed into the bathroom wall, fully naked, and he had his arms over each of my shoulders so I couldn't leave the position. He started screaming in my face. I turned my head, but that only made him put his mouth right up to my ear that was facing him.

"You whore! You never loved Alex. When you climbed with me in November, you were cheating on him emotionally."

"That's not true! I needed to break up with him anyway. And I would never cheat on anyone. I'm not my mother!" I sobbed.

"You're a slut. Admit it. You cheated on him emotionally with me."

"No! I never expected to meet you. Just because we climbed together doesn't mean I cheated. I talk about deep stuff with lots of my friends. That's not emotional cheating. I broke up with him before we ever even kissed!" *Why is this happening? What is the point of this?*

"Look at me!" He grabbed my tear-streaked face and turned it toward his. "Say it: 'I'm a slut.' Do it, right now." He stared at me intently, rage in his eyes.

I was so scared and vulnerable, standing there naked. Trapped. I wanted out of the situation more than anything I'd ever wanted in my life. I was learning that the only way to potentially appease him was not by arguing with his psychotic claims, but by agreeing with him, even if it was a lie. Anything to get him to calm down. He was too far gone.

"Fine! I'm sorry! I'm sorry . . ." I cried, holding my arms over my bare chest.

"No! You need to say it! Fucking say it, Fallon!"

"No . . ." I choked out between sobs. "Please don't do this."

He slammed his hands against the wall on either side of my head. "Say it."

"Okay! I'm a slut! Are you happy?"

He looked at me in disgust, left the bathroom, and started hitting himself on the head again. I shut the bathroom door, put my hand over my mouth, and fell to my knees. I turned on the shower water to drown out my sobs. I felt so violated. It was a lot easier to be sympathetic and sweet during his mental breaks when I wasn't the target. When I became the enemy in his head, helping him was the last thing I wanted to do.

When I was done showering, I got dressed, and as soon as I came out of the bathroom, the fighting continued. He was just as unhinged, yelling insults and accusations at me as he hit himself.

"Look at what you make me do to myself!" *Thud, thud, thud.* "Aren't you glad I don't do this to you instead?!" *Thud, thud, thud.*

I looked away, horrified. I tried to remind myself that the suffering from the imbalances in his brain was far greater than the challenge I faced by listening to him lose his mind. But in the moment, that was little consolation as the nightmare in front of me intensified.

"Aren't you going to stop me? You never fucking loved me! If you loved me, you wouldn't do this to me! This is *you* doing this to me . . ." His shouting faded into tortured crying.

I went over to the couch and tried to hold his arms down so he wouldn't punch himself. He was stronger than me, and strained against me. He contorted his neck, and pulled back so he'd be closer to the wall. Sweat soaked his shirt. He started slamming his head into the wall.

"Dan! You have to stop. Please! Don't do this. It's going to be okay. Try to take some deep breaths." He seemed not to hear me.

"I just . . . I can't . . . I'm so alone." His voice was quiet now, and his eyes were vacant, like he was very far away. His head knocked more gently against the wall now, tears streaming down his face.

"Breathe, Dan. Calm down. What can I do for you?"

"Nothing. You're a bitch." He got up and went over to the stove. He filled a pot with water, added rice and lentils, and set it on a burner.

Just like that, it was over. It was like when a storm suddenly stops, and you tilt your head up to the sky, surprised to find no more rain falling down. He had finally escaped the spiral, and was cooking dinner like nothing had happened. My mind was spinning with everything he'd said, the implications of his words.

I felt a small shift within, a slight hardening of my heart with the realization that no one was coming to save me. For the time being, I needed to protect myself. I didn't have a way out, so I had to play the game. Our relationship had reached a turning point, and there was no going back to how we used to be. Not after what he'd said. Not after what he'd done. I composed myself.

We ate dinner, and Dan apologized profusely. His apology meant little to me, but I accepted it. We looked up the weather forecast, and talked about the patterns, wind, precipitation, and what it meant for climbing. We messaged our families to update them, and of course I didn't mention the fight. I told them everything was going great, and focused on the beauty of the landscape.

When we went to bed, I turned away from him and tried not to touch him, which bothered him. I couldn't stomach being close to him. I had to figure out how to survive this, one way or another.

CHAPTER 10

VENOM

January 22 – 24, 2017

The Chevy Classic blew down the dirt road out of town, destined for the Río Electrico trailhead. We had hulking packs ready for the gear carry, and full bellies from breakfast at Cúrcuma, a local vegetarian joint. I pointed my camera out the car window for the entire half hour drive, excited to see new views of the landscape, mountains, and rivers. Most climbers had to walk, hitchhike, or pay a taxi in order to get to this trailhead, but we thankfully had the rental car, which simplified our logistics.

The trail begins with a river crossing, then wanders through an open flat stretch of gravel. It slowly grades into the forest in the valley, always paralleling the river. In the forest, I was surprised at the lack of underbrush—it was like someone had planted thick trees at intervals of a few feet, with nothing between them, just a soft, short bed of green grass. The weather was moody, with indecisive clouds lightening their loads intermittently. The trees were relatively small, but provided welcome shelter from rain and wind.

We padded along the gentle trail for a few miles until it opened up onto the banks of the river, exiting the trees. We reached Piedra del Fraile, a privately-owned *refugio* that serves drinks and food, and offers expensive beds for the night for trekkers.

"This place is a fucking scam. You're supposed to pay them a fee when you hike through, but I avoid it as much as I can. Let's go inside this time though. Fuck the rain."

Inside, Dan sipped on a beer while we watched the downpour. The weather was worsening, so we opted not to carry our packs all the way up to Piedra Negra, which would be our basecamp. Dan pointed out the rocky slope we'd have to trudge up next time: steep, with thousands of feet of elevation gain. I knew I hadn't been training enough prior to the trip. *My poor legs. I'm so screwed.*

We stashed our bags at the edge of the forest and hiked out. Our spirits were high, almost as if the fight had never happened. He was in a good mood, and I didn't question it—I just tried to ride with it for as long as possible, enjoying the fun and grateful that everything seemed better between us.

We wandered El Chaltén and bought food that we'd need in order to become established up at our camp. With all of my allergies, it was difficult to find options that I could eat. I discovered *dulce de leche*, a sugary treat. I ate it straight out of the container like an energy gel. I didn't have many other options for quick sugar. It became my favorite snack, along with gluten free *alfajores*, Argentinian pastries that consist of two cookies separated by a filling (which was typically *dulce de leche*). Otherwise, I was stuck with rice, lentils, and almonds from an overpriced natural foods store, while Dan got all the variety he could ever want or need from a regular market. It was essential for us to bring enough food to give us time to wait out storms and then be fueled for a potential summit attempt when the time came.

We ducked into random cafes for coffee and downtime. On days spent in town, I wrote in my travel journal, dutifully jotting down every detail, while Dan reviewed photos from his camera.

As we got more familiar with El Chaltén, we made friends with the street dogs. Dan would get right down in the dirt and cuddle them, scratching behind their ears and talking to them in a cute voice. Whenever we saw our favorite dogs, he'd run up to them and tussle with them in the middle of the deserted roads. Watching Dan with the dogs reminded me that he could be loving, gentle, and sweet. I thought maybe his previous meltdown was a random one-off triggered by sleep deprivation, and that we'd be good for the rest of the trip. I felt hopeful as I watched him tangle with the scruffy pack on the dusty roads, tails wagging on every dog and a huge grin on Dan's face.

That night, Dan got us a new place to stay: a lovely rental with an open second floor, with two extra beds in a loft above the other bedroom, kitchen, bathroom, and dining table. It felt extravagant compared to the typical hostels in town, where you bunked with other travelers and used grimy communal bathrooms.

"We shouldn't need too many more nights in town, Perdy. I think we'll be up on the mountain for most nights here pretty soon. Might as well be comfortable for now." He smiled at me as he made dinner. His expensive taste was out of my price range, and I wondered how he had enough money to pay for something so fancy. *Guess his parents are hooking him up. We belong with the dirtbags at the regular hostels.*

"It's really nice, thanks. Definitely better than freezing our butts off in the tent up there." I paused, walking over to help him wipe off the counter where he'd spilled some sauce. "Man, you're a messy chef!" I said lightheartedly, laughing.

He was not amused. "Fuck, I can't do anything right."

"I didn't mean it like that, babe. I was just playing around."

"Nah, that was so rude." His voice got louder. "How could you be such an ungrateful bitch?"

"I promise I was just joking. Pongo . . ." I looked at him, using his nickname in the hope that he'd see I meant no harm. "I really am grateful to be here, and I'm sure this dinner will be great."

"You don't appreciate anything I do for you. I get you this nice ass rental, make you dinner, and what do you do? Insult me!" He slammed down the spoon he was cooking with. "I can't deal with this. Fuck this."

He stomped out of the apartment. I wasn't sure how long he'd be gone, but I was nervous for his return. I ate in silence and took my nightly antibiotic. Throughout my body, my tendons screamed in pain. He startled me when he came back with a bottle of Malbec. He'd spiraled during his errand.

"You never appreciate anything! I fucking bend over backwards for you. I take you here to this goddamn beautiful place. Put you up in a fancy room. Feed you. Shower you with love. I never get my love reciprocated from anyone!" He chugged from the bottle and took an Ambien.

It reminded me of my mom's attitude when I was a kid. She was always demanding gratitude for all of the "sacrifices" she'd made. I never could figure out what she'd given up, besides giving up on being a decent mother to us and leaving. All I could think of was her suffocating control, forcing me to miss climbing competitions to attend useless Girl Scout events with her (that I wholeheartedly loathed) despite my protests, and constantly making negative comments about my weight and appearance.

I tried to assure Dan that I was grateful, and remind him that I thanked him often for what he did for me. I shifted into de-escalation mode, navigating what he needed to hear in order to chill out, talking as sweetly and calmly as I could.

Nothing worked.

I zoned out while he yelled at me and threw things around the apartment. If I could just feel like I wasn't actually there, then it wasn't so bad. Dissociation meant survival.

I remembered when I was a little girl, there was a big wooden cabinet in our living room that was mostly empty. I'd crawl inside and shut the doors, tucking my knees under my chin and hugging my scrawny legs to myself. I'd close my eyes and just pretend to not exist. I did this regularly as a kid. My sisters would always poke fun at me when they caught me in the cabinet. In hindsight, maybe I just needed an escape sometimes. These were my earliest memories of dissociation, and the skill was serving me now to endure Dan's breakdown.

We ended up sleeping in separate beds. He was up in the loft, and I was down on the main floor, but since it was all one big open room, he could hear me and see part of the downstairs area. I cried silently in bed. I hadn't meant my comment to hurt him. *How do I keep fucking this up? I don't know what to say. He's just so volatile. Explosive. One spark, and it all goes to shit. I don't know how to make him not hate me.*

I longed for the early period of our relationship, when everything had been easy, and the days were full of climbing, sunshine, and laughter. So much had happened in the two months since we'd first met. The loving, fun side of Dan seemed to disappear in pieces, a slow attrition as the walls hiding his mental illness and addiction crumbled in front of me.

I thought he was going to dump me, leave me in the street the next morning to fend for myself. I devised a plan. I already had gear stashed up in the mountains now, so I set out hiking clothes for the morning. I intended to quietly pack early in the morning and leave with everything I had. I'd hitchhike up to the trailhead, get my gear down, and then take a bus elsewhere. It was over for sure. I was solemn, reserved, and felt deeply alone. The fear rose in my throat, but I pushed it down, resolved to leave.

The next morning, my alarm went off early. I quietly changed into my hiking outfit. I accepted that my plan was the only way. I was determined to reclaim my autonomy and get back all of my stuff. If he thought I was an ungrateful bitch, then surely it must be better for me to leave him alone. As I tried to creep out the door, Dan got up. He was just as livid as the night before.

"What are you doing? Trying to sneak off without me? Leave me here alone?" He was seething. "How could you?"

"You said I was ungrateful, so I figured I'd be doing you a favor by leaving. All I do is make you mad. Let me go. I'll get my stuff and not bother you anymore. You can find a better partner for Fitz Roy than me, anyway," I reasoned.

"No! You do not get to give up on this right now. Do you know how much time and money I invested to come here last year, and we didn't even fucking make it to the base of the climb because of the weather?! I'm not letting that happen again." He shook his head. "We have to do this, and you're coming with me."

"Dan, please, we both know this is not gonna work. I can't stand feeling like I always react wrongly to you."

"Fuck, dude, I can't believe you were gonna go up there and—what? Just retrieve all your shit and then leave? That makes me want to fucking die! You're committed to this! There is way too much riding on this." His eyes got wilder as the psychosis settled in. He hugged himself with his arms, rubbing his hands up and down his forearms as he blocked the front door.

"Please don't make me do this . . ." I begged. My resolve to carry out my plan lessened with each thing he yelled at me.

"Look, Fallon, we have way more gear, we're more prepared than I was last year, and you're a better partner. You don't get to just leave now!" His voice rose as he started shoving things into a backpack. "This is my goal, and you're coming with me even if you don't want to. You don't have a choice! Get a fucking bag and start putting gear in it!" he yelled while motioning to our pile of equipment. "We're going up to do a gear carry *now*!" he commanded.

The thought of moving more of my gear even farther up the mountain scared me. The more established we were at higher elevations, the more committed I'd be, and the less chance I'd have to get out. *I don't want to be stuck up there with him acting like I'm his climbing slave.*

"C'mon! Get your shit together!" He tossed me a bag and pointed to the gear we needed to bring up. I weighed my options. Trying to run didn't seem possible. He'd just come after me, and then what? Where would I go? He'd catch me easily, and then he'd be even angrier. I reluctantly started putting equipment into the pack, and my cries turned to sobs.

"You're coming with me whether you like it or not! You're mine, dammit, and you're going to help me get up that mountain because that's why we're fucking here. I can't fail again!"

"I'm not your climbing slave," I protested, even as I followed his orders. "Dan, let me leave. You said I'm ungrateful. Just let me go." I looked longingly at the door.

"Yes, you are. Keep putting shit in your pack and shut up."

What the fuck. He really thinks I'm his climbing slave. How do I get out of this? I don't want to go up the mountain with this lunatic. I didn't want to think of the consequences if I refused.

Dan frantically threw things into his bag, smoked some weed, and popped an Adderall. He looked like a wild animal, enraged, determined, and ready to attack anything that got in his way. With ragged breaths and shaky hands, I finished packing my bag, filled my water bottles, and laced up my shoes. We loaded our packs into the rental car, and Dan rocketed out of El Chaltén, his erratic driving mirroring the hurricane churning in his mind. A cloud of dust rose behind us as he went double the speed limit on the dirt road to the trailhead.

"Fuck! Look at this perfect weather!" He pointed up at Fitz Roy. The entire range was baking in the sun with only pure blue skies above. It was calm, with little wind—ideal climbing weather. "We should fucking be up there! If you'd helped me with that gear carry the first day, and been a better partner, then we'd already be established up there, and we could fucking go for the summit! But no. You ruined everything!" he screamed as he maneuvered the corners on the winding road.

He was completely out of control, and I faced away as far as I could in the passenger seat, trying to create space, apologizing through my tears. "Dan, please, it's not my fault! I'm sorry!"

"We never get weather windows like this in Patagonia! How could we possibly be wasting this? We came too late! If you were a man, we wouldn't have had this problem! A male would've helped me carry all the gear in the first two days, and we could be up there climbing already! You useless bitch!"

"I can't control that I'm a girl! You're the one who told me I'd be the perfect partner for Patagonia and that I'd be ready for this! If you wanted a guy, you should've brought a fucking guy! I'm sorry I got a UTI, and that it rained, and that we had to buy food in town, but I can't control any of those things."

He slid off the dirt road at the trailhead and parked the car.

"Get out! It's time to go!" He shouted orders at me. We put on our packs, and he took the lead. He started punching himself in the head as he walked. I was horrified, and could barely keep up with him. As soon as we entered the forest, he took one of his ice axes off his backpack.

"You bitch! You fucked all of this up!" He chucked the ice axe with astounding force, and it ricocheted off a tree trunk. He retrieved it like it was some kind of fucked up boomerang.

"I can't fucking put up with this anymore! I want to die! This isn't fair!" He threw the ice axe again. I stayed behind him so I wouldn't be in the target range. Over and over, he screamed, hucked the ice axe, retrieved it, and repeated. I cried as I hiked, hoping someone would come along the trail and witness his behavior.

Suddenly, he stopped, and his rage melted into sadness. He let his pack drop to the ground, and then he curled up on a boulder in the fetal position. He was whimpering, muttering indecipherable words, and contorting himself into odd shapes. He'd lift up his head, and then slam it back into the rock. He clawed at his own skin and pulled hard on his clothing. I approached him warily, not wanting to set him off, but also unable to tolerate watching him do this to himself. As I got closer, he screamed at me to get away. I backed off and waited, watching from a safe distance.

"I hurt myself so I don't have to hurt you. Why do you do this to me . . . ?" his voice trailed off as his head bounced up and down on the boulder. I was appalled and hurt, and didn't know how to intervene; frankly, I didn't even want to at this point. Dan's strange behavior was totally disturbing and freaked me out. My tendons were starting to hurt even more, and I could feel a deep ache in my forearms, hips, knees, and ankles. The emotional and physical pain overlapped in my body.

After a few minutes, he got up, put his pack on, and kept walking up the trail. He swung his ice axe angrily, and it *thumped* as the blade sunk into tree bark. He'd yank it out and brandish it aggressively as he screamed insults at me. Fear swelled within me until it was bigger than my own body, finding a release only in my tears and shakiness. I tried to dissociate from what was happening, but it was all too raw, undeniably happening to me right here in the woods.

"You cunt! I fucking hate you! You're the most incompetent person I've ever met! You're not a fucking climber. You're an ungrateful slut." He spit the words at me.

Eventually he saw people coming down the trail, and it was like a switch was flipped—immediately, a calm washed over him. He looked completely normal, and the ice axe lazily swung by his side. I wiped my tears, incredulous at how easily he could just turn it on and off. The hikers passed us without thinking anything of it. I secretly hoped one of them noticed what was happening. As soon as they were out of sight, Dan's rampage resumed. I struggled to keep up with him.

He looked at me in disgust. "Ya know, you really look like a man when you wear your hair in a ponytail. You sound like a dude when you talk about climbing too." He mocked me, trying to imitate my speech. "You think you're so strong. You're not. You're not even hot either. You're not that pretty girl I wanted."

I'd never seen someone look me in the eye with such hatred. His words felt like knives to the gut. How could he have gone from adoring me, complimenting me, and talking up my climbing, to *this*? Was this what he'd thought all along? Why did it matter if I looked pretty when I was trying to climb hard? I slowed down my pace as tears streamed down my face, wanting to fall back in the hope that he would continue ahead without me.

"You don't have a fucking chance at Fitz Roy. You're just a manly nerd! Geology this, science that. Give me a break." He pointed at the rocks all around us and then looked at me and scowled. "God, you look horrible without makeup on. You know, it's hard to be nice to you when you look ugly." He started walking backwards so he could face me as he harangued me. "You're just a comp climber. The high-pointing you did was so lame. You're no alpinist," he scoffed, planting his ice axe into another innocent tree.

I kept asking myself why in the world I was carrying more gear up this mountain with this awful person when I just wanted to leave more than anything. It was as if I could feel the venom in his words poisoning me, pulsing through my veins like a toxin dead set on stopping my heart. I wanted to disappear. The variety of insults was overwhelming, each one making me more insecure, more worn down, more hollow.

"Please, then why am I going with you? If you think I suck and I have no chance?" I asked nervously, my voice breaking.

"Because we came all the way here! So much time and money wasted! I am not failing again. I'm going to get to the top no matter fucking what! And you're helping me, bitch!"

I was crying uncontrollably and couldn't form a response.

"Jesus, you're such an ugly crier. It's seriously hard to be nice to you when you look ugly. You're so pathetic," he laughed.

The miles dragged on. This trail felt like a hell I couldn't escape. I gave up on trying to respond to him or reason with him. His mental state was too precarious, so I just cried and kept my mouth shut, hoping his brain would put a halt to his tirade. Every time a hiking party passed us, Dan put on his fake air of calm, nodded at the people as they walked by, and then went right back to screaming as soon as they were out of sight. If he had such good control to be able to turn off his rage at the drop of a hat, then why did he have to continue the breakdown? I couldn't understand.

I felt like livestock being led to the slaughter.

We retrieved our previously stashed gear near Piedra del Fraile and rearranged the bags so we could fit everything for the slog up to basecamp. I started up the long, rocky slope for the first time, my thighs burning, my shoulders aching with the weight of the various packs stacked on my back.

My heart felt odd, and it kept fluttering and skipping beats. I'd stop and gasp, scared by the sudden arrhythmias. I put my hand on my chest, wishing I could reset my heart. I'd been at much higher elevations before and never had this problem, so it must have been from another cause. I didn't know what was happening, but I had to keep going up. There was hardly a trail. The path wound around small streams of glacial snowmelt. I tried to step on rocks, but often had to trudge straight up through soggy dirt covered in spongy green vegetation. My shoes soaked through almost instantly.

Some European climbers descended the trail, and told us what was happening higher on the mountain. "Oh, very bad ice fall. Sun is making everything melt. Too many climbers in the *Supercanaleta*, ice falling on each other. No one getting the summit." The climbers looked like sturdy men, outfitted in the nicest lightweight gear and neon layers. They were solid, trustworthy. I was grateful that my oversized gas station sunglasses were hiding my puffy, red eyes.

I looked at Dan. He had been so upset that we weren't climbing in this perfect weather, yet the sun had created new issues of its own. Since we intended on a rock route, we needed to wait for it to finish thawing out. *Looks like it wasn't my fault after all. It wouldn't be ready for us yet anyway.* I tried to reassure Dan of this, but he just shot me a glare, not wanting to blow up at me in front of these other climbers. We thanked them for the info, and they continued down.

I gazed up at this new view of Fitz Roy, Mermoz, and Guillaumet, amazed at the formidable walls of rock rising out of the massif. Looking back when I needed to catch my breath, I saw the Río Electrico valley unfold below me, swaths of gray gravel cut by the frigid braided stream, with colossal snowy mountains rising up on the other side of it. As we gained elevation, I saw the Southern Patagonian Ice Field spilling over between sharp spires in the distance; the map showed the Chilean border cutting across the ice nearby.

It was one of the most interesting, dramatic alpine environments I'd ever been in, but I was distracted by Dan's meltdown. We had about a thousand feet of elevation gain left to get to Piedra Negra, but Dan decided he'd had enough. *Ironic, considering he was hell bent on getting established and in position for a climbing attempt.* A small cave created by large boulders leaning against one another provided a hidden place to stash our gear. We arranged the bags, wrapping them up in the rainfly of the tent to protect them.

Without saying anything to me, Dan took off down the trail. I followed at my regular speed. The swampy, muddy, loose talus was even worse on the downhill than it had been on the trek up. My soaked shoes slid down the rocks into small pools of water. Dan got farther away from me, becoming just an ant below, and I was grateful to be alone, free of his torturous screams and nasty insults. I felt a pressure in my chest loosen as the distance between us increased, but I still couldn't stop crying. I'd never felt so broken, so bullied, so used. The hike down passed in a blur of tears, my body trying to process its anguish.

He was waiting for me near the river at the bottom of the steep section, and I hiked right past him without making eye contact. I could hardly believe all the terrible things he'd said to me on the hike in; it was impossible to even look at him.

He followed right behind me. I could tell that he was calmer now and had emerged from the spiral, but I wanted nothing to do with him.

"Fallon, I'm sorry. I didn't mean anything I said. Seriously."

I was hesitant, as if I was sizing up a dog that had savagely bit me but now wanted to cuddle. I kept walking while staring straight ahead at the trail. *Asshole.*

"Please, Fallon, talk to me. I'm so sorry. I lost it. You know how my bipolar is sometimes."

"The things you called me . . ." I shook my head. "Everything you said hurt me a lot. Swinging the ice axe around was terrifying. Just because you have bipolar doesn't mean you get to take things out on me. Who the hell do you think you are to be able to insult me like you did? Why did you say all of those things?" I asked, my voice scratchy from crying.

"You're right. I'm so sorry."

I kept hiking, my hands balled into fists. What if I told him what was wrong, and then it set him off again? I needed to tread carefully to avoid another breakdown. My nerves couldn't handle it, so I proceeded with extreme reluctance.

"You can't call me things like that. Bitch, cunt, slut, ugly, manly . . . You just can't. It was horrible. I couldn't even help you. I thought you loved me. Having bipolar doesn't mean you get to be so evil to someone. That's a *choice* you made, to say all of that." I was heartbroken. I explained to him how hard it had been to watch his violence, to witness the full capacity of his rage. I was traumatized by how he'd so quickly turned into a monster, and since he was being receptive, I told him how I felt.

"I promise I won't say those things to you again. It's like my brain plays tricks on me and tells me to say and do bad things. When I'm in it, I don't have control. It's hard to explain . . ." He sounded apologetic, but I was skeptical.

"Do you know how horrible it was? Sorry doesn't cut it, dude! You were so scary. I don't want to be here with you. It was awful." I let out a trembling breath.

He reached for my hand, desperate to make amends, but I pulled away. Some sins can't be forgiven.

All I could see in my head was him possessed, hitting his head, throwing the ice axe, whimpering on the rock, vicious words flying out of his mouth. When I looked at Dan now, with his puppy dog eyes and kind demeanor, it was hard to believe this was the same person. It was so confusing. My thoughts were disjointed and unable to form an assessment, but I knew deep down that I had lost most of my trust in him. I could never look at him the same with the knowledge of what he really thought of me. The despicable words he said could never be taken back. I was overwhelmed with the urge to get out of there, to plot my escape, but felt helpless and stuck.

As I told him what was wrong with what he'd done, he apologized profusely and nodded along like he was on board. I was glad to get an apology, but it didn't feel like enough to make up for what I'd had to endure. Relief had washed over me when his tirade had ended, but the hours of deranged images still played in my mind repeatedly to the soundtrack of his echoing insults.

We made it back to town and got cleaned up. I stopped at a store to buy some aspirin—I was worried about my heart after the bizarre arrhythmias I'd experienced on the gear carry. I was nervous about my stomach ulcer from the ibuprofen, my tendon pain from the antibiotics, and various other health issues. *Why is my body doing this to me?*

Dan took me out to dinner at El Viejo Nando, one of the nicest restaurants in town. He said it was the least he could do to make up for his behavior. I ate rosemary potatoes and one of the best steaks of my life—Argentinian beef was famous for a reason. We chatted in the soft warm light of the restaurant, Dan acting normal while I tried to wrap my head around the fact that this was the same person as the monster who attacked me earlier in the day. Was it possible to still love this Dan while putting up with his dark side?

After dinner, we walked down the street so he could buy cigarettes. He'd run out of American Spirits and now had to smoke whatever he could find at the *quioscos*. Whatever brand it was, he usually complained about the tobacco being too harsh and the price being too high, but he sucked them down all the same. The wind never stopped, so we'd huddle together to block it long enough for him to get a light. He was almost out of weed already as well, which shocked me based on how much he'd managed to smuggle down here.

While I waited for him to smoke, I made an Instagram post with a photo I'd taken up in the mountains. He read it over and shook his head. "No, no, no. You should say *this* instead." He took my phone and edited the caption with his version. I was too tired to argue.

We stopped to listen to live music by a band of nomadic Chilean musicians. It was enchanting, full of life and color. The hippies and the Euros and the climbers all danced together in the dirt in the shadows of the Fitz Roy massif under the setting sun. This was what I'd imagined travel would be like. They swayed with their instruments, picking up on each other's cues, their baggy patterned clothes flowing as they moved, engrossed in their music. I tried to get lost in the music with them, eager to escape my new reality.

CHAPTER 11

PAMPAS FOR PORRO

January 2017

I dropped my remaining bags down next to the bunk bed on a rough wooden floor. I looked up to see another woman on the top bunk. She greeted me and we introduced ourselves. I gave her a weak smile, exhausted from my ordeal, and she went back to reading. I sat on the bottom bunk and looked out the window at the mountains. I wrung my hands together. *Is he going to find me?* I put my head in my hands, feeling my chapped lips and puffy eyes.

Despite Dan's attempts at an apology the previous night, I couldn't shake the experience of his rampage on the gear carry. He had struck me with his words and his aggression. I still couldn't process all he had said to me, but in the morning, I'd decided to leave. I didn't feel safe with him. Enough was enough. I'd gathered the belongings I still had in town and walked to a different hostel. I paid in cash at the front desk and booked myself a dorm bed in this shared room. It had been a bold move, my bravest yet. I checked my iPhone to make sure my location was still turned off.

I didn't know what to do, so I kept looking out the window and thinking about my next steps. I wanted to get far away from Dan. I thought about buying a bus ticket. I'd met some cyclists who had biked down the length of Patagonia, and they'd mentioned there was a bus route that followed a similar path. I imagined myself getting on the bus alone, feeling the relief with every additional mile of distance between me and Dan. Being alone sounded fabulous.

I laid back on the bed and looked at my phone, searching up bus routes and other options. I journaled for a while, celebrating my newfound independence, and then organized everything in my bags. I needed some time to let myself relax and try to think clearly about my plan. I needed to get into the mountains first to get my stuff back, and then I could get out of here.

After a couple hours, I heard footsteps outside the door. Dan opened the door and my heart jumped out of my chest. He saw the other woman, and then told me, "Come here." I tried to stay calm and powerful, and kept my head held high as I followed him into the hallway. I didn't want to let him make me feel lesser anymore.

"What do you want?" I said, trying to sound aloof.

"You can't just run off on your own. It's not safe. You need to come back with me."

"It's not safe? Really?" I laughed. "As if I'm safe with *you*. Or did you forget about yesterday already?"

He rolled his eyes. "Get your stuff."

"No. I'm on my own path now. You should leave me alone." I turned to go back into the room, determined to be done with this asshole once and for all.

"Fallon, I'm not asking. You're going to grab your bags, and go back to my hostel with me," he instructed.

"Oh yeah? What if I don't?" I challenged him. I could see he was surprised by my lack of acquiescence. In a public place, he usually wouldn't pull anything, so it was safer to talk back here than in a private setting. He was too prideful to embarrass himself in front of other people typically. I was emboldened by my choice to leave and wanted to keep momentum. I thought other people in this hostel would protect me if it came to that.

He went back into the room and shouldered my bags. I protested and told him to drop my stuff. When he didn't, I tried to pull my backpack off of him, but he twisted and easily shrugged me off. He walked out with my bags and I followed him.

"Stop! I'm not going with you!" I raised my voice now in the hopes that it would make him listen. Apparently, today was a rare day where he didn't care about causing a scene in public. Maybe my actions had actually made him realize how serious I was about leaving.

"Yes, you are! Stop being ridiculous! You don't just get to abandon me." He walked down the stairs toward the lobby and communal kitchen. "Remember, you don't have a choice, Fallon. You're my partner and you're climbing with me!" he half-yelled, trying to rein himself in but failing.

Back to the climbing slave order, I thought. I felt a pang of dread as my autonomy slipped away again.

"Please, Dan! Stop! I don't want to go with you. Just let me leave." He didn't stop. "Jesus! Fucking stop, okay?" I pleaded. I wanted to knock him to the ground, but I knew I couldn't.

We were next to the communal kitchen now where a few trekkers were sipping maté together. They glanced up, semi-intrigued by the drama. Dan shot them a *mind-your-own-business* glare, and they went back to their conversation. They seemed relatively unconcerned. I didn't want to cry, but I felt a lump in my throat. I wanted to keep my power so badly, but I was failing.

"Dan. I'm staying here. I already paid. Leave me alone!" I said, trying to hide the desperation in my voice. He ignored me and walked out of the hostel with all of my stuff. I looked around frantically for someone to back me up, but was out of luck. They paid me no mind. I ran out after him.

He trudged down the gravel road toward the main strip. I walked behind him, trying to think fast for a solution. How could I make him listen? He walked into a cafe, dropped my bags on the ground, and sat at a table.

For a couple hours, he argued with me about the situation. I defended myself, reminded him of his unacceptable behavior, and fought for my freedom, but I ultimately lost. He made it very clear that he wasn't going to let me leave. If I tried, he would track me down. My power had been sapped, and now I was stuck again. *I should've gone straight to the bus station instead of the hostel*, I thought. I kicked myself for the missed opportunity.

No matter where I went or what I tried, he was going to find me, and he was going to win. I felt shackled.

Dan showed me the Reddit app on his phone, a post pulled up about where to find weed in Argentina. He was down to his last bowl of bud and was itching to resupply.

"I don't know why I can't seem to get any here in Chaltén. Assholes, I guess. But this guy is saying I could find weed in Río Gallegos. The weather looks shit here anyway, so there's no point in rotting in the tent up there. Let's take a road trip and go find out."

"Do you have the gas money for that? It sounds kinda sketchy . . ."

"Fallon, it'll be fine! We'll make it fun. I need weed, you know that. It's my medicine. I don't wanna have another breakdown like before. Weed helps me stay calm so I don't have to be like that again." I shuddered, remembering his behavior.

Most of our gear was stashed up on the mountain, so we loaded up what we had left into the rental car, bought Red Bull at the local market, and queued up our favorite Spotify playlist. The gas station on the edge of town had a long line, but before we knew it, we were speeding down the highway toward El Calafate.

He sang along to "Jumper" by Third Eye Blind as the plains whizzed by out the window, quickly passing by the large lakes and arriving back to El Calafate. I messaged my roommates about where we were going, and I did some research from my phone about the tendon pain I'd been having. It turned out that the antibiotic I was on, Ciprofloxacin, was known to cause tendon problems, among other serious side effects. It's especially bad for folks who have connective tissue problems (like my hEDS). *Fuck. Isn't that just the icing on the shit cake of this trip?*

We were about to venture into new territory, jetting southeast all the way across Argentina to the Atlantic coast. Río Gallegos is a port town six hours from El Chaltén, and one of the southernmost cities in the country.

The desolate *pampas*—vast flat plains—stretched out before us. Dan ignored the speed limit signs as miles and miles passed without seeing another vehicle. He stopped to pull over and pee in the dirt, not worried about being spotted. We continued down the highway, transported deeper into this landscape so different than the alpine mountain environment we'd just been in.

Rheas, ostrich-like birds with long legs, ran across the open expanses. I'd never seen anything like it in the wild. Dan was afraid of the rheas, and as I crept closer for a video of one, he yelled at me to stop and come back to the car. I just laughed. What was the bird going to do? There was no need to be afraid.

Occasionally we passed *estancias*, rural estates coming and going in blink-and-miss-it towns that were rarely labeled on the GPS. For the most part, the lonely road seemed to be leading us nowhere as the dry scenery remained the same. Everything was beige and tan: the dirt, the arid plants, the scarce wildlife blending into a monochromatic world.

We rounded a bend in the highway, and suddenly we were at a surprise military checkpoint. Armed soldiers and police motioned for us to get out of the car. Dan started sweating, and told me to play it cool.

"*¿De dónde vienes?*" one of the officers asked us as they inspected our passports.

"El Chaltén. *Somos andenistas,*" I explained. Men with huge guns popped the trunk of the rental car and started pulling out our backpacks. The officer looked me up and down, having a hard time imagining a young American girl in a sundress as a mountain climber.

"*¿A dónde vas ahora?*" he continued.

"*Río Gallegos. Queremos ver el país. Argentina es muy linda,*" I said with a big smile, trying to seem like a nonthreatening tourist. The interviewing officer looked over at Dan, who was intently watching the others rifle through our bags, shifting his weight from side to side in his Converse.

The officer asked us a few more questions, and when they were satisfied with their vehicle search, we were allowed to go.

"Oh thank God. Fuck the cops and the feds. That was spooky," Dan said as we drove away. He turned the music back up, lit a cigarette, and continued on the two-lane road across the plains. Slowly, our surroundings turned more and more urban. Billboards popped up along the bleak gray road, more gas stations, dilapidated buildings, and streetlights appeared, and the road started widening into a proper city highway.

On the outskirts of the city, we passed another military checkpoint, where we had to repeat the process: out of the car, bags searched, answer the typical questions in Spanish. I was becoming more confident every day since I was forced to practice constantly, but I knew I still sounded like a beginner.

It was afternoon already as we entered the city. Confusing signs and road patterns gave us a navigational challenge, but we eventually reached the Plaza San Martín, which, according to Dan's Reddit search, was a centrally located spot to find a variety of drugs from *chicos*, young kids connected to the local dealers. Brick paths cut across a large grassy area spotted with trees and benches. A statue of San Martín on a horse dominated the center of the plaza, and groups of kids hung out around it. They seemed like they'd just gotten out of school for the day, and they socialized and flirted.

We approached a group of boys at one of the benches. One of the *chicos*, about 13 years old, was wearing a hat with a pot leaf design on it.

"*Hola, ¿qué tal?*" we greeted them, knowing full well that we looked like any other white tourists. I had lots of tattoos showing because of my skimpy dress, my long brown hair perfectly straightened on either side of full eye makeup, and Dan wore a t-shirt, Prana jeans, and a five o'clock shadow.

The kids were surprisingly friendly and patient with our Spanish speaking. The main leader of the group was named Martin—go figure, with the name of the plaza.

After a bit of confused, slow conversation, Martin said he had a friend who could hook us up with *porro*, but we'd have to wait a bit. At first, it sounded like this friend was going to come to meet us at the plaza. We waited awkwardly, with this group of about seven boys, trying to make small talk. They were all Argentinian, dressed like punk teens, and were chain smoking cigarettes. They asked us about climbing, and then challenged us to climb a tree. Dan clambered up easily. I didn't want to climb above them in my dress, so I did some pullups on a branch instead. They were amazed at our small display, and we laughed with them.

Eventually, using WhatsApp to text his friend, Martin told us it would be just a little longer. We watched a group of break dancers perform in one corner of the plaza. An hour passed, and Dan and I were starting to get suspicious. We took a walk a few blocks to the ocean and back while everyone waited on the hookup. Martin then said it would be necessary for us to go to his friend to get the weed.

Our rental car could seat four people, but the back seat was filled with our remaining luggage. I moved things as much as I could and squeezed into the back. Martin and his friend Luis half-sat on each other shoved into the front passenger seat while Dan drove. Martin shouted out *derecho*, *derecha*, or *izquierda* at every intersection to guide us through the busy city. We left downtown for a more run-down residential area, and finally arrived at the drug dealer's location of choice. I waited in the car with Luis, while Dan was escorted inside a nearby building by Martin.

I made nervous conversation with Luis in Spanish, hoping he wasn't going to try to pull anything since I was alone. We were in a bad part of town, but I tried to maintain a confident vibe. After what felt like an hour, Dan emerged again with Martin. I tried to ask him how it went inside, but he shook his head, his eyes wide, and gave me a knowing look that said, "We'll discuss later, let's get out of here." The drug dealer kids wanted to go to the beach to smoke together before being dropped back off at the plaza—it was basic etiquette to share, apparently.

We pulled up to a deserted concrete building near the Atlantic Ocean on the edge of Río Gallegos. The boys chose a raunchy rap song and let the music pour out of the car, laughing as they cranked the radio up. Dan and the boys passed around a joint, smoked cigarettes, and drank beers while I sat half in the car, half out with the door open. The boys were shocked I didn't want to smoke pot when offered. I wasn't sure how to explain its negative effects on me in Spanish, so I just shrugged.

The sun shone on us and the air smelled of salt. I remember trying to commit the moment into memory since it was such an odd situation. Here I was, an Idaho girl, the daughter of a cop, at the end of the world, driving around with drug dealers, basking in the sunshine with a man I had only known for a couple months. I looked out over the ocean. The last time I'd been to the Atlantic, it was in New Jersey, and the water had been warm and an inviting blue, pleasant for swimming. This water was choppy, gray, and cold. I pondered how many miles it was to Antarctica, and wondered if I'd ever go farther south on the earth than this in my lifetime.

When the joint ran out, we drove back to the plaza and dropped the boys off.

"Holy shit, dude, that was not cool!" Dan was heightened, his voice betraying his fear now that we were alone again. "I went in there, right? And the guys in there were way older than Martin. They were scary fucking dudes, strung out on coke, high off their asses. They tried to get me to buy coke, but I just kept thinking about how coke almost fucking killed me, ya know, and I couldn't do it. I got barely any weed, and it's absolute shit, and Martin and his buddy smoked half of it just now!"

He'd spent 1000 pesos for a tiny amount of the shittiest weed in South America: Paraguayan brick weed, dark and full of seeds and stems. It only looked like it would last for a few bowls, and I was curious what his long-term plan was. It surely wouldn't last him till the end of the trip, however long it was going to be. He unwrapped it from the plastic to show me. The bud looked disgusting, and was a far cry from the beautiful green flower we were used to in the States.

"They fuckin' scammed me 'cause I'm a white guy. This sucks. I mean, it's good to have some pot, but shit. That was a lot of money. It probably has barely any THC. Christ. Let's get out of here. This city is gross and there's too many tweakers."

We drove away from the plaza and parked to get into the trunk of the car to grab some clothes. The sun was about to go down, and the temperature was dropping. We finished up in the trunk, closed it, and got back in the front to drive to El Chaltén.

"Hey, babe, where's the car key?" Dan asked, searching the front seats. We looked together for a few minutes, and then it dawned on us. The key was locked in the trunk. We played with levers on the back seat, but it was a secure trunk—we couldn't access it from the main cab of the car. *Fuck, fuck, fuck.* It was getting dark, and we were locked out of the car in a random city. There were no cafes or places to get WiFi nearby. Since we couldn't use our phones to look up a locksmith, we decided to lock the front of the car to protect our other belongings.

We set out together down the road, in a direction that looked like a safer neighborhood. After walking for a while under the buzz of power lines, we found a group of adults painting a driveway bright pink. They looked trustworthy enough. In broken Spanish, we told them about our problem. I didn't know the word for locksmith, but one of the men pulled out a cell phone and dialed one for us. We thanked them and sat on the curb while they kept painting the driveway.

The locksmith appeared after ten minutes. He only had one seat available, so I hopped in to show him where to drive to get to the locked car while Dan ran along the road. The locksmith had no issue using the driver window to unlock the front of the car. We showed him how we couldn't get into the trunk from the cab, and after a few attempts, he agreed. He set to work on the trunk's lock with no success.

After dozens of tries, we were getting discouraged, and he seemed to be feeling incapable too. It was getting late, and he tried key after key from a big toolbox. *Shit, this is annoying.* Finally, he found the magic key and the trunk opened.

We drove back out of town and miraculously got through both security checkpoints without issue. One of the officers recognized us and was suspicious that we had arrived and left within the span of a single evening, but soon enough it was just me, Dan, the Chevy Classic, American music, Argentinian snacks, and the stars of the southern hemisphere lighting up the sky above us.

When we stopped to pee, I tilted my head back to take in the view of the stars. Out in the middle of nowhere, with no light pollution, we were afforded a full display of the night sky. There were so many constellations I didn't recognize.

"Man, really makes you think about how puny we are in the universe, ya know?" I said. I thought about a class I'd taken recently on geologic time. "It's crazy to think about how the light from the stars we see is actually from millions of years ago. Since they're so far away in space, it takes a long time to reach us. Like, some of the light we see originated back when there were still dinosaurs around and even way older than that too," I rambled, full of awe.

"Damn, you gotta stop with that shit. Too existential. Looking up at the stars freaks me out, dude. I can't handle that," Dan said, zipping up his fly, casting his eyes down, and opening the driver door. I took in a last view of the stars and hopped back in the car with him.

In the middle of the night, we made it back to El Calafate and decided to crash until morning. Dan booked a hostel for the night from his phone, but when we arrived, the front desk worker told us we'd accidentally put in the wrong reservation date since it was after midnight. He couldn't do much to help us, but welcomed us to sleep in the common area. There was still a group of people partying in the dining room, and he told us that the cleaning crew would come at 6:00 a.m. We didn't have another option, and figured the people hanging out in the dining room would leave soon since it was already so late.

Dan bought a beer and we sat on the porch with the hostel worker. The man pulled out a guitar and played us a song he'd written. We sat there on the wooden porch in the night, smoke and the sound of the guitar mixing in the air. The invisible dances within the visible. I passively watched dogs fight in the street and scurry away when the occasional taxi passed by them. These dogs didn't seem as friendly as the pack in El Chaltén. I found myself nodding off next to Dan.

It was almost 4:00 a.m., and people were still hanging out in the common room where we were supposed to sleep. Knowing we'd have to leave it at 6:00 a.m. anyway for the cleaners, we decided to try to sleep in the cramped car instead. The seats only leaned back so far, and it was a totally sleepless, uncomfortable night. When the sun rose, we both felt dreadful. Our bodies hurt from trying to rest in the awkward seats.

Feeling like zombies, we drove back to El Chaltén, not knowing it would be our last time driving that stretch of highway. As we got closer to town, Dan perked up and elbowed me.

"Fallon! Look! There's Fitz Roy!" It looked just like the classic photos I'd admired from home for years: the highway pointing straight at the vertical mountains, each peak spearing the skyline just like the Patagonia brand logo. I'd seen the mountains close up, but this was the real quintessential view of the range. It was a breathtaking panorama. It had been too cloudy when we'd driven this road previously, but the mostly clear skies now were giving me the show of a lifetime.

The wind blasted us as we tried in vain to hold our cameras steady to snap photos of each other. We couldn't hear each other over the incessant wind. We'd jump back in the car to drive a bit farther, singing along and clicking away on our cameras before we'd get out yet again. I looked over at Dan at one point, intently focused on his camera, and saw a large scar on the side of his head I'd never noticed before—the wind was ruffling his hair just so to reveal it.

Dan shot a perfect photo of me walking along the road in my favorite dress, camera in hand, hair blowing in the wind, Fitz Roy rising up directly above me. I examined that photo and hardly recognized myself. I thought about myself as a little girl, spinning the globe, thinking I would never be privileged enough to travel to these exciting places as I looked them up in my dad's encyclopedias. Even daring to dream about visiting far-off places felt absurd back then. I looked at this photo through the eyes of that little girl, and I felt proud to be here.

CHAPTER 12

WITHDRAWALS

January 2017

I found myself on the soggy talus slope once again, my neck craning up at Fitz Roy, watching the high winds blow clouds over the summits as if the weather gods hit fast forward on the atmosphere. It looked like the mountains were running giant smoke machines as violent white clouds billowed off the peaks. The steady onslaught made a loud rumbling sound, constant and booming, accentuated by whooshing gusts that nearly knocked me to the ground. Small snowflakes blew around erratically, confused by the sun peeking through the chaotic, ever-moving clouds.

Dan labored uphill in front me, burdened by the weight of the haul bag. We had grabbed our stashed gear in the rocks on the hike up, and we made slow progress under our heavy loads. Dan wasn't far ahead of me, but the wind made it impossible to hear each other.

I got my bearings at Piedra Negra, noticing all of the climbers' tents scattered around within the black boulders. We dropped our gear—this would be our basecamp, and all of our equipment was finally here. The first real phase was complete. We were closer than ever now to Guillaumet, the northernmost major peak in the range. Because of the high winds, we didn't stay long. As soon as we'd claimed a spot with our gear, we ran back down the mountain. The weather forecast for the next few days looked bad for climbing, so there was no point in waiting around up there.

Dan was pleased to have all of the gear carries finished, and was stoked to descend with no pack. He smiled and howled as we ran down together. I wasn't supposed to run because of my hip problems, but I joined him anyway, feeling intensely euphoric. I got lost in the movement, planting one foot after the other, purely focused on watching for rocks, roots, or other obstacles in the path. I was amazed at how free it felt, to be without a pack, feet moving as fast as possible, plummeting down the swampy trail with the wind whipping my hair. The wind energized us, the storm hastening our manic descent. I laughed ecstatically. Partway down, a rainbow appeared right ahead of us, framing the Río Electrico valley below, and it felt like things were looking up.

Back in El Chaltén, we waited for a few days, anxiously checking the weather multiple times a day to see if we could have a weather window to climb soon. I was still wary of Dan because of our previous fights, but since I was stuck on this mission with him regardless, I figured I should try to enjoy it when he was being pleasant. We walked the streets, stopping for food, coffee, or wine. I still couldn't drink legally back home, so the novelty of being able to order my own drink was satisfying. Dan and I sat next to each other at a bar, and I sipped Malbec with my head on his shoulder and his arm around my waist. The ambient sound of rain coupled with the low light in the bar was soothing, cozy. These moments of intimacy were comforting in such an unfamiliar environment. When Dan was angry and spiraling, I was the recipient of the unstoppable chaos, but when he was calm and loving, I tried to lean into it and milk it for as long as possible.

At random hostels, we'd hang out with other travelers while slacklining and poring over the guidebook. When people learned we were American, their demeanor would change. The news was dominated by Trump's early presidency and ridiculous behavior and commentary. We'd have to quickly clarify that we were ashamed of Trump, and that we hadn't voted for him. After that, they would nod in agreement and then keep talking with us.

Everyone seemed to have guitars, and music was the constant background noise to the common topic of conversation: no one was climbing, and no one was summiting anything that season. Climbers from all over the world complained about the storms and avalanches, and we were no different. Everyone was waiting for a weather window.

At one hostel, we found a book exchange. I left behind the book I'd just finished reading and grabbed an autobiography by Barack Obama. For the remainder of the trip, Dan and I alternated reading the book out loud to each other. The pages were falling out and we lost more and more of the book as the trip progressed. It was reassuring to hold on to the voice of a leader, since we hated the current situation waiting for us back home. When we weren't reading to each other, or journaling, we'd talk about our plans and dreams for the future.

"Perdy, let's just stay in Argentina. For, like, a long time. I'll start a refugee camp for all the people who need it since Trump is turning them away from the States. Fuck Trump. We'll teach them how to climb, and live off the land. Look! I mean, c'mon. Building materials are cheap here! I bet my Dad'll fund it if I can come up with a legit business plan. It'll be perfect. I've always wanted to live down here." Dan was fixated on starting this climbing camp for refugees, and talked about it at any opportunity. He made it sound like a real possibility. I doubted his follow through on another big idea.

I'd started the trip with minimal money, and had used what little I had left for food and my failed attempt to get my own hostel. Dan seemed to not be worried about his finances though, as I watched him down bottle after bottle of Malbec, packs of cigarettes, coffees, and Red Bulls. He thought he'd be able to build an entire business? It was a dubious plan, but I kept my mouth shut. I preferred his manic states over his depressive ones solely for the reason that he treated me better. I knew he couldn't control it, but I wanted to ride out this high for as long as I could. It was easier to travel with someone who was positive, enthusiastic, hopeful, and, most importantly, kind to me.

Eventually, the updated forecast showed a few days of potentially promising weather before a big snowstorm. I messaged my family and roommates to tell them I'd be heading up the mountain and likely unable to respond for a few days. I was deeply afraid of questing beyond basecamp, but it was go time.

There's some courage involved in the act of staring into a storm, feeling the earth rumble below your approach shoes, swallowing hard, and crossing the river anyway. The water at the trailhead acted as a gateway to the rugged world, where a threshold is crossed—the symbolic starting line of a commitment in the mountains.

At this point, our trail routine felt intensely familiar: the river crossing, the swath of gravel, the gentle forest, sneaking past Fraile to avoid paying a fee, and finally toiling straight up the mucky talus slope to Piedra Negra. My brain should've known better than to keep moving up the mountain with Dan toward menacing clouds, yet here we were. We tried to yell to each other in the howling wind, realizing our suffered noise would never be captured by human ears. We cried out in frustration at the weather, hoping it would clear once we climbed higher. Blind reliance on the weather forecast required faith.

We set up the tent as flurries collected on our hoods and shoulders. There was zero visibility because of the snow. The summit of Fitz Roy was concealed behind the wall of clouds, and I could imagine his presence, god-like in the landscape.

We got settled in, and placed our packs under boulders and in the tent vestibule. We had all of the clothes, gear, and supplies we would need for an attempt. Food was the one exception. Although I'd found a few options I could eat, my allergies and limited money had made things difficult. I had a pathetic amount of food. I surveyed my stash and realized I'd have to ration it out if it needed to last more than a couple days. Usually I was more prepared for things like this, but food had been one hurdle I hadn't been able to fully figure out.

Dan fired up the stove and cooked us a pot of rice and lentils. Strong gusts of wind threatened to cave in the tent walls, so we were vigilant to keep the stove from getting knocked over. I had spent countless nights of my life in tents just like this, surrounded by the familiar colorful glow of the nylon, my legs comfortably cocooned in my sleeping bag.

Being stuck in a tent is a curious experience; since you can't see outside, you can imagine yourself to be anywhere in the world. I could very well picture myself on any of the other mountains I'd climbed in my life. I thought back to my time in tents through the years. Shivering from getting soaked in a storm on Kings Peak in

Utah on my first ever backpacking trip at 15. Freezing on the glacier on Mount Rainier when I was 16, venturing out in the night to pee while squatting over my crampons in the dark. Waiting for a weather window to summit Gannett Peak in Wyoming when I was 17 and listening to powerful thunderstorms shake the earth for days. I was typically claustrophobic, but tents didn't bother me. Tents were a safe haven in an otherwise brutal environment.

After we finished eating, Dan rummaged through his pack. It was starting to get dark outside, a subtle change since the storm clouds had already been blocking so much sunlight during the day.

"Fuck, dude. I don't have any pills with me. I must've left them in the car! Fuck me." He was getting agitated, so I helped him search through the bags. No luck.

"I don't have Ambien. No Xanax. No Seroquel. I don't know what the fuck to do. I can't function. I can't sleep without those pills. This is bad." His voice was panicky.

"What should we do? Do you have weed at least?"

"I only have like one bowl left of that Paraguayan brick shit. It's not gonna be enough. I haven't even really had any the last couple days anyway 'cause I was trying to save it. Fuck, dude!" He pushed his pack away in frustration. "I'm gonna get the sweats. It's gonna be dangerous. If I soak through my clothes and sleeping bag, I could get super cold. It's already been hours since I had anything. I was banking on having those meds."

He fidgeted around, and I could sense his dismay. I didn't have a solution, so I asked how I could help.

"Just . . . be a good partner. Take care of me. Here, take a video for me." He handed me his big camera and I started rolling. He spent a few minutes explaining the situation to the camera. Passionately, he described how he wanted to climb Fitz Roy more than anything, and he wasn't going to let forgetting his pills negate his ability to attempt the climb. I was relieved to hear his determination, but deep down I was concerned. I had never seen him off the pills; they were his bread and butter. I thought he sounded ridiculous in his monologue, but of course I didn't comment on it. When he was finished, I stopped recording. It was getting late.

I had brought my smallest book, *Brave New World*, knowing that having some kind of entertainment can be helpful when you're stuck in a tent. I started to drift off to sleep to him reading out loud as the temperature dropped and I shivered in my sleeping bag. Snow piled up around us as wind battered the tent, collapsing the walls.

"And if ever, by some unlucky chance, anything unpleasant should somehow happen, why, there's always soma to give you a holiday from the facts. And there's always soma to calm your anger, to reconcile you to your enemies, to make you patient and long-suffering."

Dan paused to shake the tent, knocking off snow. His hands were already jittery from withdrawals, and I could see him sweating. I hadn't realized just how dependent he was on those pills. Could it really happen so quickly? He smoked a cigarette, but his body was craving more than just nicotine. The smoke was thick in the small space, lit up only by the beam of his headlamp.

He continued reading. "In the past you could only accomplish these things by making a great effort and after years of hard moral training. Now, you swallow two or three half-gramme tablets, and there you are. Anybody can be virtuous now. You can carry at least half your morality about in a bottle . . ."

My eyelids grew heavy as the roof of the tent sagged in with more snow.

An hour later, he woke me up, irritated that I'd fallen asleep without discussing the plan for the morning.

I understood my mistake and felt regret for letting myself drift off. As an alpine climbing partner, it's crucial to agree on a plan prior to any climbing attempt. If I had stayed asleep, we wouldn't have known if we were going to start our push that night, or if we were going to take a rest day. He was furious.

"You don't want to do this climb, do you?" A bead of sweat crept down across his jugular.

Of course I don't want to do this, I thought. *You made me come with you as your climbing slave. No wonder you couldn't summit last year; you're a disaster.* Instead, I lied to him. I managed to come out of my stupor enough to convince him that I did indeed care, and to apologize for my negligence.

He'd given up on me. "Yeah. Whatever. You don't even care, so just go back to sleep, for fuck's sake."

Deep down, I resented him for forcing me to be here, for thinking that he could control me. Angering him more terrified me since I'd seen him transform at a moment's notice. I woke up fully so we could discuss weather, the route, the glacier, and other determining factors. It was still heavily snowing outside and we decided that we shouldn't set off up the unfamiliar glacier in the dark. We'd re-evaluate in the morning.

Although I was upset, exhaustion beat emotion, and I slept through a cold night of high winds and snow. I woke up intermittently during the worst gusts, my arms shooting out of my sleeping bag to support the imploding tent walls. It was practically an involuntary reflex after enduring so many windy nights in tents. My hands automatically rocketed out to the tent walls to brace against the wind, praying the tent poles were strong enough to withstand it. For these brief periods where I was half-awake, I saw Dan shaking on top of his sleeping bag, his shirt soaked with sweat from benzo withdrawals.

In the morning, we unzipped the door to find relatively clear skies. We left camp with 65-pound packs, crossing over huge boulder fields and slabby crystalline outcrops between two alpine lakes nestled under glaciers. The rocky summits of Guillaumet, Mermoz, and Fitz Roy towered far above, resembling volatile deities of the geologic world.

Dan darted ahead of me, typical because of my painful hip, out of shape lungs, and tendon pain from the antibiotics. I was alone in the complex of ice and rock, breathing hard. Above one of the lakes, I had to cross an exposed, narrow, rocky ledge with an overhanging block above it. A sheer cliff dropped off below the ledge toward the glacial lake. I had to lean to avoid hitting my head on the overhanging wall above me. The tip of my ice axe on the outside of my backpack got caught on the block above me, and I was knocked off my feet.

I was suddenly upside down, half-laying on my backpack that was also pulling me down, with my heavy mountain boots floating in the air above me, and my arms somehow incredulously holding on to the grippy rock. My climbing reflexes must have saved me by allowing me to automatically latch on. I hung high above the lake, upside down on my back like a flipped-over turtle, supported only by my arms straining at my sides. The water below was seafoam green from its glacial rock flour content, and I saw the surface shimmering as blood rushed to my head.

I knew Dan was too far away and couldn't see or hear me, so I had to do something to save myself from falling down the cliff. My internal risk assessment kicked in. If I let go, I was doomed for an icy swim in the lake far below, surely with broken bones, and would drown from the weight of the backpack . . .

I shut off the worst case scenario imagery. Mustering my strength, I did the hardest, most awkward pullup of my life while trying to dig in with my heels. I wriggled back onto the ledge, my adrenaline pumping. *Holy shit. I got so lucky.* This was supposed to be a more mundane part of the ascent, but it was a good reminder that steep, exposed scrambling terrain can still be hazardous.

I continued up the outcrops and huge boulders littered below the first small glacier under Paso del Cuadrado. Dan and I regrouped at the base of the glacier to get out our crampons and ice axes. It looked like more of a small snowfield than a proper glacier, so I naively didn't think there would be any crevasses. The angle was some of the steepest snow I had ever been on, but I felt comfortable with my skills. Dan charged up the snow slope, too impatient to wait for me. *How is he so fast? With how much he smokes? Agh!* Soon he was just a tiny dot approaching the ridge above.

Step, step, plant the axe. Repeat. I made steady progress, and couldn't help but smile. I hadn't been on a glacier in a couple years, and I enjoyed the feeling of moving on snow again. It was much warmer than the previous night, with a mixture of blue sky and clouds above.

As the angle steepened, the poor snow conditions became challenging. The top centimeter was composed of useless snow crystals lying on top of rock-solid ice. The snow from last night must not have accumulated here—probably too windy and steep. I couldn't kick a step into the thin top layer of snow to make a mini-platform for my foot, and I couldn't quite get the crampons to dig into the underlying ice. I kicked my crampons in as hard as I could at the angle of the slope, but my crampons were made for mountaineering, not ice climbing. I couldn't gain purchase in the miniscule snow layer or in the ice with my crampons or with my ice axe. I immediately felt incredibly insecure, like I was going to slide down the slope at any moment. I cursed Dan for not roping up with me, and took deep breaths to try to stay calm.

I could smack the ice axe pick in occasionally, but otherwise I resorted to using it as a third balance point. I was performing a delicate, dangerous dance on the glacier: all at once staying in balance with my two foot placements, moving my axe up, trying not to let the heavy backpack throw me off, bracing against the wind, and trying to get whatever purchase I could to safely move uphill on my own.

I noticed my crampon straps were slowly coming loose. Now I had to contend with rattly crampons on top of my other difficulties, because the slope was too steep to fix them; I could neither sit down nor take off my backpack to lean over. I was wearing borrowed mountaineering boots with my old crampons that had been set to different rental boots years ago. I had made the mistake of not adjusting the metal foot piece because it had looked like the right size, and when I put the crampons on initially, they felt snug and secure. I was regretting my complacency now.

To complicate matters, I also realized that there were, indeed, crevasses. What I'd foolishly thought were just oddly colored stripes on the snowfield were actually gaping crevasses veiled by a small amount of snow, making their surface slightly indented. As I climbed, I probed the slope in front of me with my ice axe, able to locate the fissures when the world dropped away and open space appeared. I would glance right and left for a clearer view of the stripes cutting the snow like giant stretch marks to give me clues. When I arrived at one, I would gingerly step across, struggling to establish myself on the ice above with my loose crampons and dull axe.

Sometimes the crevasses were too large to step across, so I had to walk on the unsubstantial snow bridges, like unsupported roofs perilously topping each fissure. In these instances, my foot would punch through and I would be horrified—I had one shitty crampon placement on the solid ice below me, one leg dangling in the abyss, and extremely limited ability to use my axe to pull myself up on the uphill side. I imagined I was as lightweight as a feather, and cautiously moved my limbs and axe to regain purchase above each crevasse. It scared the hell out of me to be dangling over a crevasse, unroped, trying to pull up on a single ice axe that was barely sunk in. *This is fucked up. We really should've roped up. I wish I had proper ice climbing tools.* I cursed my naivete.

Shaken, I eventually made it up to the rock section above the glacier, and Dan and I finished the final scramble together to Paso del Cuadrado. We crested the ridge, and the scene that unfolded before us surpassed our wildest dreams. This view of Patagonia was undoubtedly the most breathtaking landscape I had ever had the privilege to lay my eyes on. We both broke down into tears, in awe of the majesty.

Looking out over the alpine paradise, to our left we had a new perspective of Guillaumet, Mermoz, and Fitz Roy: thousands of feet of rock and snow, the true scale of the peaks revealed by the enormous slopes falling away below the main rock faces. Slightly right of those lay a massive glacial valley, and farther out, a perfect view of the Torre Group. Straight ahead rose the striking, pointed Aguja Pollone, and right of that was the ice cap creeping its tongues of white and blue over the edge of dramatic cliffs. In every direction, the scale was grand.

But then the harsh reality hit us: since we'd crested the pass, we finally had a good view of our intended route "Maté, Porro, y Todo lo Demás" on the North Pillar. Most of the route was covered in a thick layer of rime ice. The bottom section that wasn't coated in rime would be at risk for heavy icefall as the top pitches melted out.

We evaluated the approach to the base of the route. We'd have to drop down a long slope of tricky, technical ice and rock, and then traverse the main glacier for some distance. The glacier below us looked rotten and ablated, rife with penitentes and huge crevasses. Above the glacier, the approach to the North Pillar would involve snow climbing thousands of feet. Just days before, other climbers had told us about the avalanches frequently occurring on those slopes. We adjusted our gaze upward. The route itself, thousands of feet of granite crack climbing with no fixed anchors or gear, was covered in ice with an even icier headwall lying above the North Pillar to the summit of Fitz Roy.

Our hearts sank. It looked impossible, and we both knew it, but didn't want to initially admit it. There was no way in hell this climb was going to happen. We didn't have ice climbing gear or advanced mixed climbing experience—we had come for rock climbing, and Dan had been dead set on this specific route. We reached a mutual understanding that this was the highest we'd be going, especially since a big storm was coming in the forecast.

We thought about stashing our load of gear up there, but after more discussion, we decided to go back to Piedra Negra with all our equipment. It was heartbreaking, to stand in such a beautiful place and know we wouldn't be exploring it any further. We took photos and marveled at the topography. I was surprised that Dan was willing to throw in the towel that easily after being so adamant about summiting no matter what. The conditions were horrible enough to check his stubborn hubris, and even he had to acknowledge there are some things beyond our control.

Defeated but also amazed at the beauty, we hiked back down. I told Dan about my crevasse issues on the way up. This time on the glacier, we stayed closer to the edge with the rocks, skirting around most of the crevasses. We got back to the tent and decided to hike out with a single load of gear. It was too much to carry out in one load, and we held on to the false hope that there would be a weather window for an attempt to climb a different, smaller objective as a consolation prize after the next storm. We chatted with other climbers at Piedra Negra, and heard disappointing tales from them, not surprised that other parties had been turned away from their objectives too.

We deconstructed the tent, shoved our sleeping bags into their stuff sacks, and loaded up our packs for the first gear carry down. Dan pulled ahead as always. I was grateful for the alone time and experienced a range of emotions. When I was tired and my tendons screamed for a break, I let my pack slump to the ground, and I laid down right there in the trail. I looked up at the sky, blinking when raindrops hit my face. They mixed in with my tears as I grieved how poorly everything seemed to be going: the trip, the weather, the relationship, and my health. I took deep breaths into my belly like I'd learned in a yoga class in college, feeling the dirt under my back as my chest expanded and deflated with each breath. My feet ached. My nose was cold. *Why am I here?* I stared into the sky and found no answers.

After all of that, it was over. Dan's stubbornness, his determination to climb the mountain at all costs, his investment of time and money, and his insane orders for me to support him, had amounted to running out of drugs and turning around because of bad conditions. I could hardly believe I'd only gotten to see the route for such a brief amount of time, but was secretly relieved that it had been coated in ice and plagued by avalanches. I shuddered at the thought of what would've happened had we continued up the climb and bivied while Dan went through withdrawals.

CHAPTER 13

MAKE ME A BIRD

February 2017

Our sleep was abruptly interrupted by a knock on the door.

"*Buenos dias. Por favor, abre la puerta,*" a woman's voice said hesitantly. We rolled out of bed, groggy from the long hike out the day before. She continued, more worried this time. "*La policía está aquí.*" That sure woke us up. We opened the door to find the hostel front desk worker, Mikaila, standing there with a distressed look on her face.

"Your car," she explained, and led us to the front lobby. We threw open the front door and stepped out onto the dirt road to find the rental car totaled where it had been parked last night.

"Ohhh shit. Shit. Shit. Shit," Dan panicked. We ran over to the car and saw that the driver's side was totally smashed in, as well as the trunk.

The police were eager to find out what had happened, and asked us if we did it.

We'd been sleeping and hadn't heard anything. We explained to them that we'd left the car parked overnight in perfect condition, and knew nothing about who had crashed into it and left it there on the street.

I walked over to the car and noticed that the cab was open since the doors had been smashed in. I opened the back door all the way and started searching through the stuff we'd left in the car overnight. Dan joined me, and we made a depressing realization: my cameras were gone. The night before, we'd gotten in late and I hadn't carried in much of my stuff since I was so tired. El Chaltén seemed relatively safe, so I didn't think break-ins would be an issue. The thief took both of my cameras and all of the memory cards. I immediately burst into tears, knowing I would never again see my photos and videos from the mountain. I was crushed at the loss.

"Fuck this, dude. This is so stupid! I can't believe we have to deal with this," Dan complained, rightfully pissed off. We also discovered that the aux cord to play music in the car had been stolen as well. From what we could tell, nothing else was missing, but our gear was so scattered at that point that it was difficult to say with any certainty. We stretched our sore muscles while waiting out on the street, unsure of how to deal with the situation.

After talking with the police for a little while, they went back to the station. We moved all of the rest of our belongings from the rental car into the hostel so they wouldn't be at risk of being stolen too.

The mangled car sat on the street, fully exposed. Dan called the rental car company, Hertz, and explained what had happened. They said they'd have to send out a company representative from El Calafate to look at the damage and find a way to transport the car. We'd still be responsible for the additional days of rental and for repairing the damages, which was a huge financial blow.

For the next couple days, our life became a nightmare of meetings at the police station and with Hertz. None of the police officers spoke English, so Dan and I used our best Spanish skills to communicate. I had limited knowledge of the legal and technical terms we needed, so I heavily relied on a translation app on my phone, which slowed the process. We didn't have a better option.

The first day at the police station, they interrogated us about the car: where we rented it, what we'd been using it for, and how we had parked it that night. We answered all of their questions. It seemed like they still didn't know who had crashed into us. Dan and I thought it was abundantly clear that whoever crashed into a parked car should be the one to receive punishment and responsibility for damages, but they made everything sound ambiguous. I told them about my missing cameras, and they said they would keep an eye out for them, though it was unlikely they'd be able to find them. They told us to come back the next day for updates.

We left the station haggard and overwhelmed. Dan yelled out in frustration as he smoked a cigarette on the street, kicking the dirt with his Converse. At an empty restaurant, we were seated by a window and ordered food. Dan practically chugged a Quilmes and ordered another. I couldn't blame him.

I kept my head down, depressed about my cameras. It was all I could think about. My dad had given me the DSLR, and it was one of my prized possessions. For the rest of the trip, I found myself always glancing around in cafes, on the street, at hostels, trying to spot my cameras, hoping I could apprehend the thief. *Why didn't they at least leave the memory cards? I mean, take the cameras I guess, but c'mon! The memory cards too! I want my photos!* Bargaining didn't get me anywhere though. I looked outside at the gloomy day, windy and spitting rain.

Later that night at the hostel, Dan took my phone and read some messages between me and my dad. My dad was understandably worried about me, even with my glossed-over version of recent events. I can't remember what exact message set him off, but Dan got pissed.

"He shouldn't be telling you what to do! This is not gonna fly."

"Dan, it's fine. Don't worry about it," I said, reaching to get my phone back.

"No, you're mine, not his! I'm going to call him!" he said forcefully. He jumped back with my phone, typed my dad's number into his own phone, and then hit the call button. He pocketed my phone and stepped out of the room. When I tried to follow, he stopped me, and shut the door. He started pacing up and down an empty part of the hostel hallway while talking to my dad.

I panicked. What was he saying? This was so uncool. Now my dad was going to worry even more. I cautiously cracked the door open and strained to listen to what he was saying. I only caught snippets of his side of the conversation. I could tell he kept cutting my dad off, and making threats. I overheard him say things to the effect of "she's mine, back off," "I can take care of her," "she can make her own decisions," "she doesn't need you anymore," and "you don't get to do anything about this, she's with me." My heart sank every time he raised his voice at my dad. Dan interrupted him constantly, trying to claim power, and he was gesticulating as he paced. My dad didn't deserve this.

I imagined myself lunging out into the hallway, knocking the phone out of his hand, snatching back my phone, pushing him to the ground, and telling him to never try that shit again. But I wasn't nearly ballsy enough. I'd seen what he was capable of, and I was uninterested in facing his anger. I secretly hoped my dad was about to orchestrate a ridiculous rescue like the movie *Taken*, but I knew that wasn't going to happen.

The next day, we were back at the police station. The cops had changed their tune—apparently they'd known all along who had crashed into the rental car. At first they wouldn't fully tell us about it. They sat us down at a table in a back room, and an officer slid a paper across to us. It was a statement, in Spanish, about what had happened. He motioned for us to sign it. Dan and I looked at each other, confused. We read through the document carefully, using my translation app when needed, and realized that it contained a bunch of lies.

"We're not signing this! This isn't true!" Dan pushed the paper back to the cop. "Can we write our own statement about what happened? It's really not that complicated." The officer shook his head. We pointed out the inaccuracies, baffled at where they'd come up with parts of the story. After much discussion in Spanglish with multiple officers, we learned that a local woman named Claudia had crashed into our car in the middle of the night. She was claiming it had been parked improperly, and that's why she'd hit it.

"Oh, I see. So this woman is blaming it on us so she doesn't have to face responsibility. That's fucking rich . . ." Dan was livid. We assured them that the car had been properly parked all the way on the edge of the dirt road outside the hostel, just like everyone else's. For hours, we labored over the document they wanted us to sign, but we refused.

"We were asleep, for Chrissakes! This is not our fault. This lady needs to pay." Dan and I were in agreement on this. I couldn't fathom how the cops thought it might be our fault whatsoever. We left the station again, annoyed at how long everything was taking. I braced myself for the freezing, blowing rain every time we had to go outside.

"Shit, we're spending so much money to just sit here in town and deal with this. Like, we can't leave or go back up the mountain. So we gotta keep buying food and hostels. And now Hertz is on my back asking for tons of money. This sucks," Dan said between puffs of a cigarette.

We walked over to one of the only ATMs in town and stood in a long line. There was always a long line. When we got to the machine, we had to pay a fee, and then we'd always choose the option to withdraw the max amount of cash: 1500 pesos (around $100 at the time). The cash crisis was getting worse, and everyone was nervous about it. I was reliant on Dan for larger expenses at this point since my account was almost fully drained. Dan had been out of weed for a while now, and was heavily leaning on nicotine and alcohol to pick up the slack. I put my arm around him as we walked, grateful to share body heat, unsure of how to help.

We found ourselves back at the station for a third day. There was news: Claudia had admitted to being drunk and hitting our car. But they weren't going to hold her responsible because she was a local, and didn't want to have to pay for it. *Ahh, the sweet smell of corruption!*

"What do you want us to do? Hertz is demanding all of this money from me, and she should be the one responsible!" Dan wasn't going to give in to them. I helped with translating, and eventually they gave us some advice. They gave us the name of the pizza place where Claudia worked, and told us to go talk to her. They warned us that she also didn't speak any English. If we wanted her to pay for the damages, then we'd have to go visit and intimidate her to give us the money. I thought back to my childhood with my dad as a police officer. I couldn't imagine something like this happening in the States; I had to laugh at how ridiculous it sounded, but apparently it was our best option.

We went to a cafe and drafted a letter to Claudia together. We didn't want to have to explain it verbally in case we messed something up, so we spent a long time analyzing our letter, making sure it was clear with what had happened and what we needed. We explained in the letter that we were traveling climbers, didn't have enough money left to pay off Hertz, and that since it hadn't been our fault, we shouldn't be the ones responsible to pay for it. I also wrote about my missing cameras and asked her to return them if she'd been the one to take them or know who had them.

That night, we walked over to the pizza place. It was dark and cold—the deep cold that pricks at your cheeks and the tip of your nose and makes you shove your hands deeper in your coat pockets—and the restaurant was located on the edge of town. In the parking lot, we noticed a beat up black car that had clearly been in a recent accident, and realized it must be hers. We were seated and asked for Claudia. Soon, a middle-aged waitress approached us and asked for our order. We handed her the letter, and the blood drained from her face. She motioned for us to follow her back to a private, empty corner of the restaurant.

As soon as she saw that we were asking for money, she made up an excuse that there had been something in the road, and she'd swerved to avoid it. We raised our eyebrows. *Seriously?* Then she accused us of having parked the car too far out into the roadway.

We emphasized that we had been sleeping and that she had ruined our parked rental car—this was on her, not us. I asked her about the cameras and she shook her head. Someone else must have come after the crash and stolen them when they saw the opportunity.

Claudia held up a finger to tell us to wait a minute. She returned with a piece of paper, a pen, and a stack of pesos.

She was very focused on what she was writing. It turned out to be a contract, complete with the date, the amount of money being exchanged, and so on. She said she was poor too, and could only give us 5,000 pesos (a little over $300). Hertz had been asking Dan for around 30,000 pesos (nearly $2,000), so this was hardly a fraction of the bill. Regardless, Dan was just pleased to receive any kind of money from her.

Claudia called over one of her coworkers and handed them a small digital camera. After we signed her impromptu contract, she made us pose for a photo with one of us shaking her hand while the other clearly held up the contract and the stack of cash splayed out so the amount was evident. This must've been her way of proving the exchange, her own record of accountability.

Dan and I walked out of the restaurant and couldn't contain our laughter. He pocketed the cash and we howled together as we walked down the road. We were in stitches and tears rolled down our cheeks. The whole situation had been so absurd, and the photo at the end was the icing on the cake. I'd pay good money today for a chance to see that photo again. Dan and I hadn't laughed that hard together in a long time. Everything was shitty, and I partially felt bad for Claudia, but somehow this scenario provided much needed comic relief.

"Jesus, Fallon! That was hilarious. Let's go out to eat." We stopped at a restaurant on our way back to the hostel. Dan and I stuffed ourselves with beef and vegetables, and he paid with some of the cash from Claudia. The trip was still fucked, but in the soft yellow light of the restaurant, laughing over our steaks, it seemed like maybe, just maybe, we could get through anything together.

The next day, Hertz sent out their representative to meet with us. In the lobby of the hostel, we gathered with Pablo from Hertz, a few police officers, and Mikaila from the hostel front desk. We knew slightly more Spanish than they knew English, and the discussion was a broken mixture of the two languages.

After clarifying what had happened, Pablo demanded the money from Dan for the extra days of the rental, the damages, and the cost of transport back to El Calafate. When Dan argued with him over the amount, their voices rose in a heated argument.

Pablo spit in Dan's face.

My jaw dropped and I looked to the police officers to see if they were going to do anything about it. They sat there, clearly content with wanting to protect their own. Dan yelled at Pablo, but held back to avoid getting arrested.

When the meeting adjourned, Dan had lost the argument, and paid the money to Hertz. I wasn't sure how he was affording all of this, but I figured his rich parents back home must be helping him despite his denial otherwise.

"They scammed us. I can't believe how much I had to pay when I did nothing wrong! And he got away with spitting in my face!" Dan sneered.

"Yeah, that was shitty and unfair. I'm glad it's over. I'm still just sad about the cameras . . ." I said softly, fixated on my loss.

"Let's get our stuff down from camp and get the fuck out of here."

The next morning, we tried to hitchhike into the Río Electrico trailhead. Dan was extremely upset about the rental car situation, and felt distraught.

"God, Fallon, I can't believe Pablo spit in my face and the cops didn't do shit about it! I had to pay him so much money. I wanna fucking die! Losing our chance to summit, dealing with this shit, it's just too much!" he yelled angrily as we walked the dirt road toward the trailhead.

"I know, it sucks. We can't change it now though. We just need to go up one more time to get the rest of our stuff, and then we can leave," I reminded him as gently as I could, trying to help him avoid a complete spiral. It was too late though—the wheels were in motion and he was escalating as we walked up the road.

He picked up a rock from the side of the road. "I hate this! Nothing is working!" He hit himself in the head with the rock. I tried to grab it from him, but he yanked his arm away and quickened his pace.

"Dan, stop! Please!" I begged him. He threw the rock off to the side of the road and started punching his head instead. "You don't have to do this!"

"Yeah, I do! I can't stop it! You're such a bitch, I can't fucking stand you! I want to die!" he wailed. *Here we go again*, I thought. He stopped in his tracks, and got right up to my face: "Everything is your fault. I hate this!"

"Yeah, well I fucking hate this too! I don't know how to help you!" I cried as he kept walking away from me, his fist steadily making contact with his skull. I was running out of patience.

"Of course you can't help me! You're just a slut. What would you know about comforting me?! You never help me. You'll never find someone who loves you like I do. You just want to hurt me," he blithered on, feeling sorry for himself. I wasn't even sure what I'd done most recently to deserve this. I suppose he wanted to blame me for all that had gone wrong on this trip, even things out of my control like the weather, the drugs, and the rental car fiasco.

When people encountered us on the road, it was incredibly awkward. We weren't hidden in the trees this time; everyone could see what was happening. I was clearly distressed, but they paid us no mind. Dan at least had the decency to pause his self-harm until other people had passed us, resuming as soon as they were out of sight. I didn't like the way that this was becoming a pattern, and I yearned to be anywhere but here.

I thought of my favorite movie, *Forrest Gump*, where Jenny says, "Dear God, make me a bird. So I could fly far. Far far away from here." I used to think about that scene when I was a kid, subjected to my mother's rage during my brief visits to her. I remember her lip shaking, the smell of vodka on her breath, as she screamed and called me a little shit. I wondered how she could hate her own daughter so much. Since I lived with my dad, I usually was only exposed to her outbursts on the phone; her yelling always had a time limit before she'd throw her landline phone, smashing it into oblivion, and the line would click off, freeing me from the call. I wished I was a bird then just like I did now, but I had no such luck in either situation. Dan's ranting and punching continued on as I forced my feet to keep moving down the road.

The best I could do was leave mentally, so I withdrew into myself, remembering a quote from Marcus Aurelius, a Stoic philosopher I love, about how the mind is our best fortress, our guaranteed place to retreat into reason and calm regardless of external circumstances. My dissociation had become an essential defense mechanism as I endured Dan's episodes. I could pretend like I wasn't there, and check myself out mentally to try to tune out his insults and violence. It only worked up until a point, but it was better than nothing. Anything was better than fully living in this nightmare.

I stopped to drink some water and sat on the side of the road. Dan had calmed himself down, like a toddler finally crying their way through a tantrum, and he plopped himself next to me in the dirt, leaning over to lay in my lap. I was sickened at first, not wanting to be face to face after the hurtful things he'd said. It was getting harder and harder to be sympathetic toward him, but I knew that being cold was only going to prolong his episode. I swallowed my own hurt to try to help him ease his own. We were both crying, and I held him with as much tenderness as I could muster despite my disgust for him. He apologized to me with a hoarse voice and I noticed his dark hair was slightly tinged with blood—must've been from the rock. My heart ached for him, for his unstoppable internal conflict.

The touch comforted him, and he escaped the episode. We kept walking up the road, awkward now after what had just occurred. I never knew how to handle the transition from being the target of his spirals to suddenly not fighting. It never really went back to normal, whatever that meant by now. I could inexplicably feel myself within his grip, under his control, and I couldn't for the life of me figure out how to break the cycle.

The tears had stopped flowing, and we walked with our thumbs out. Finally, someone picked us up, and we hitched to the trailhead.

The flat portion of the hike passed by quickly. Dan wanted space, and I was grateful for it. The hike into Río Electrico was idyllic, with the angular boulders jutting out of the river and green trees sheltering the gentle floodplain. When I first came here, it was inspiring with its beauty. Now, it felt haunted by memories. I noticed the marks from the ice axe in some of the trees I passed from Dan's previous rage, and my stomach churned.

As I ascended the slope up toward Piedra Negra, I realized that I hadn't seen Dan in quite some time. He was far ahead of me now, totally out of sight. I looked all around me at the mountainside: the talus tumbling down for thousands of feet, crisscrossed by the tiny rivulets of glacial snowmelt, partially covered by the spongy green vegetation underfoot. My thighs burned with the gradient. I was the only one on this entire section of the mountain. I felt my throat getting tight; the urge to cry became harder to ignore.

I finally let it all out. I glared up at Fitz Roy, cursing the mountain and kicking the rocks in my path. "I hate hiking! I hate this fucking trail! I hate Dan! I never want to hike again! I hate having wet shoes! I hate being cold! I just want to rock climb in the sunshine!" I screamed as loud as I could.

I sobbed uncontrollably, and my pace slowed to an imperceptible crawl in my sorrow. I dragged my feet on the trail, losing the will to move them another step. The level of suffering I was experiencing went beyond the objective reality of going up this mountain under my own power; it was representative of all that had brought me to this very spot.

"Get me the fuck out of here! Goddammit! I hate heavy packs! I promise I will never hike again! I'm done! I hate this!" I yelled out all my other grievances in my anguish. My hair was wet, a mixture of sweat and intermittent rain, and I bitterly brushed it out of my eyes. I felt wild. I felt like I could release everything I'd been bottling up under my stoic exoskeleton.

My voice became raspy from yelling that no one else would ever hear. The mountains above me were wholly unperturbed by my dramatic meltdown as I flopped down on a rock, devoid of motivation. *I came all the way here for nothing.* I could find no reason worthy of hiking the rest of the way up just to have to face Dan once again, after everything he'd said and done. *You're weak. You look like a man. You're an ugly nerd. You have no chance. You ruin everything.* I felt the unbearable weight of inadequacy and defeat crushing me.

All I could do was cry. My tendons hurt. My hip hurt. My stomach hurt. My heartbeat felt off. I no longer wanted to hike, or to be responsible for my own decisions. I begged for death on the spot. I lay on the rock, curled up, crying, swearing to myself that I would never again hike for fun.

I dreaded having to finish the hike back up to camp, but I got cold just resting there. I didn't have any layers with me; we'd already carried that stuff off the mountain on our last trip down, and I didn't want any extra weight on the way up since we'd be carrying all of the rest of the gear out this time. Ten minutes or an hour could have passed on that rock. I was so upset that I had no concept of time. The cold forced me back to my feet, and I staggered my way up the rest of the slope at a snail's pace, sobbing the entire time—the body-wrenching, silently painful sobs of an unsolvable situation. Step after step, my chest heaving, I let everything out of me in a profound release.

When I stumbled into basecamp, I located the gear I'd left previously. Dan approached me, visibly annoyed by how long it had taken me to get up there. He tried to yell at me, but I was so deep in my own misery that his words had no impact. When he realized that nothing he said would hurt me more than the pain I was already experiencing, he stopped, and we did a site check to make sure we had everything packed.

"Hey, while we're up here, I'm going to run over to the glacier and get some drone footage. I carried it all the way up here, and I think it would be super pretty to fly it over the glacier and then have it pop out at that amazing view at Paso del Cuadrado," he explained, opening up the drone case. "Keep watch for me, yeah? Drones aren't technically allowed here."

We hiked up toward the glacier, and deposited our packs at the rocky saddle between the alpine lakes. Dan wanted to take advantage of the beautiful evening light to capture spectacular drone footage of the peaks and glaciers. I was exhausted physically and emotionally, so I stayed behind while Dan practically ran up the complex of fourth-class rock toward the toe of the glacier.

I watched the drone buzz above him briefly, and then take off on an acrobatic aerial journey. He flew the drone high above the ice, watching the camera from his phone, adjusting the angle as needed to get the shots he had envisioned. The light was fading as dusk approached and the sun dipped low in the sky. He needed a few takes; the drone went up to the pass, popped above the ridge to the view of the mountains and ice cap, returned back down the glacier in sweeping arcs, and then began its climb again.

It was perfectly quiet except for the buzzing of the drone and the never-ending *whoosh* and rumble of the winds at these higher elevations. I envied the drone: the ease with which it ascended, weightless, shooting up the glacier in a fraction of the time that the hazardous climb had taken me. I longed for the freedom it felt even as the strong winds mercilessly buffeted it from side to side.

I wished to be like that drone. "Dear God, make me a bird. So I could fly far. Far far away from here."

CHAPTER 14

QUICKSAND

February 2017

Carrying the last of our gear in bulging packs, we started our final descent from the mountain in a defeated retreat under the cover of darkness. Dan left me in the dust in his eagerness to get off the mountain. My stomach was angry and I had to stop frequently to allow it to empty—not ideal on an exposed, rocky mountainside, but at least no one else was there to witness it. *C'est la vie.*

About halfway down the steep slope, I met up with Dan. He was wincing in pain and told me he'd fucked up some ligaments in his ankle. He'd rolled it on a rock while trail running down, and now he didn't know what to do. He was out of weed and desperate for relief. We didn't have any pain meds with us since those had been carried off in our previous trip down the mountain.

I felt helpless and wished I had something to ease his pain. His pack must have weighed over 75 pounds, overloaded with the rest of the gear we needed to take down. To make matters worse, his stomach was also protesting just like mine. Over five miles remained to get back to the trailhead, and since we no longer had the rental car, we faced an additional long walk on the road back to town.

"Just go ahead of me, okay? I don't want you to hear my screams as I walk," he instructed me as he struggled to descend on his injured ankle. It made sense in theory, but didn't work out since I didn't want to be on my own in the dark, and I felt compelled to help him as he hobbled along.

We stumbled through the somber forest in the pitch black, sheltered by the trees for the very last time. Hours dragged on, punctuated only by many urgent stops for our exploding stomachs. We were out of food and water, had no extra warm layers, and didn't have the tent or sleeping equipment—those had all been carried down on our previous trip out. Our careless lack of preparation is unacceptable and shocking to me now when I look back.

I thought briefly about drinking the river water, but without a filter and already experiencing an upset stomach, I couldn't bring myself to do it. By the time we crossed the river for one final time and limped into the trailhead, utterly spent, it was well after midnight. We collapsed on our packs and both of us broke down into tears, alone in the dark in this remote countryside. I lay on my pack, looking up at the unfamiliar constellations, finding no answers as usual. All I felt was pain, exhaustion, and the stark reality of isolation.

The road was deserted, rendering hitchhiking impossible, and we couldn't call a taxi from town. We decided to abandon our huge packs and limp to the nearest rural hostel, El Pilar, about a mile down the dirt road.

We were barely functioning at this point due to hunger, dehydration, fatigue, the cold, and whatever stomach bug we had caught. I cursed myself for not bringing another jacket, and tortured myself with thoughts of curling up in the tent we didn't have with us. Dan struggled with his ankle, my hip was throbbing, and both of us were on the brink of passing out. We walked the mile in a foggy half-consciousness.

In a delirium, we reached the hostel. I made the soul-crushing mistake of getting my hopes up before we knocked. No one answered the door of the building, and all of the lights were out. We walked around the hostel grounds, banging on windows and doors, calling out for someone—anyone—to help us as we shivered. In an outbuilding, a woman miraculously answered the door, but shortly after seeing us and exchanging a few words, she waved us off and left us to fend for ourselves. I couldn't blame her. If two grungy strangers showed up on my doorstep in the middle of the night, I wouldn't let them in either. I felt uneasy about trespassing as we circumnavigated the main building, but we were desperate for help. No one heard us, or if they did, they ignored us.

Nada. We were on our own, unable to limp additional hours back to El Chaltén, over nine miles away.

There were two front doors of the main hostel—one to the outside, then a tiny entryway, and then the door to get inside the building. The first door was unlocked, so we had a small area partially sheltered from the wind, but unheated. The second door was locked, so we couldn't get into the actual building.

Dan decided to pull the thread-thin curtains off the windows as insulation against the ground, but it didn't do much of anything. They were thin as doilies. We spread out these meager white curtains with their intricate lacy texture, and huddled together on the rough concrete. It was bitterly cold. With no insulation, I shivered and rubbed my limbs. I hunkered down on my side, the hard floor unforgiving on my sick, aching body. My throat felt raw from the lack of water and the intermittent crying.

Being out of food and water, and so physically fatigued, added to the difficulties. The ground stole all of our remaining heat, and we each had just the one unsubstantial layer we'd been wearing on the hike. I begged for the sweet relief of sleep, but it eluded me. Suffering and exhaustion overcame me. I stopped shivering and made no further effort to keep myself warm. I was too spent to actively prevent the mild hypothermia from setting in as the ground stole any heat.

Time passed in a sluggish haze as my brain became confused, and I found myself unable to properly talk or move. I felt like I was in a dreamlike, frigid state wading through quicksand, as if the world had become too heavy and too tired. I gave up and succumbed to the cold, drifting off into the metaphorical quicksand for a few hours.

At some point, Dan must have observed how desperately cold I was in my meager hiking outfit, freezing there on the ground next to him. He left the small entryway and quested off into the night to gather some branches and make a fire. He returned and forced me to get up, helping me to my feet like I was drunk. We limped outside, and huddled in thorn bushes around the tiny flames. We passed the rest of the night half-lying in the bushes, trying to scavenge enough fuel from nearby plants to keep the tiny fire going. I watched the fire in a trance, rotating over time so different parts of my body could warm up slightly in turn, but my core temperature never seemed to increase. The fire was too small. The haze and quicksand-feeling pressed in on me as the cold settled deep within me. Never fully sleeping, never alert, just sick and hollow.

The sun finally dawned after the coldest night of my life. Sunrise lit up Fitz Roy in a magical display of coral and crimson. We knocked again on the front door of the hostel, and this time, an employee answered and ushered us inside. He let us sit on the couch by a fireplace even though we were totally filthy and had no money to offer him. I wondered if any other climbers had ever shown up on the doorstep here with the hope of warmth and water, but then realized that was unlikely—we were idiots for not having a tent and layers with us. The couch and warmth felt luxurious after lying on cold concrete and then dirt. He gave us tea, and I expressed my gratitude as the warm water graced my throat. Dan and I must have looked horrendous.

We waited there, exhausted, ready to go back to El Chaltén to lick our wounds. It was still early in the morning, but as soon as businesses started to open, the hostel called a taxi for us. An hour passed, we were picked up, driven back up to the trailhead to retrieve our packs, and then dropped off in town.

We reserved a final hostel in El Chaltén, and bought bus tickets to El Calafate for the next day. Zombified, we sat at a cafe on our laptops and looked at weather reports and the drone footage from the previous night. Dan bought us coffees, and then he made a post on Instagram with this caption:

> "I failed on Fitz Roy. Two years in a row I failed on Fitz Roy. The pain. The sense of loss. The anger. The amount of times I've screamed FUCK into 70 mph winds that just didn't give a shit. I can't express the hurt. It sounds ridiculous. But we gave up everything for this, and we lost. Traveling is so hard. Dragging hundreds of pounds of gear down a mountain you've walked 7 times in two weeks. Watching the weather smile at you leaving. Fitz's middle-finger. There's no way to convey the sense

of shame, failure, and honest depression. Last night we dropped our packs at Rio Electrico around 1:00 AM. No movement in my right ankle, I hobble another mile and a half with my right arm around Fallon for support. We finally arrive, but there's nobody awake at Pilar to take us to El Chaltén. Another three hour walk. So I build us a fire. We'd hoped for wine, and maybe a consolatory meal. Instead we shiver and moan and bitch at the night to turn to day. They say a watched pot never boils. But I watched one of the most desperate nights of my life . . . every second of it . . . turn to day. As it always has, and, as I trust it always will. Words can't share the sense of loss we feel. But we've cut our losses, and we're moving north for better weather. Hope all is well back home."

After updating my family and roommates with a watered-down version where I skipped over the bad parts, I searched for my journal to write about the experience, but realized I couldn't find it anywhere. I tore apart all of my packs, asked Dan if he'd seen it, and then asked the cafe employees if they'd received a lost and found journal. No luck.

We'd be leaving El Chaltén for the final time in the morning, and I had to accept that my journal was gone. *First my cameras, now my journal too? Fuck.* It felt like I was being robbed of my memories. *But maybe that's for the best . . . ? No, I want to be able to relive what's happened and remember how I felt at the time.* I started a new document on my laptop and started to write everything I could remember while it was fresh. As painful as it was, I didn't want to forget.

"You know, I think having children is, like, the ultimate optimism. You have to believe you can bring them into a better world in the future," Dan said as the landscape zoomed past outside the bus window. I wasn't feeling so optimistic after yesterday's events.

"Mmm, maybe. I don't want kids. There's too many people already. You gotta spend so much money and time on them for decades. And giving birth sounds like shit," I countered, making a fake barfing noise.

"Nah man, when I have a son, I'm going to name him Dean. Like the Kerouac character in *On the Road*. And like Dean Potter," Dan said confidently. I thought about how he behaved when things went wrong, and internally shuddered at the thought of him ever being a parent. He was feeling thoughtful that day and wanted to dive into a deep conversation. My brain and body were still recovering from the freezing night, and I felt low. I didn't want to get into this stuff, but there was nothing else to do on this bus ride.

Dan droned on faux-philosophically about life plans, kids, and careers.

"One of my professors at the U calls me Hem, like for Hemingway. She said my writing was just like him. I need to get writing again. Maybe I can do that for work," he wondered out loud as he fidgeted with a pack of cigarettes, pulling one in and out of the pack repeatedly. I agreed passively to indulge him, but internally I was rolling my eyes. I couldn't stomach his bullshit anymore.

He was bummed about our failure on Fitz Roy, like he'd expressed in his social media post, but it seemed like his mania was providing him with ample distractions to ignore what had happened. I was worried about what would come next for us, but grateful to be off the mountain and alive, with all my gear back. Thinking about the distant future sounded like an unproductive exercise when I couldn't even predict what would happen the next day.

I resigned myself to go along with Dan since I had no money, and felt like I was out of options and energy. Surviving meant indulging his every desire and decision. When we arrived in El Calafate, Dan's mood darkened.

"Let's go over to the Hertz shop. I wanna kill Pablo. He deserves whatever is coming to him, that dirty motherfucker." Dan was dead set on finding Pablo and getting revenge for the rental car fiasco. "I could get a knife, and get him outside, and fuck him up. He won't stand a chance." Dan looked determined, and I was concerned about the violent fantasy coming to fruition. Murder seemed like a harsh punishment for Pablo's transgressions of overcharging us for an accident that wasn't our fault and spitting in Dan's face.

We dropped our bags off at a hostel, ate lunch, and walked over to Hertz. Dan spent some time plotting and stewing. Eventually, he got himself hyped up and went inside. I sat on a bench in the plaza waiting for him, worried about what he'd do, absent-mindedly rubbing my sore hip and watching people walk by on the road. It smelled like rain and gasoline. Dan emerged with a scowl on his face.

"Guess fucking what? Pablo wasn't here." I breathed a sigh of relief as Dan continued. "They didn't even have to tow the rental back here. They were able to drive it back from Chaltén! It must not have actually been totaled if they were able to drive it back. He lied to me! Fuck, I can't believe he charged me that much." He put his hand to his forehead and pushed back his hair, pissed off.

That evening, he went back to the Hertz for a stake out, watching to see if Pablo would show up. He waited nearby with rocks ready—to throw or clobber, I wasn't sure. Thankfully, nothing happened.

Dan and I discussed what to do next. He was out of weed and prescriptions, and wanted to go north to climb. Since I had no money left, I wanted to completely throw in the towel and go home.

"No, Fallon, we lugged all that big wall shit down here for Cochamó and Frey. I bet the weather will be better up north in Bariloche. Let's buy our flights."

I explained to him that my new credit card needed to stay empty for the eventual flight back to the States, and that I had nothing left for the flight to Bariloche. We had a serious talk about money, and I had to defend my situation. I'd only had a month to prepare for the trip, had to buy a passport and loads of gear, had put the original flight on my other credit card, and hadn't had enough time to work and save up for this. He'd been the one urging me to come down here with him on such short notice.

He reluctantly agreed to help me if I could meet certain conditions, like supporting his climbing goals, and he chastised me about my financial situation. There was nothing I could do, and we both knew that. I was cornered, and despite feeling enraged and worried, I had to placate him. He had the money, and therefore all the power too. He said we could get jobs teaching English in Bariloche to make some money. Dan begrudgingly bought both our flights. We walked around a street market in the endless search for weed, and he had no success.

In the morning, before I got up, Dan made another social media post:

"Grateful for this girl that follows me up and down glaciers. It must be nearly impossible to put up with me. Honestly, I know it's impossible. By now, I know myself. I'm hard to date. I ask too much of people; I wear them down. She literally bleeds from both hands and knees, following or finishing my leads. Climbing with Fallon, I push myself to the point of tears. I look behind me, to make sure she's alright, and she's smiling. I ask her to learn a second language, and now she speaks it better than I do. Then, after a long day out, she's everything else I need. Beautiful. Curls. Lashes. Eyes. Like . . . Disney princess. Lady . . . With this tramp. I'm often irritable, moody, and, at my best, (let's get real) I can be kind of obnoxious. Like lemme tell you EVERYTHING I know and EVERYTHING I don't. I'm passionate but then melancholic. Manic-depressive. She listens, with patience far beyond me. She inspires me. Some of my most beautiful thoughts were only thought because she was loving enough to listen. And then she sits with me in silence when I'm tortured by my thoughts. I'm amazed to have found someone so patient with me; so forgiving of my many shortcomings; so understanding of my disorder. I don't use that word lightly. Perhaps, it's time I opened up about bipolar disorder. If anything, so I can remind myself . . . to be better toward those of you who've found it in your hearts to love me, despite my countless flaws. No girl's ever treated me this well. I've learned that my time with people often burns like a fuse, but . . . Fallon's been something of a candle. This post is yours babe. I love you. You've actually seen me at my worst. You know that; I know that. But the best is yet to come. Thank you for roping up with this wreckage of a soloist, and for reminding me that two climb way harder than one. At your service, hun. Wake up. Let's get a drink."

I was surprised by his change of tone after he'd berated me the day before. I guessed he was finally acknowledging self-awareness of his behavior and habits, and the words gave me hope: for him, for me, for us. I also wondered if the post was just for appearances, or if it was genuine. Maybe a mix of both. Either way, it didn't make a difference in my current situation. Before we knew it, we were shoving our carry-on bags into the overhead bin of a tiny plane to San Carlos de Bariloche, saying goodbye to the southern part of Patagonia for the last time.

CHAPTER 15

SANGRE

February 2017

Bariloche greeted us with the beautiful Lago Nahuel Huapi glittering blue next to Swiss-style buildings and an ornate cathedral. Chocolate shops lined the cobblestoned streets, and live musicians brought violin crescendos into mountain air filled with the aroma of lavender being bundled for sale by artisans. Tourists mingled with locals at quaint restaurants and bars. We fell into step among this romantic town, grateful for a change of pace and scenery. It was a much larger city than El Chaltén, with far more amenities.

Dan found us a nice hotel downtown for our first night. He hoped we'd only need one night, and then we could head up to Frey, the local climbing area in Nahuel Huapi National Park. When we got up to our room in the hotel, his mood soured and he confronted me.

"I just paid so much for this room. I wish you could help," he grumbled as he dropped a backpack next to the bed.

"I'm sorry. I didn't *want* to run out of money. You and I both know that I couldn't save up enough for this. I don't know what to do." I sighed. "Thanks for getting us a hotel. From now on, let's find cheaper places to stay. Or just camp or something."

"Yeah. I just wanted to get us somewhere comfortable after the hell we went through up there. Dude, I wish I had weed. I've been out for so long now, I can't handle it!" Dan sat on the bed. His leg bounced up and down. He ran his hand through his hair over and over.

"Well, hopefully you can find some weed soon. There's gotta be some around here . . . I mean, there's so many skiers and hiker tourist types here, ya know."

"I can't fucking stand this! I need weed! I don't have money to support us both! I have to figure out how to get scripts here too. I wanna fucking die!" he yelled.

I felt the familiar sinking feeling in my gut. I knew what was coming.

He started pacing back and forth in the room, working himself up into a rage. "So much of this is your fault! You stupid bitch!" His fist made contact with his skull in a steady rhythm. "I want to die!"

I closed my eyes and took a deep breath. I was torn between being pissed off at these never-ending insults, and feeling concerned for him as he harmed himself. *Why do I always find myself in this situation? He's so mean to me that I don't want to even help him. But I don't want him to hurt himself either. I need to stand up for myself.*

"Dan! You have to stop. I can't handle this. It hurts a lot . . ." I hesitated but kept going anyway. "I don't want to be insulted by my boyfriend. I deserve better than this. I thought you loved me. Stop hurting yourself!" I said as sternly as I could manage. Inside, I was terrified, but I pretended to have a backbone with the hope of self-preservation.

"Oh, it hurts *you*?! You know that I hurt myself and break shit because I can't hit you! You ruin everything!" He tugged at his shirt violently and tore the fabric. He was suffering so much inside that he wanted to break free, and the shirt was the closest thing he could destroy to try to free himself from his own prison.

I was exhausted from traveling, managing each of our problems, and stressing over money and my food allergies; I had little patience. Normally, I tried to be sweet to help calm him down and make myself less of a target. Not this time.

"You can't blame this on me! And you can't blame this on bipolar either! Being bipolar doesn't mean you have to hurt either of us. You're using it as a crutch. It's just an excuse for your shitty behavior!" I yelled back. I was getting bold now, and I felt a rush of power.

"That's not true! How dare you say that. You don't get it! You slut! I hate you!" he screamed as he threw things at me. I rarely fought back, so my resistance had fanned the flames of his fury. He slumped down against a wall, and then fully onto the floor. He lifted his head and dropped it as hard as he could onto the hardwood, over and over.

"You can't do this to me! I don't want to see this. I'm going to call the police. You need help that I can't give you!" I said, out of other options.

"You're my girlfriend. You need to help me, not hand me over to the cops! I'll fucking kill myself if you call the cops!" he shouted back, still banging his head against the floor. I tried to stop him from doing this, but whenever I got near him, he pushed me away. It was useless to intervene.

"I need wine! That's my best bet of calming down. You need to go buy me wine! I can't go out like this."

I looked outside—it was dark. "Dan, I don't want to go out in the city alone at night to buy wine. That's a bad idea. I don't think it would be safe."

"No! You have to go buy me wine, bitch! After all I've done for you, you can't do this one small thing for me? Wine is the only other thing that could help me since I don't have weed!"

I argued with him a bit more, but he won. He handed me a stack of pesos, and I grabbed my purse and left. My hands shook. I went downstairs and asked the folks at the hotel lobby where I could find wine nearby. They explained that it was past the hour they could sell alcohol in the city. *Shit.* Despite their warning, I went out onto the street and looked left and right. I spotted the lights of a *quiosco* a couple blocks away, and I walked there quickly with my head held high. I wanted to act confident so I wouldn't be a target.

When I got to the *quiosco*, I received the same news: it was too late to sell alcohol. I pleaded with the cashier, and wondered if they could hear the desperation in my voice. I didn't want to return empty handed. They refused, so I bought some chocolate as a last resort, and booked it back to the hotel.

When I got to the room, Dan looked hopeful at first, but as soon as he saw I didn't have the wine, he exploded. I explained what had happened, and offered up the chocolate, but that wasn't good enough.

"What the fuck, Fallon! You have to find me wine! That's literally all I'm asking for. It's so simple! There must be wine in this city. Go back out there and find me some!"

I felt stuck. I knew I wouldn't be able to find him anything to drink, but he was adamant. He went into the bathroom, pushed a towel up against the slit at the bottom of the door, and smoked a cigarette, carefully blowing the smoke out the tiny window above the shower. I hoped smoking would calm him down, but it seemed to have little effect.

"When I get out of here, you need to be back with a fucking bottle of wine!" His yell was muffled by the door.

I left the room again, knowing I wouldn't have any luck, but at least I'd be able to tell him I tried. That's all I could really do.

I passed by the front lobby and found myself alone on the street once again. I let out a heavy sigh and wiped the tears off my cheeks. I looked around and enjoyed the relative silence—this part of downtown was quiet at this time of night. I didn't want to be alone out here, but I didn't want to go back and face Dan without the wine either. I set off in the opposite direction this time, wandering around with dwindling hope as I faced the same fate at more stores. My efforts were in vain.

Eventually, I had to go back to the hotel. I craved sleep. I didn't want to have to listen to Dan's rampage anymore, and I was sick of his shit. I hoped that he'd knocked himself out or fallen asleep in my absence. When I came back, he was even angrier.

"How could you fail on such an easy fucking task? You're so incompetent! You can't do anything!" He scratched himself while hurling more insults at me.

"I hate you! You make me want to die!" he shouted, his neck straining as he beat his head more. I wondered how his brain could inflict so much trauma on itself. "I don't even want to sleep next to you!" he added. *Yeah, me neither, asshole.*

"Fine! I'll just buy my flight home to the States then. I saved that other credit card so I can get home. Is that what you want? Then you don't have to put up with me if you hate me so much. I'm just a burden! I'll fucking leave. I was excited about the climbing here, but I don't want to deal with this anymore. I'm done!" I yelled back.

"You're not going anywhere! I won't let you. You are going to stay right here, you cunt!" he threw things at me again, and while I cowered to avoid getting hit, he lunged for my purse. "You can't leave without your ID and passport!"

I cried out of exhaustion and fear. I felt deeply depleted and helpless. Anything was better than staying here enduring his abuse, but I was trapped. I dissociated to cope. *I can't get out of this, so I might as well just try to tune it out till he gets it out of his system.* I let my eyes unfocus and glaze over, and tried to not hear what he was yelling at me. *This has nothing to do with me. He's just sick,* I tried to remind myself.

The hotel room became a blur: the bed, the dresser, the lamp, the desk, all of our bags, the mess from Dan's psychotic break, all of it fading together into a dream.

I am not here. This is not happening.

I could hear noise from his yelling, from things breaking, from objects hitting the wall, but I chose not to differentiate. It was just noise. All of it was just noise. I distracted myself with other thoughts.

Dan hated that I wouldn't respond to him. He got right up next to me and yelled in my ear. I could feel the heat and moisture from his breath, but I chose not to hear what he said. I did not need to discern or listen or take in whatever he was saying or doing. I sat there like a statue, forcing my brain to stay turned off, begging for sleep to come.

The sun came first.

He eventually calmed himself down enough to sleep for part of the morning. When we got up, his eyes were puffy, his knuckles raw, his head bruised. I could barely look at him. The day passed in a haze: getting coffee and sitting on a cafe patio, walking along the shore of the deep blue lake, touring the cathedral covered in stained glass windows, sampling incredible chocolate from cute shops, and talking to locals at a street market while Dan searched for weed. He bought a small necklace with a cross pendant on it and started to wear it every day. Neither of us was religious. He claimed he was wearing it to help him blend in since everyone here was Catholic. It made no sense to me, and seemed like a waste of money. *Why aren't we heading up to climb?* I wondered. Since he wouldn't let me leave, and I didn't have any money, I wanted to at least go climbing.

I wanted to appreciate the idyllic city and beauty around me, but I was too on edge. I was walking on eggshells so as not to set him off again. Whenever I needed food, he had to buy it for me, and I died a little bit inside knowing that he had control of my needs as essential as food and shelter.

The hotel was too expensive to stay long term, and Dan was set on us staying in Bariloche indefinitely. He booked us a rental to use as a home base on the outskirts of town. We passed a welcome sign that said "Bienvenido al Barrio Junta Vecinal San Francisco II y III." As I looked around at the trash and dilapidated brick buildings in the neighborhood, I didn't feel very welcome. The taxi rumbled down the dirt road and deposited us in front of a two-story concrete building partially concealing a junkyard out back. High fences surrounded the plot and a little black dog ran up to greet us as we strained under our gear-filled luggage.

At the door, a plump older woman was pleased to see us. She introduced herself as Marta and ushered us inside.

In Spanish, she explained that her son had built the house and managed the rental, and she lived upstairs. He was traveling right now, so if we needed anything, we could ask her. She prepared maté and we all sipped on the hot tea. Our rental on the lower floor was modest and had low ceilings. Marta spoke no English, but was eager to chat with us in our limited Spanish nonetheless. I was slowly improving my skills.

Once we were settled in, we started searching for English teaching jobs on our laptops. After some applications and emails, we set out to get laundry done and buy groceries to stock up at the new place. We walked on dirt roads out of the neighborhood, down a long paved hill, and into town. At the laundromat, I was reluctant to hand over my technical climbing clothing. I worried they'd damage it somehow with high heat or harsh soap, but I surrendered the stuff sack anyway. Anxiety about my belongings was ever-present.

We wandered over to the markets in town, where Dan struck up conversations with anyone who looked like they might sell weed. I tried to distance myself from him as I admired the jewelry, paintings, and other wares from the merchants. Everywhere we went downtown, there was live music. Dan found someone to share a joint with him on the beach, but he hadn't been able to buy bud to take with him. We moseyed back to the rental, picking up our clean laundry on the way. We cooked dinner and checked the weather: the forecast for Frey showed complete rain all the way down the screen.

"Man, I feel really bloated. My stomach hurts," I complained. Dan brushed me off and we went to bed in our new temporary home.

In the morning, my bowels forced me out of bed and I ran to the toilet. My stomach unleashed its fury as I grimaced in pain. I couldn't bring myself to eat breakfast. I looked down at my bloated belly, appalled, feeling it contort itself. I ran back to the bathroom in agony, conceding to the urgent need of my digestive system to empty itself. I groaned and crossed my arms over my abdomen, hoping this would be the last time.

It was not the last time. The shits started to arrive with increasing frequency until they came every few minutes. "I feel weak," I told Dan, "like I'm going to pass out." My knees buckled and my face paled. Dan ran out onto the street looking for help. He hailed down some cops, and then helped me into one of their cars. Bariloche flew by as the police car raced to the hospital.

When we arrived, we had to wait in a lobby to check in. Since we were American, we'd have to pay out of pocket. I had no money, so Dan produced the cash.

"¿Dónde está el baño?" I asked urgently. A nurse pointed me to the bathroom and I rushed over to it. When I was done, Dan told me that there was a wait for a bed. I slumped into a vinyl chair, feeling my heart pound and sweat collect on my brow. Every couple of minutes, I ran back to the bathroom. One time, it was occupied, and the nurse explained in Spanish that someone was collecting a urine sample. I stood there, running out of time, and asked if there was another bathroom. She shook her head. This was the only toilet in the hospital.

My gut jumped and twisted in a fantastic choreography of illness. I made it just in time once the other patient exited. My head spun as I sat on the toilet, the room blurry in my wooziness. When I looked down, I was surprised to see the toilet was full of blood. *Oh fuck. This is not good.* I impatiently waited back in the lobby, nervous about what was happening to me.

Eventually, a nurse led us back to a room filled with hospital beds, and motioned to an empty one. I crawled onto it, clutching my stomach. It felt like I was digesting thorns and my abdomen had ballooned up, making my skin taut.

Almost immediately, I had to go back to the bathroom again. I sobbed on the toilet. The shits were becoming more painful, more bloody, and more frequent. Life was draining out of me one drop at a time, and I started to lose touch with reality over the ensuing hours.

I collapsed back on the hospital bed and shivered violently. My heart beat like a hummingbird. In my confusion, with goosebumps all over my body, I flashed back to my recent mild hypothermia. *My poor body*, I thought. I was too lost and dizzy to do anything about it, but Dan demanded they bring me a blanket. "Godammit, why won't anyone help us in this fucking place?"

After much delay, an unwashed blanket was tossed toward my bed, and Dan gingerly covered me in it. I was grateful for it, and too far gone to worry about it being dirty. The hospital was underprepared and understaffed. Dan ran out to grab me Gatorade and returned quickly.

I was dehydrated from hours of losing fluids. A few nurses struggled to get a needle in my arm for an IV. I cried from the added pain of the needles. Their five failed attempts were more painful than all of my tattoos combined. The insides of my elbows were bloody, raw battle scenes. I took a bathroom break and returned. Finally, the IV went in, and fluids flowed into me. A nurse explained in Spanish that the IV bag needed to stay over my head when I got out of the hospital bed to go to the bathroom.

"Why is this happening to me? What is this?" I moaned. Dan tried to comfort me, and swore off the hospital workers for not helping me enough. He sang to me gently and held my hand as I thrashed around, unable to get comfortable. He scooted up against me to try to give me some of his body heat since I was still shivering.

The knives in my stomach made me curl up into a ball. The inevitable urge returned, and I cast off the scratchy blanket as Dan snatched the IV bag and we rushed toward the toilet. I cursed the cheap toilet paper for making everything even more painful. It felt like this was never going to end. I was in such distress that I could hardly bother to worry about how disgusted Dan must have been as he watched me shit blood over and over.

Eventually, the doctors had me collect a stool sample to send off for testing. When I returned to the bed, I was fading even more, my face's pallor a reflection of my inward struggle. Dan tried desperately to get in touch with my family as I writhed in pain.

Often, the singular bathroom was occupied. While we waited eagerly outside the door, I was too weak to stand, so Dan had to hold me up with one hand while his other hand held up the bag of saline.

I became lost in a sea of pain, weakness, and drowsiness, adrift in my affliction. I longed for death and wished he would pay me a visit. "Please, I don't want to feel this anymore. Just let me die. Come on!" I imagined myself begging for death to come, summoning him telepathically as I succumbed to hypovolemia. I became irritated with death for making me wait. Each time I got out of bed to run to the toilet, my anger intensified. I groaned as I made the trip back and forth and caught a glimpse of the blood each time before I could flush it out of sight. I wasn't thinking logically enough to remain stoic through the illness; my body was shutting down and I surrendered to the misery.

I lost track of time. My only way to measure its passing was by counting how many trips I had made to the toilet. The bag of saline had run out a dozen shits ago. The bag now looked vacuum-sealed, devoid of every drop that had been greedily sucked out of it by my withering body. I faded in and out of consciousness, shivering under the dirty blanket, waiting to find out what was wrong with me.

"Ay-col-ee," the nurse seemed to say when she returned with news. I wracked my brain. *Huh? What is Ay-col-ee?* Dan and I spoke with her, confused by what she was trying to tell us. After much bewilderment, it dawned on me. My Spanish was fuzzy in my current state, but the pronunciation of vowels finally clicked.

I had E. coli. It was causing hemorrhagic dysentery, which explained the blood. They gave me Ciprofloxacin (incidentally, it was the same antibiotic I'd taken for my UTI which had given me tendon problems) and something to help with the stomach cramping. I later found out that antibiotics aren't necessarily the best treatment, but I didn't know that at the time.

"Let's get the fuck out of here. This hospital is unsanitary." Dan made a grossed out face. "Now that we know what's wrong, let's just call docs in the US to help guide treatment. At least at the Airbnb you'll have blankets and your own toilet." We left in a taxi, and I collapsed into bed back at our rental. The rest of the day passed in a complete blur.

The next day, though I still had diarrhea, it was no longer bloody. I was able to drink water and Gatorade. Eventually, I added back in small portions of mild foods. I still suffered from stomach cramps, fatigue, and weakness for the next week. Dan ran out on errands, looking for weed, wine, and food. I lay in bed, recovering, reading books when I could, and using my laptop to search for local English teaching jobs. I felt pressure to pull my weight since I had no money. Dan looked at some longer term apartments for rent and even checked out a motorcycle. He was bored of the long walk to get into town.

Marta came down to check on us one day. She became concerned when she learned of my illness. She held up a finger and went outside. After a few minutes, she returned with some green leaves in her hand, heated up water on the stove, and pushed the mug of mystery tea toward me on the wooden table. I was skeptical but drank it to be polite.

Next, she pulled out a piece of long fabric. Her expression implied that she was about to do something important and serious. She took my hands and folded the fabric in a careful manner around them while reciting a prayer in Spanish. Her voice was grave and maternal. When she was done, she gave me a gentle smile and sat with me for a time. I was honored by her kindness.

After she left, I was back to the lonely confines of the bed for long stretches of time. Dan would come in and blame me for getting sick since it was delaying our climbing plans and wasting money. I lay there exhausted and in pain as he yelled at me for ruining the trip. I had no emotional capacity left to defend myself. He'd been sweet and caring in the hospital, but now he was annoyed with me. He told me I needed to try harder to get better, and find a job so I could start contributing to our life in Bariloche.

One night, he cooked a nice meal, and offered me some of the food. The serving on the plate was far too large for my stomach's current capabilities. I took a bite and was assaulted by spiciness. My weak GI tract couldn't handle spice yet. When I told him I couldn't eat it, he yelled at me and called me ungrateful, and wouldn't talk to me the rest of the night.

After a few more days, I was well enough to walk around town with Dan for short periods of time, but I had to sit and take breaks often. We went to a quaint chocolate shop—even thinking about eating chocolate made me queasy—and then emerged next to the lake. I sat on a bench looking out at the water, hearing its small waves lap at the shore.

"Dude, when are you gonna be better?" Dan asked.

I shook my head. "I don't know. I feel like trash. This sucks."

"Well . . . The weather still looks horrible and rainy at Frey and Cochamó. Let's do something else while we wait," Dan said. "I heard I might be able to find weed down in El Bolsón. There's a bunch of hippies there apparently. Let's spend Valentine's Day there."

CHAPTER 16

VALENTINE

February 2017

Lucky Strike smoke, secondhand, swirled in my lungs as I labored under the weight of my bags. I spoke hurried Spanish to an unfamiliar man sipping a Quilmes, the smell of beer as overwhelming as it was sticky on my sandals from walking the streets of Bariloche.

"*¿Es este el lugar para el autobús que viaja al Bolsón?*"

I was unsure of myself, but he appreciated my linguistic effort. Although I was confused by his slang, I processed enough of his response to understand: yes, this is the bus stop for El Bolsón. The man's daughter scurried past me with wide eyes, her small hands grasping a packet of sweet *dulce de leche*.

I squinted at my ticket, concentrating to ensure I was reading it correctly. I'd relied on Dan to buy our tickets since I was still financially dependent on him. Money in my bank account was a distant dream by now, and I had just a few pesos floating around in my purse. I inched away as Dan steadily puffed his cigarette, avoiding eye contact. I was surrounded by a crowd, but loneliness was my primary emotion.

Externally, I was burdened by my 70-liter backpack on my front, Dan's giant climbing haul bag on my back, the Portaledge on one shoulder, and my carry-on pack awkwardly hanging from my elbow. Dan and I were the only white people at the bus station. I shifted uncomfortably on the sidewalk, my knees sore from gear carries, my heart heavy with lessons, and my stomach still doing cartwheels from the hemorrhagic E. coli.

Dan stamped out his cigarette with his Converse, and muttered, "Fuck." My skin crawled from the eyes watching me from every direction. Our absurd amount of climbing equipment and expedition gear made us a walking spectacle.

"Go get me a beer, will ya?" Dan asked, handing me some pesos. I dropped the bags, walked inside to a grimy counter, and returned with a Quilmes. Dan downed it and threw the bottle in the trash. It was Valentine's Day. *How romantic!*

A rickety two-tiered bus parted the herd of waiting people, who swooped up their belongings in preparation for boarding. I exchanged a knowing look with Dan. We handed off our bags to the driver and he tossed them into a compartment below the cabin. I stepped onto the bus, grateful to escape the bustle of the station and the weight of our gear.

The driver steered the bus south, and for two hours, I watched the scenery out the window: emerald forests, jagged mountains, deep rivers. I ran to the cramped bathroom at the back of the bus a few times, still reeling from my illness.

We found ourselves in a new environment. El Bolsón was a small town, visited mostly for its outdoor activities, nestled in a river valley under a rugged ridgeline of mountains. They felt miniature compared to Fitz Roy. We stood in line at a bank for Dan to max out the ATM cash withdrawal, and then beelined it for the street market.

The market was the main attraction in town. Rundown booths lined the streets, and artisans sat behind their tables, carefully watching the tourists handling their products. Threadbare tapestries were draped overhead to provide shade and weak protection from potential rain. Kids ran all over the place and hippies smoked while sitting under trees in the grass of the park.

Dan was easily able to find weed, and bought an ornate wooden pipe. I realized I hadn't bought any kind of souvenir from this trip to bring home with me. I walked the aisle of the market, looking side to side at my options. I found a leather belt with an intricate geometric pattern made by a local craftsman, and he punched the holes in it according to my waist size. I paid with the last few pesos I could scrounge together from my purse plus some from Dan. I really couldn't afford non-essentials (or anything for that matter), but it was cheap and I was happy to have something permanent, local, and handmade to keep from Argentina. Plus, I needed a belt anyway—my pants were too loose after the weight loss from my dysentery recovery.

As we exited the market, I took a video. Dan smiled into my phone camera and said, "It's the high times farmer's market. It's the coolest thing ever." He winked and we kept walking.

Weed in hand, Dan happily lit up while sitting on the concrete edge of a big fountain. His mood change was immediate: he was the most relaxed I'd seen him in a long time. He slid over next to me on the fountain edge and put his arm around me.

"Will you be my Valentine?" he said playfully.

I laughed and nodded, and we kissed. He was scruffy from not shaving for a while. Dark brown hairs extended across his face, jaw, and neck. Hand in hand, we walked the streets of El Bolsón, taking it all in. He took me out to dinner at a nice restaurant to celebrate. My stomach was still sensitive, but I managed to eat a bit while Dan had his typical Malbec and steak. I popped one of my antibiotics with the meal. When we stepped outside, the sky was aflame with vibrant hues of pink and purple like cotton candy. I gasped. The depth of the cloud layers and saturation of the colors was breathtaking.

"Pink for Valentine's Day. It's perfect!"

Dusk descended in a beige haze, the intensity of the magenta sunset now faded. After an unremarkable night in a hostel, we packed up to head back to Bariloche. On the lawn outside, a black-faced ibis was poking around in the grass. I ran over to it with delight while Dan cautioned against it. It was like the rhea encounter all over again.

"Stay away from that thing! Look how long and pointy its beak is!"

I ignored him. Sitting down at a safe distance, I admired the bird's elegant beak, bright red feet, and earthy feathers. I'd never seen anything quite like it, and it was a welcome moment of natural beauty.

Our return to Bariloche was anticlimactic. Rain fell, and the extended forecast was still showing rain, and only rain. Dan managed to get some of his prescriptions refilled at a pharmacy in town. The return of the meds plus weed made him much more pleasant, and I wondered if things would be okay again. We kept applying to English teaching jobs and looked at apartments, but nothing panned out. Dan was holding on to hope that we could find a way to stay long term. We figured out the bus system, and spent hours walking the city too. Money was burning up fast as we killed time not climbing. Finally, we had a hard discussion about what was coming next.

"I still feel kinda sick. I think my body might take a while to fully recover from all of that," I admitted. "It also sucks being out of money. I don't wanna be a burden on you, hun. I thought the English jobs were gonna be easy to find based on what you said . . ."

"Yeah, I dunno why no one emailed us back. It's super weird. Also, the weather is such shit," Dan said, showing me the weather app on his phone. "I mean, it's just rain and rain and rain. Fuck this."

"Doesn't seem like we're gonna be able to wait this out. I don't know what to do. It would be a lot easier for me to make money back home and just dirtbag."

"Dude. I wanted to make a *life* down here with you." He looked at me with disappointment in his eyes. "Like, we could have done some real shit here. Nothing worked out. This trip was such a failure. Not even close on Fitz. And we didn't even get to *see* Frey or Cochamó. I don't know what I'm gonna tell folks back home." He shook his head and flicked at his cigarette. I could hear the shame in his words.

"I'm sorry. So much of this was my fault . . ." I thought about my illness, my lack of money, how shitty I'd been as a partner.

"Let's go home. We can't wait out this weather. Just don't break up with me when we're back, okay?" He grabbed my knee and stared off into space as he took a drag. We got our phones out and booked the flights for the next day. Ashleigh had messaged me the information for my new credit card, and I carefully copied over the numbers into the airline checkout page. The flight was $1,300. *Ouch. No choice though.*

A cocktail of relief and wariness welled up inside me. I didn't know what I was going to do back home. It was the first time in my adult life I wasn't enrolled in college. Upon my return, I'd have no money. Two nearly maxed-out credit cards. No job lined up. Things had gone wrong so quickly. I kicked myself for my decisions, and became internally angered with Dan for coercing me into this trip. He'd made me think that everything would be okay, and he had been deeply wrong. Now I was in a shit position. I dared not voice it to him.

I wasn't sure how he'd handle the transition. Sinister flashbacks of Dan hitting himself and screaming at me replayed in my head every day. I fantasized about breaking up with him as soon as we arrived back on US soil, but I knew it wouldn't be that simple. He knew it too, and I could see his gears turning, trying to figure out how to maintain control over me.

Deep down, he must have known how unacceptable his behavior had been. I think it scared him. It scared him that he was capable of acting in such a terrifying way. And it scared him because he knew it had pushed me away and filled me with fear and resentment. I'd tried to leave, and threatened to on multiple occasions, and now I'd have the opportunity to follow through. He must have felt very nervous about that.

He'd dug his own grave. It was hard to console him after I'd been treated so poorly. At times, I had to play the game and feign sweetness to prevent further blow ups in the interest of self-preservation. But internally, I was raging and cold, plotting my escape. I simultaneously felt tethered to him and like I never wanted to see him again.

My path had taken an unexpected, convoluted detour. I had strayed too far and now I was broken. Everything felt like a dream, but at the same time, I was acutely aware of what was happening. I was operating on red alert for a chance to rid myself of Dan. All I could think about was getting away from him. A peculiar mix of dissociation and hypervigilance yanked my nervous system back and forth while my head swam with ideas.

We flew to Buenos Aires and then home to the US, with heavy hearts, empty bank accounts, and haunted memories. I arrived home shell-shocked and weary.

PART 3

THE WEST

(iii)
the third time death kissed me
i wandered among
spires with rough granite
towering above
i climbed alone till i was
filled with the Mojave
the desert spilled over the brim
gray crystals under hand and foot
and by the time
i was on the top
i cried
i cried
i lay under the light of the sun
i had no room for death anymore
so i sent him away—
next day on the highway
broken window
i clawed for a handle
screamed into sand
bled onto shards of glass

upon escape, trudged
on the open road
big blue sky above
thu-thump in eardrums
ran between Joshua trees
fell into the grit
collapsed in death's arms
asked him
"why is this so heavy?"
he told me,
"everyone feels the weight,
sweet child"
he kissed me on the nose
gently set me down
on the yellow line
in the middle of the road

CHAPTER 17

KNIFE AND HAMMER

February – April 2017

These are the things I knew to be true during my return to life at home.

Dan blamed me for 90% of the trip's failure.

I needed to make money.

I was not the same person I had been when I'd left.

Lastly, and most importantly, I needed to rock climb.

The most shocking part of returning to the States, besides Trump being in office, was the grocery stores. I had spent my entire life taking for granted the vast selection, high quality, and beautifully stocked shelves of American grocery stores. In Argentina, even the best markets had been relatively small, with a limited variety and almost nothing safe for my food allergies. Now, even with allergies and virtually no budget, I could eat like a king. I wandered the aisles salivating, in awe of the presentation and options. I hadn't realized how much of the trip I had spent deeply hungry. Eating was a sweet relief.

My fantasy about breaking up with Dan as soon as I landed was not realized. We spent the first few days climbing together around St. George, desperate to touch rock after being deprived for so long, before he begrudgingly drove me back to northern Utah in his truck. The entire drive, he kept asking me for reassurance that I wasn't going to leave him. I lied and said I wouldn't, but deep down

I felt conflicted, and delayed action.

I wish I could say that my return to home life was normal, but it was not. I awkwardly rejoined my roommates in Logan, who knew something was off, and I left frequently to go on climbing trips with Dan. When people asked me about what happened in Patagonia, I didn't know what to tell them. I felt ashamed that we hadn't been able to climb anything, but I also knew that a lot of it wasn't within my control. *I went through all of that, and for what?* It was easiest to blame the bad weather and my illness, and change the subject.

By the beginning of March, we were in Indian Creek, UT, only able to complete a couple climbs before we emerged from the tent the next morning to a solemn blanket of snow covering the desert. The Six Shooters were frosted red towers spearing the gray sky, and the sagebrush and rabbitbrush sat dormant under their winter coats. Dan slammed his truck door shut, blasted the heater, and sulked at the impossibility of climbing before pointing us north to return home.

I got hired as a substitute teacher in Logan, and started subbing every day I could. I was grateful for the opportunity. I was barely 20, but I made sure not to tell the high schoolers that I was only a few years older than them. After all, I was almost done with college. Subbing was a perfect fit for me: I excelled in school, loved working with kids, and thrived with the flexible schedule.

I usually got bored at other jobs because of the repetition. Not the case with subbing. Every day was a new adventure. I would show up to different schools, have to locate random classrooms, and teach new subjects all the time. It suited me because of this unpredictable variety. The kids liked me because I was young and not on a power trip to try to control them. I would tell them, "If you're cool, I'll be cool," and they appreciated the mutual respect. I rarely had any students with behavioral problems because of this, and as they sat there completing their work, I got to read books and work on my writing.

Dan and I became (mostly) weekend warriors. With subbing, I could choose my schedule and take time off whenever I wanted, but I tried to maximize the days I worked since I needed the money so badly. The pay was only $65 a day, but I didn't care. It was a relaxing job, and my first paycheck felt so good—now I could pay rent at the end of the month and feed myself.

By mid-March, Dan and I were back for more desert climbing, eager to escape the depressing wintry scene of the Wasatch. In Moab, we fought our way up Indian Creek splitters, and then wrecked ourselves projecting the Crackhouse: a sandstone cave with a low roof split by perfect roof cracks. It was my first time there, and I sensed the magic of the place, so wonderfully tucked away in the canyon country. I could hardly link moves on it back then, and relied on Dan for beta and spotting. It was my first time on a true roof crack, and I was hooked as I battled for every foot of progress while dangling in the cave, torquing my hands and feet to their limits until I'd inevitably slip out and land on a crash pad. Dan idolized Dean Potter, and I looked up to Steph Davis, so the Crackhouse felt like holy ground. He pointed out the best jams to me, and I stood in awe of the length of the climb, astounded that people could actually climb it from start to finish without falling.

Dan and I had easily fallen back into step together in our Utah life. Things were less complicated than they were in Argentina, and for a while, I thought that maybe the stress of the trip was what had triggered his meltdowns. Now that he had a job, a steady flow of weed and prescriptions, and plenty of rock climbing, he was mostly back to the Dan I'd fallen in love with before the trip. We ran around the southern Utah desert together, dodging snow and cops, listening to Blitzen Trapper and Blind Pilot, and getting our climbing fix.

I didn't have time to overthink it. I worked and slept just enough to support our climbing habit, and we were so focused that we could hardly examine our relationship. You don't always end up talking much when there's a hundred feet of rope separating you from each other. I figured if things stayed the same, but didn't get worse, then it would be okay and I could stay with him. I'm not sure what mental gymnastics I did at the time to brush aside his previous attacks, but he must have told me something convincing that blamed it on his mental illness.

Because of work and weather, we couldn't always drive south, so we spent a significant amount of time climbing in the mountains of the Wasatch as well. One day in March, we went up Little Cottonwood Canyon, and Dan hopped on 'The Green Adjective,' a route that starts off with a miniscule seam and slick granite. He placed a microcam and slipped off a couple moves later. I leaned my weight back into the belay to catch him since he was still close to the ground, but the cam popped out, and we tumbled down the granite hillside together in a chaotic jumble of limbs, rope, and gear. When we stopped, I assessed the damage. Besides some bruises and scrapes, we were mostly okay, with two exceptions: my right hand and wrist, and Dan's elbow.

Dan finished the lead, I gave it a toprope, and then we climbed some other nearby routes. I surprised myself by almost sending 'All Chalk and No Action,' a crimpy 5.12a, even with my wrist pain. Dan tried to lead it after me, but couldn't finish it, so I had to lead the entire thing a second time to retrieve the quickdraws. (I finally returned for a send in 2024.) My hand and wrist were getting progressively worse, and I had trouble opening and closing my hand. I belayed with just my left hand as Dan quested up another climb.

Suddenly, I heard a boom reminiscent of a train crash. I looked down at the highway expecting to see a pile up of cars. The sound continued and I searched across the canyon on the north-facing slope to see a massive avalanche cascading down a gully. For minutes, it continued its roar, a slurry of snow, trees, and boulders carving out a path down the mountain. As it thundered on, we remained still, shaken by its power and sheer noise level. I'd never been so close to an avalanche before, even in Patagonia. The waterfall of dirty snow astonished me, and I could hardly focus on belaying as Dan resumed climbing. *Glad we're on this side of the canyon and not over there . . .*

My hand and wrist pain became too hard to ignore, so I got an X-ray back in town, and was sent home with a brace and pain meds. The next week, we found ourselves in American Fork, crossing slick logs over a river gorged with snowmelt to reach a cave to climb in. Then we were back cragging in Little Cottonwood, greedy for more pitches on granite, manically zig-zagging our way across the Wasatch.

At the very end of March, we drove down to St. George for a weekend climbing trip. Dan caught a virus, and was sick when he woke up on April 1. Fever, chills, muscle aches, and nausea took their turns on a rotation in his body. I offered him DayQuil, ibuprofen, blankets, hot packs, water, and food.

We went to an urgent care facility, but the wait was three hours, so we left. We stopped at the grocery store for some food, and when I remarked that it was too warm outside for me to want to eat soup, it pissed him off. I told him I'd make it with him and he could eat it, but I'd get something different for myself. I didn't think it was a big deal, and I apologized since it upset him, but it triggered a horrible episode.

I wish it had been an April Fool's joke, but unfortunately it was all too real. My apology fell on deaf ears. The rest of the car ride was silent. Back at his parents' desert house, he went into the bedroom, and I went to the dining room with my laptop. I wanted a break from his dramatics. Best to keep to myself and work on my computer until his overreaction subsided. He emerged with the key to his truck.

"Pack up your shit. Drive my truck back to Lehi. Put your shit in your car, leave, and never come back," he said resolutely. I raised my eyebrows. *Get out and never come back . . . because I told him I didn't want to eat soup?* He was dead serious.

"Get your shit. Now!" he yelled, holding out the key for me. *Here's my out. I used to want this!* I thought. I didn't protest.

I pushed my chair back from the table, snatched the key from him, and gathered my belongings. I packed up and carried everything to the garage. I took his stuff out of the truck and set it on the garage floor, not wanting to take anything from him during my drive back north. I packed the truck's cab with my bags since I knew the drive would be rainy and snowy.

At this point, I knew how Dan operated under his disorder. I had every intention of following his directions, and knew that disagreeing wouldn't get me anywhere. I pretended to be sad. Inside, I was secretly rejoicing. Our climbing bender had made it easier to ignore the chasm between us, but I still felt upset about how he'd treated me in Patagonia, and had been waiting for the right time to get out.

Once everything was in the truck, he came into the garage.

"You won't even fight for us, will you?"

"You told me to leave! Now you're mad I didn't try to stay? What the fuck do you want?" I was confused and torn.

He started in again with the insults that always accompanied his psychosis. "You're pathetic. You couldn't even offer me more than bread and water when I'm on my deathbed?"

I rolled my eyes. *Deathbed? Really?* He had a minor virus like a cold or flu. Or maybe he was having side effects from drugs he didn't tell me about. I wasn't sure. I didn't know what to believe anymore. My grasp on reality had been steadily slipping away ever since the first time he'd screamed in my face.

"I thought you were too nauseous for anything besides a BRAT diet. How was I supposed to know you wanted other stuff? I'm sorry."

"C'mon Fallon, that's a lie. Do better," he said, disappointed. "I wanted Powerade and better food. How hard would that have been?" He walked back into the house, and I followed him.

"If you wanted other shit, why didn't you say so? I can't read your mind. We went to the grocery store—you could've just said something."

"You bitch! I read *your* mind when you had dysentery and got you what you needed."

I thought back to all of the times he yelled at me and called me lazy and ungrateful while I was recovering. He had been supportive in the hospital, but back at the AirBnb, he had only made things worse. He was delusional and continued his tirade.

"You're a shitty girlfriend. You don't deserve me."

"Fine! Then let me leave. Clearly my effort is unappreciated," I retorted, annoyed with him. "I can't be what you want me to be."

He started throwing decorative pine cones from a basket across the house, shattering them on the tile and sending tiny wood pieces everywhere.

"I'm not dealing with this. I'm gonna go." I walked the hallway to the garage. He dropped on the floor, wrapped himself around my leg like a toddler, and begged me to stay. I pulled away and tried to yank my leg free. "Jesus Christ. You told me to go! Fucking let me go, Dan. Please!"

He pulled harder on my leg and started banging his head on the ground and hitting himself. I looked down at him and felt sad for him, but not a sadness borne of love—it was a sadness like when you see a tweaker outside a gas station and you feel bad for their situation as you observe them talking into the void and scratching themselves. Too far gone. Not worth engaging. I was out of compassion. He took back the car key and locked my stuff in the cab of the truck so I couldn't get to it, and he grabbed my phone from the front seat.

The night before, a fellow climber had texted me asking about conditions in Zion. I'd replied with an explanation of the snow and rain that were preventing climbing for a couple days. Dan was jealous when he read the exchange.

"Who the fuck is this guy? Why is he in your phone contacts? You shouldn't be texting other men!"

"It's my boss from the climbing gym. Look at the texts, Dan! We literally only talked about conditions. Scroll through the conversation. There's clearly nothing going on there. You're so paranoid!"

"You're the worst! I can't trust you. You can't take care of me like a woman should. You're too young!" he shrieked. He threw a backpack across the bedroom, breaking a piece of wicker furniture and sending shards all over the room in brilliant trajectories. I screamed and backed away.

"Stop, Dan! You're destroying everything! I just want to leave. Give me back the key."

"I hate you! You make me wanna die! You're a fucking child, and you always say the wrong thing." He flipped over the couches in the front room, and then smashed his head into the wall. I'd never seen so much violence from him. I guessed since it was his parents' house, he didn't feel as bad about breaking things. It's not like they would charge him for the damage like a hotel. They were so rich, they probably wouldn't notice the cost of the repairs. He continued his riot, throwing and smashing things with no rhyme or reason. I watched, horrified, trying to stay out of his path of destruction.

"I'm going to call the cops if you don't let me leave! I don't deserve this!" I protested.

He got in my face. "No you fucking won't." He smelled awful and I crinkled my nose at him.

"Yes, I will! You need professional help. I want to leave. Give me back my phone and the keys," I demanded through my tears. "I'm not going to be your hostage!"

"Professional help? They never help me! They just tie me down and inject me with shit and make everything worse. You're my girlfriend! I need *your* help! You fucking owe me!" he cried.

We were back in the garage now because I wanted to get in the truck and leave. He banged his head on the car window and body, trying to smash a window and knock himself out. *Thud. Thud.* He was too strong to be stopped, and I wailed in fear. He got pissed because the garage door was cracked open and he worried a neighbor would hear and call the cops.

"Give me my phone! Unlock the truck!"

"No! I don't want you to call anyone. I don't trust you, bitch! I want to die!" There was a toolbox on the side of the garage. He was drenched in sweat and had a feral look on his face like a scared animal. He picked up a hammer and held it to his head, tapping it along his skull, testing his aim. *Whack.* It made contact with a sickening noise. I cringed.

"No!" I lunged for the hammer and threw it across the garage away from him.

He picked up another hammer off the tool bench. "I'll just fucking hit myself in the head with this until I die!" he laughed, unhinged. "Wouldn't you like to see that?" Sweat was pouring down his face and neck, soaking his torn shirt.

"No, no, no, no! You can't do that. Stop! You're sick. You don't have to do this. You need to calm down, Dan!" I talked him out of it and we went back inside the house.

There was a long knife with a red handle and silver blade sitting on the kitchen counter that he used to poke holes in Red Bull cans for smoking weed. He ran over to it and held the knife up to his throat in front of the kitchen sink.

"If you leave, I'll fucking do it, Fallon. I want to die. If you leave me, or if you call the cops, I'll just slit it. It'll be so easy," he said, miming the motion.

Time slowed down and adrenaline surged in my veins. I cried in desperation.

"If you make one wrong move, it's over," he said through gritted teeth as the blade strained against his throat.

I stared into his enraged eyes. They were dripping with fear. Fear of himself. Brimming with self-hatred. I couldn't watch someone slit their own throat. I wanted to melt into a puddle of inexistence, but I couldn't let him do it. I searched my brain for a solution. I felt like I was in a movie. *How is this real life? He just ordered me to leave earlier, and now he's going to kill himself if I leave. I can't win. I'm damned if I do and damned if I don't. Wake me up from this nightmare.* Seconds passed and felt like minutes.

Thoughts ran through my head at a million miles an hour. *What do I say or do to keep him alive? I can't call 911 because I don't have my phone. Screaming will make him do it because it'll attract attention. I can't lunge for the knife because he'd slit his throat before I could reach it, a few paces away. Oh god. Please don't do it.*

Through exasperated sobs, I choked out something coercive and loving and reassuring. I pleaded with him to put the knife down and waited for his reaction. He lowered the knife from his throat, and I felt a huge weight off my chest.

He ran through the house screaming, breaking everything he could find, still holding the knife. The target didn't matter. Basket in the laundry room? Thrown against a wall and exploded to pieces.

"I want to die! I can't do this anymore! I don't trust you!" he said, stuck on a loop.

His eye was swollen and black, and he was covered in bruises from hitting himself. I was desperate to help him or get out, but I couldn't find a way without a phone or the key. I went into the garage, and he slammed the door shut behind me and locked me out of the house.

I banged on the door and he let me back in. He went into the laundry room and held the knife to his throat again. We fought over the door and I forced my way in.

"Please, Dan. We can talk about this. We can get past this. Put the knife down! This will pass. I promise things will be okay."

"No they won't! I hate you." His voice was cracking.

"I need you to put the knife down or I'm going to have to call the cops. You're not giving me a choice. You need help!" I hoped that his delirium made him forget that he still had my phone.

"If you call, I will slit your throat"—he pointed the knife at me—"kill all of the cops, and then kill myself!" he yelled, his lips trembling. Blood mixed with sweat dripped down the side of his face from a cut on his head.

My throat tightened at the prospect. "Please, Dan. Put the knife down."

"I don't want you! I want to die! You make me sick! So sick. So sick. So sick . . ." he repeated, his eyes staring far off at something I could not see. I gently took the knife from him and he crumpled to the floor and hugged his knees to his chest. I hid the knife under the kitchen sink, but it was useless because there were other knives in the kitchen. I couldn't hide them all.

I went back to where he was rocking on the floor.

"I just want Powerade and good food. Why can't you just go get that for me?" he said, shaking.

"I can do that! Give me the key and I'll go get it for you."

"No! I don't trust you. You'll just leave me. You don't care," he wailed.

"You can come with me. But not like this. You'd have to get cleaned up."

I led him to the bathroom and he took a shower. The water rinsed the blood off his head and neck like a deranged baptism. Now with my phone back, I left the bathroom and texted his dad a warning message about Dan's psychotic state. My heart racing, I texted a friend and told them things were really messed up right now, but instructed them not to respond. I immediately deleted the texts so Dan wouldn't see them.

When Dan emerged and got dressed, he was surprised to see me.

"I thought you'd run off with the car. I don't want to be with you, bitch," he said apathetically. He got in the truck and tried to leave. I ran out after the truck and yelled at him through the window.

"Let me get my stuff out first! I don't want you to leave with all my stuff!" My bags were still in the truck cab. The thought of losing everything terrified me. I had so little left in my life beyond these few possessions. He tried to lock the door, but I was faster. I pulled open the door and grabbed everything. Shoes, food, climbing gear, and clothes spilled out onto the driveway in the dark desert night.

"Stop causing a scene," he hissed at me, looking around at the other large houses sitting quietly on the street behind their manicured landscaping. I wondered if any of the neighbors had heard his screams and bangs from inside the house and garage earlier.

I dragged my bags back into the garage and he closed the garage door.

He came back inside and said he couldn't trust that I wouldn't leave—why else would I want my stuff?

"Please, I wanted it just in case. I don't know how long you'll be gone. It scares me to be separated from my stuff. Like my EpiPen was in there. I need to have that with me all the time. You know how it is." Of course, in reality, I wanted to escape.

Satisfied with my answer, he finally left. I pulled up the phone number for the local taxi service on my phone. I tried to calculate how long his errand would take, and how long it would take a taxi to get to the house. My thumb hovered over the call button, but I couldn't bring myself to do it.

I still don't know exactly what compelled me not to press call. The cycle of abuse had fried the wiring in my brain, and my decisions were no longer rational. He'd fucked with me so much that I couldn't bring myself to leave even when the opportunity was right in front of me. I felt the need to stay and watch over him. To make sure he didn't die. I knew it wasn't my responsibility, yet I stayed anyway. I'd been carefully conditioned and manipulated to the point where I didn't know what my life was without him.

It was an effort not to press the call button. I felt like a captive, but it was my own fault, so I hated myself for it. I hated myself for giving up my previous life for this nightmare. I hated that I was too afraid to leave. What if he came after me and found me? I wanted nothing more than to destroy him, yet I couldn't leave him; his claws were too deep in me.

I waited in the house, hoping he was calming himself down. He returned late into the night. I was exhausted, but grateful he hadn't killed himself. I took a shower and went to bed.

He came into the bedroom and apologized. I had the exact same feeling I'd felt so many times before—like a mean dog had bit me and now wanted to cuddle me. I inspected his black eye and swollen face, and we hugged. It felt forced. The last thing I wanted was to be this close to him, but he was craving the comfort of touch. I felt traumatized and wanted nothing to do with him. My skin crawled.

In bed alone, I tossed and turned and found myself breaking

down in sobs throughout the night, too disturbed to really sleep. I wished I'd been able to leave in the truck when he'd originally told me to, before it had all gone awry. When I did drift off, I'd have visions of the knife and the hammer, and startle myself back into consciousness.

CHAPTER 18

PSYCH WARD

April 2017

Dan and I resumed our typical schedule of Red Bull and rock climbing. Things were awkward. He got upset with me when I was able to boulder harder than him in Moe's Valley, the local bouldering area in southwest Utah. It rained again, so we bailed back to Salt Lake. On the way, he apologized for the previous night. He showed me a song called "That Wasn't Me" by Brandi Carlile.

"I hope this helps you understand. When I'm like that . . . It's not me. I'm not in control." He turned the volume dial and motioned for me to listen. The music came through the speakers accompanied by the squeak of the truck's windshield wipers.

I listened to the song. It made sense why he related to it, but it didn't feel like it excused his behavior. *So he can just absolve himself by claiming it's "not him"? That doesn't seem fair.*

"She gets it, Fallon. I'm gonna get better. I can beat this." He rubbed my knee.

"Okay." I gave him a weak smile and passively watched central Utah pass by outside. I wanted to believe him, but I didn't. I'd been so wrong about Dan. I was literally and figuratively not in the driver seat for my life anymore.

We climbed in Big Cottonwood Canyon in a windstorm. The wind tangled my hair as I ran it out dozens of feet between pieces of protection on a cruiser multi-pitch up the quartzite, feeling disconnected from my body, unconcerned about falling. I couldn't bring myself to care about my own safety. I mechanically went through the motions of rock climbing without any real awareness of what was happening, just letting my body do what it knows how to do. This was a stark contrast to my first day of climbing with Dan months before, when I'd been so nervous about my trad climbing skills. Now I was running it out without a care in the world, not second guessing myself at all.

Spring break arrived for my school district, so I couldn't substitute teach that week.

I got a message from Dan while I was in Logan: "I'm having a really hard time. I feel terrible physically and emotionally again. I don't think I'm actually dangerous, but I know I'm not okay either. I don't expect you to wanna see me anymore, kid. I really don't. I'm not well right now. I'm sorry."

I was glad he was acknowledging it, but I knew that wasn't enough to change his behavior.

I went to the doctor when I couldn't stop hacking up green mucus. Bronchitis. I mustered what little energy I had to follow through on a prior commitment to volunteer at a science event at the university, where I was still technically an Ambassador for the College of Science even though I'd taken the semester off from classes. It felt reassuring to be back on campus; I'd missed it. When my colleagues saw how sick I was, they quickly sent me home.

The next day, I was supposed to meet up with my sister Bryn, who had been completing a medical school rotation in Salt Lake City, and then I had plans to go climb with Dan. A restless night of coughing left me feeling horrible. I texted him that I needed to bail on climbing that day, and he became inflamed.

"If you feel so sick, why did you go to that event last night? You can do that but you're suddenly too sick to come climb with me? Whatever, dude," he texted me. I responded and explained how I had been sent home, and that I'd gotten sicker throughout the night. Plus, it was snowing between Logan and Salt Lake, so driving down wouldn't be safe anyway. He spiraled.

Dozens of texts rolled in on my phone. He was on the attack, calling me awful names, freaking out, telling me to fuck off, saying he didn't want to be with me. It seemed like nothing would placate him or change his mind. No matter how fast I texted back, it was no match for his manic speed. The messages were never ending. He told me that he hated me and that I had ruined his Saturday.

I'd had enough. I texted him back, "Fine. I wish you the best. If this is it, then goodbye! I'm done." I was too sick to deal with his tantrum and take his abuse even via text messages.

At first, there was sweet silence from my phone. *Maybe it worked.* I felt relieved.

Then I received a string of texts: "You can't do this to me! You BITCH! You don't just get to leave me!! I'm going to kill myself because of you!"

The constant suicide threats were exhausting. It was starting to seem like the boy who cried wolf, and I could tell he was using it as a manipulation tactic. Still, I didn't want to have his death on my conscience. I was too sick to drive down to him, and the roads were too snowy, so I continued messaging him in a foolish effort to keep him alive. I texted his dad and told him I was concerned. Mark drove up from Lehi, found Dan in Salt Lake City, and started following him around in his car.

"I have my 9 mil gun. I'm going to do it tonight! Just wait and see," Dan texted me.

Once he realized I'd alerted his dad, he was even more pissed. "I can't trust you! How could you tell my dad about this!"

Dan talked to his dad and convinced him to go back to Lehi. Mark was an enabler and a complete pushover—I couldn't believe he left when his son was struggling so much. Dan had him wrapped around his finger. If his own dad couldn't help him, and was driven away so easily, who was left to save him?

Things escalated, and Dan called me on the phone. I had lost my voice from the bronchitis, so while he screamed at me, I furiously typed my responses over text. I didn't want him to die even as he verbally attacked me.

Through the phone, he screamed at me, "I'm going to come see you in Logan. And I'm gonna kill myself on your porch! So you can see what you do to me. You'll have to watch it!" I started panicking. My whole body shook uncontrollably.

"Dan! You can't do that. I'll call the cops on you! They'll stop you!" I typed.

"You cunt. I told you, if you ever call the cops, I'll kill you, and them, and myself!"

Then he said he'd drive into oncoming traffic to kill himself. Then it was the gun again. He was out of his mind, out of control. There was a new method every moment and I couldn't keep up. The spiral sucked him in deeper and deeper.

By the evening, he'd given up hope that I would come down to Salt Lake to save him. He told me he'd been drinking. Hysterical, intoxicated sobs crackled through the phone.

"Fallon. I'm serious," he told me, his voice breaking, "I'm going to do it. I'm gonna shoot myself." I pleaded with him over text, and then he said he was going to come up to Logan to see me. I imagined him driving drunk on the icy roads in the dark to kill himself on my porch.

I broke down. My hands were tied. I couldn't handle this on my own just by texting him. I had to report this. I called the police and gave them a description of him and his location. Calling the cops was one of the scariest things I'd done, since he threatened to kill me if I did it. The distance gave me the courage to do it. After a few anxious minutes of waiting, the police followed up with me.

They had him. It was out of my hands now.

I took a healthy dose of NyQuil and cried myself to sleep.

The next morning, I was horrified when I checked my phone. I had received hundreds of texts from Dan, in addition to missed calls, voicemails, and video messages. He had been outrageously hysterical all night long. He said they had busted him for marijuana, and then booked him into the psych ward, tackled him, strapped him down, and injected him without his consent. In his video messages, I hardly recognized him. He lay in a gown on a white hospital bed in a tiny, empty sterile room that had a small window on its locked door. He turned the phone around to show his face. Puffy eyes and a ghostly facial expression stared at me through the glowing screen.

He cursed me for calling the police. "Look at where they put me. Look at what they've done to me. This is worse than rape," he cried with a hoarse throat, "and it's all your fault that I'm here. You called. *This* is what happens when the cops come." The video ended.

He had begged me all night to help him get out, but I'd been sleeping. His voicemails were almost incomprehensible, pierced by the despondent voice breaking through the sobs. He ricocheted between rage and sorrow. He blamed me for all of it.

I spoke with his dad, and decided to go down to the hospital to visit before he was transferred to a different building. Despite all he'd done to me, I felt like I needed to help him and show him kindness. He was clearly suffering. I was unsure of where we stood, but I wanted to see him for some reason I couldn't quite explain. We had a strong dysfunctional bond by this point, and he reiterated that it was my duty as his girlfriend to take care of him, so I obeyed.

Dan didn't understand the emotional trauma and distress I had been through the previous day by spending over eleven hours on the phone with him while he was suicidal. Calling the cops had been my last resort to ensure his safety. My wheels spun on icy sections of the highway, spitting up the salt and muck that had accumulated all winter.

I arrived at the University of Utah hospital, where Mark stood outside the entrance. We left footprints in the slush as we walked in together past dozens of security guards, doctors, and nurses. Dan was now in a plain room that contained only a hospital bed with restraints, a medical monitoring machine, and a chair for a visitor. He looked exhausted and was clearly doped up on some medicine the doctors had administered to calm him down. He was sleepy and not happy to see me. He wouldn't make eye contact with me at first.

Mark stepped out to let us talk.

Dan glared at me. "I can't trust you. You betrayed me. I can't believe you called the cops on me and landed me here. Against my will." He looked away in disgust.

I gave an empty apology, and hoped that he would gain something from the experience. If anything, I hoped it would be a wake-up call for him that he couldn't lie to me about having a gun, or threaten suicide when I was helpless to prevent it.

I held his hand, and I could tell that he was conflicted. He simultaneously wanted me there, but was pissed at me, and couldn't make up his mind. A nurse came in and said he was getting transferred. They rolled him out on the bed and took him to an ambulance. I asked if he wanted me to come along, and at first I thought he'd say no, but he wanted me to come after all.

We rode over to a different part of the medical complex, where high security entrances were blocked by guards. We were granted access for only a minute with Dan, and then they carted him off with little notice.

The doctor swiftly told us, "This isn't a time for visitors." Mark got to say goodbye briefly, but I didn't get a chance before Dan was rolled into an elevator.

Dan's mom showed up and gave me and Mark a ride back to our cars at the other building. She asked me if Dan had been doing hard drugs again. I told her no, not to my knowledge. I explained his recent behavior and expressed my concern for him before getting back in my car. I didn't want to drive back to Logan just yet, because I'd only been in Salt Lake City for less than an hour.

I decided to finally visit my sister Bryn, the first I'd seen her since Christmas. We got lunch, and it was good to see her, but the conversation was tense given recent events. Dan had succeeded at isolating me from my family and friends. I felt confused by everything that had been happening. Dan's breakdowns were taking a toll on me. I didn't feel like myself anymore. I thought back to my happy days in college, running around to different classes and clubs, with a bustling social life and loads of ambition. That era had been stressful, and I'd wanted an escape, but my life now was so flat by comparison.

I felt like I had Dan and climbing, and nothing else, and that was a very precarious position to be in.

The next day, I got an unexpected message over Instagram while I was substituting. A climbing company wanted to sponsor me! I was thrilled and immediately responded. This was a dream come true. They told me their expectations for photos and articles, and I agreed to come to their store in Salt Lake City a few days later to get my shoes and gear. I heard nothing from Dan all day. *Must be locked up still.* It was a welcome break.

I finally learned that Dan was released and had gone back to his apartment. I drove down to see him so we could talk, and he immediately berated me. He was still pissed that I'd called the cops, and yelled at me for an hour. I sat quietly on the pavement behind his rental and apologized to him, trying to explain why I'd thought that was the safest option.

"I'd rather kill myself than get locked up there again. They raped me, Fallon. With their needles. They didn't get my consent for treatment. I was treated worse than an animal," he said.

I doubted that, and imagined they'd been forced to act when he wasn't compliant, but kept my mouth shut. Inside me was a raging storm, but I sat there in submission. I left early the next morning to go back to work in Logan.

A few days later, I attended a geology department awards ceremony. When I was still enrolled in the fall, I'd applied for some scholarships, and I won two of them. I walked around, chatting with peers and professors, looking at all of the research posters. It felt good to be back in the academic environment, but I felt out of place since I'd taken the semester off. I missed being in school.

These experiences where I was out of Dan's influence were rejuvenating. I felt like I could breathe again as I walked alone, a free woman on campus, my conversations and actions unmonitored and unjudged. Dan didn't like coming to Logan, and I was happy that I mostly got to keep it to myself. I loved going up into the Bear River Mountains to hike and climb in the idyllic forest and wander along the clear river. I scarcely saw Taylor and Ashleigh since they were drowning in schoolwork and geology research. They rightfully didn't approve of my relationship with Dan, but they still cared about me, so it put them in a difficult position to observe my instability.

My sisters also did not approve of the relationship, and I got into a fight with them about it. They knew Dan was toxic, and called our relationship unstable. They encouraged me to leave him. I knew what they were saying was true, but I defended Dan nonetheless, worried about what he'd do if he ever read the text thread. The conversation with my sisters escalated and Dan found out about our fight. Sometimes, Dan would draft texts for me, or go as far as to text my sisters directly. This time, he texted my sister Shannon after learning about the argument:

> "You think she's not in a stable relationship? Fuck. Maybe if she had a family, I'd leave off. Since I know how she gets treated by her kin, I'll stick around. Screw you,

Shannon, firstly: for saying such terrible shit to my girlfriend. Secondly, for pretending like you're such an ally, like you're so good to her. You're shit to her. And I'm twice as resolved to treat her better, for seeing what she's accustomed to. You. Are. Trash. To speak to your own flesh and blood that way. And you know it. Apologize to her for your shit. You're older. And you call her a condescending bitch? That makes you one very insecure bitch. Better enter another beauty pageant soon."

His gaslighting and veiled threats only served to push me even further away from my family, isolating me more effectively. The irony was that the things he called me were far worse than anything my sisters said to me, but I dared not point that out to him. My sisters felt frustrated and angry, like they couldn't get through to me or help me out of the situation. Inside, I was screaming for help, but I didn't know how to accept it at the time.

I had to choose: ignore their advice, stay with Dan, and endure the danger of our relationship; or accept their advice, leave Dan, and be in danger of him hunting me down and taking out his wrath on me. I felt stuck. This was the central dilemma that ruled me for months, and perfectly summarizes why I couldn't fully cut the cord. Maybe Dan could get better. We could keep trying to find him the help he needed. I chose the passive option of staying.

The next weekend, Dan and I had plans to climb in St. George. On the way to meet up at his house in Lehi, I stopped in Salt Lake to pick up gear from my new sponsor. I walked out with a big box of shiny new climbing equipment and felt my heart swell with pride. I'd worked so hard for this, and thought Dan would be excited too.

Free gear would make our life and climbing that much easier, and when we'd first met, he'd been convinced he was going to make me 'famous' by taking lots of photos and videos of my climbing. That enthusiasm had tapered off, but the general sentiment was the same. Dan wanted attention, even if it was by association.

He was not happy about the sponsorship.

"I mean, yeah, it's cool I guess," he said while driving south on I-15, "but like, I've done way cooler climbing than you. I took all those photos of you that got you noticed. I should be the one with sponsors and getting free gear, not you."

I was hurt by his statement. I'd been climbing longer than him and was disappointed in his jealousy, but I started to second guess myself. *Maybe I don't deserve this.*

He rambled on through puffs of a cigarette. "Like, think about it! All that free soloing I've done. All those videos of me. Man! That should've gotten me sponsored." His delusions of grandeur were more obvious to me now than when we'd first met.

"I don't know, dude. I don't think that's always what they look at. I'm sure there are other factors involved in their choices . . ." I trailed off, torn between defending myself and not wanting to start a fight.

"You should recommend me to them. Cultivate a relationship with them. See if they'll bring me on board too. Like we're a package deal, ya know?" he said, nodding.

I hollowly agreed and turned up the music. Father John Misty's haunting voice crackled through the truck speakers.

I was treading carefully with Dan. His mental health had been crumbling lately alongside our relationship. It had caused me to slowly break down, too, and I wondered how much more I could take. *Maybe, if we both keep disintegrating, then by the end, we'll both be a pile of ashes.*

I looked over at him. He was gaunt and agitated as he stared off down the highway absent-mindedly singing along. I didn't feel attracted to him anymore. I felt none of the butterflies I had when we'd first started dating. Instead, I just imagined him with the wild look in his eyes, insulting me through the veil of his insanity, like he'd done so many times. I couldn't figure out why I was still here beside him—it felt like he owned me.

In St. George, we perked up at the nice weather. It was always so much cheerier in the desert. The warmth lifted our moods. Heat rises, and we rose with it. We climbed at Turtle Wall on sculpted overhanging sandstone. I was upset when I had to bail off a climb because of pain in my wrist. It had been a pesky recurrent sprain since that day we tumbled down the hill together in Little Cottonwood.

The next day, we hopped on 'Touchstone,' a classic big wall in Zion. We only made it two pitches up before we were held up by a rope soloist who was having a total junkshow: ropes, anchors, haul bags, and gear scattered to the winds all over a few pitches. We waited for him for a while, hanging in our harnesses, looking up at the striking blue sky juxtaposed with the sheer red rock cliffs, black condors soaring high above. When we realized the soloist wasn't budging, we rappelled the route.

'Iron Messiah' was our next objective, a commonly climbed multi-pitch in Zion. Tourists swarmed the park and the day was already sweltering. We botched the approach, but eventually found the base of the climb after navigating up sandy, loose blocks punctuated with yucca and cactus. I floated up a perfect bolted pitch of black crimpy patina, and then we snaked our way up the cracks and chimneys. The sun drew its imperceptible arc across the sky as I looked across the canyon at the dramatic Red Arch Mountain. This was where I usually felt at peace, on a cliff in the desert, but with Dan on the other end of the rope, I felt uneasy.

We needed to retreat soon in order to make the last shuttle bus. We rappelled the route in a hurry. At the top of pitch 1, Dan realized he'd left his phone on a ledge above us. We didn't have time to retrieve it, so we'd have to return the next day. We rapped the convoluted scrambling approach pitch, and the ropes got stuck when we tried to pull them. We tugged and flicked and whipped them around, but they wouldn't come free.

Dusk was settling over Zion and we only had a few minutes left to make it to the final shuttle. We knew we'd have to come back the next day to get his phone anyway, so we abandoned our ropes, threw our gear into our packs, and sprinted down the trail just in time for the last shuttle.

Less than twelve hours later, we were back at the base of the route. Our ropes were still there, along with backpacks and shoes left by another party who must have started up already. Dan free soloed up to retrieve our ropes, and belayed me up. I led the sport patina pitch again, which felt like a treat, and then I quested up the next pitch, a chimney. At the top of the pitch, I looked all over for his phone, but it wasn't anywhere on the ledge. We couldn't see the climbers that were already ahead of us, and I figured they must have grabbed it. Dan was livid, fully convinced that they had stolen it. We descended the route, this time thankfully with no stuck ropes, and heard from the other party later that day about his phone. We had to return to Zion yet again the following day to get his phone back before we took off for Joshua Tree, keeping up our intense climbing schedule.

At this point, it didn't feel like we were dating, except for the rare moments when Dan used me to satisfy his sexual urges and I laid there dissociating, robotically resigning myself to his needs to avoid a fight. We seemed more like convenient climbing partners than anything else. I was perfectly fine with that. I didn't know anyone else who could go climb with me every day, and that was what I valued above all else, so I kept rolling with it. I didn't realize that I wasn't actually rolling with it; I was being dragged along by him. None of my own needs seemed to matter anymore. I lost myself, an attrition that I was too preoccupied to digest at the time.

CHAPTER 19

NEXT TO A CORPSE

April 2017

We belted out "Like a Rolling Stone" and devoured bags of sour watermelons on our marvelous drive to Joshua Tree. At one point in a remote part of the desert, where we saw no other vehicles for hours, we encountered a section of consecutive dips in the road. Dan's truck rolled up and down the undulations, and we giggled like children on a 70 mph roller coaster across the desert, our stomachs doing somersaults.

The change in elevation over the course of the drive gave me a painful sensation in my ear. I couldn't pop my ear to fix it, and it felt like I blew out my ear drum. I'd just gotten over my bronchitis, and I was in terrible pain, but I tried to keep it together as we drew closer to the park to preserve Dan's jovial mood.

It was my first time in Joshua Tree. Massive hunks of granite were littered across a flat, dry playa as if a giant had discarded his toy blocks. Joshua trees rose up in crooked patterns, peppered between campsites and hiking trails. Wandering the park in search of Dan's friend Cooper, I felt like I'd been transported back to the '70s: weed-smoking hippies in groovy vans, Euro travelers dirtbagging under boulders, and tourists gawking up at the cliffs. We eventually found Cooper with his overpriced Westfalia van, and we migrated to nearby boulders.

I was initially overconfident, but was smacked down by the

sandbagged slabs. I tried to focus on having fun instead of sending any climbs as we bounced around Hidden Valley Campground. All of the campsites were full, so we paid some California stoners to crash their campsite. That night, my eardrum was causing me a lot of pain, and I felt exhausted as I sat silently and listened to Dan and Cooper happily chatting. I felt like a ghost eavesdropping on their conversation. *Why does Dan always do this when we're with other people?*

The next morning, I climbed with Dan and Cooper at Hemingway Wall. I was surprised by the crystalline, sharp rock that shredded my fingertips, and relished in the friction and movement. Cooper was much stronger than us, and as I admired his climbing, I wondered if Dan's jealousy applied to men too. I figured maybe men being stronger didn't aggravate him as much. He felt threatened by my climbing ability simply because I was a girl.

We drove back to the campground area to climb more, and I became disheartened when I lowered off a climb and Dan chastised me for not being able to finish it. I felt ashamed as I bailed because of wrist pain and an unshakeable fatigue. *I suck. I don't deserve to be sponsored. Why am I so tired? Why am I in this much pain?* I needed some alone time. While they kept ticking off routes, I scrambled up a different cliff in the campground and took photos of their silhouettes on top of Intersection Rock. Their bodies formed elegant shapes against a crisp blue sky.

I sat down and fell apart.

Misery and pain overwhelmed me as I fixated on my health problems. My body wasn't keeping up with me how I wanted it to, and I was incredibly frustrated. I was also running out of money again. Dan's demanding climbing schedule was keeping me from substituting enough to make ends meet, and the credit card interest alone from the unpaid Patagonia flights was outpacing my meager income. I didn't know how I'd pay rent at the end of the month or buy groceries or gas. My relationship with Dan was unpredictable and heartbreaking. I was uncertain if he even loved me anymore. It sure didn't feel like it. He made me feel like shit for being injured, and constantly put me down. It was a far cry from feeling loved.

Everything felt impossible. Even at this age, I already loved Stoic philosophy, and I tried to draw upon its wisdom, but I found myself so lost and broken that I couldn't see the light. I hadn't been able to internalize and implement its principles at this point. I thought of the quote by Marcus Aurelius: "If you are distressed by anything external, the pain is not due to the thing itself, but to your estimate of it; and this you have the power to revoke at any moment." The words rang empty as I tried to apply them to my situation.

How could I stop caring about things outside of my control when I felt stuck with a monster and confined to a broken body? How did Dan keep getting me to stay, and what was the hidden key to leaving permanently? I took his threats seriously, and dealing with the fallout was soul-crushing. I knew I needed to get away from him, but I couldn't make it happen. Was the fear of what he'd do to me if I tried to leave again really stronger than my desire for peace? These types of questions gnawed at me.

It was odd, to be on top of a gorgeous rock pile in a vast desert landscape filled with great climbing, yet feel such a deep sense of grief. It wasn't my strength that was limiting me. It was sickness and injury and abuse and poverty. I spiraled into my own despair. All at once, I was hit by a sudden urge to die. I didn't want to deal with life anymore: finding a way to escape him, enduring the pain in my body, sifting through the all-consuming sadness in my mind.

Surveying the land around me, I pondered my options. There were plenty of cliffs available, but they were mostly one or two pitches high. Not tall enough to guarantee death. I thought of the horror of surviving a fall like that and pictured my body in grotesque angles at the base baking in the relentless sun. I wished death would just carry me away. I could dissipate into the breeze, and I could be done. Tears flowed down my face in a salty cascade, stinging my sunburned cheeks. The final thread holding me to my happiness and purpose had been severed.

If I didn't have climbing, then what was left for me?

Fuck.

A foreign family approached me where I was perched. They were clearly not climbers, but they were enjoying the perfect weather and scrambling adventure nonetheless. I turned away from them, trying to conceal my face. I didn't want them to feel uncomfortable that I was depressed when they were having a fun family vacation.

When Dan and Cooper finished climbing, they scrambled up to me. I crossed my arms and was unresponsive, trying to show them my intentions with my body language. I didn't want to embarrass Dan in front of Cooper because he looked up to him. We all chatted and I downplayed my struggles while we ate around the campfire that night. I hid my depression and put on my happy-chill-girl-climber facade so I wouldn't raise concern. Inside, my brain and body were screaming at me to die.

The next day, I bouldered with Dan and Cooper. I worked on my climbing photography when it wasn't my turn to punt off something, snapping photos of them on the tricky slabs. The sharp crystals destroyed our fingertips every time we pulled onto the rock.

Dan ran out of weed, and I couldn't help but recognize the irony that the date was 4/20. He became desperate and moody, and stormed off from the boulders. I chased after him, and just like that, we left Joshua Tree in pursuit of his favorite substance.

"Fuck, dude. I'm getting the sweats. Feel." He grabbed my hand and placed it on his lower back. His shirt was soaked.

"I'm sorry, hun. I don't know what to do for you. Drink some water." I ran my fingers through my hair and pulled it up into a ponytail.

"After I was in the psych ward . . ."—he shot me an accusing glare—"the docs changed my meds. They got rid of the one that helps me with suicidal and psychotic shit."

I didn't respond. His foot was bouncing on the floor of the truck, and his hand shook as he fumbled with his pack of Spirits. He held one between his lips, lit it, and cranked the window down.

"Do you think you could call my shrink? Ya know, tell him I do better with it, or some shit. You know how it calms me down. And, man, you know what my shrink did? He fucking prescribed me antihistamines for my anxiety attacks. Can you believe that?" His eyes were pleading as much as his voice.

"Yeah, I guess I could talk to him . . . When we get home." I acquiesced hollowly, but knew I wouldn't follow through.

"God. I *need* something. Running out of bud fucking freaks me out, dude. Especially since I don't have those pills anymore."

I changed the song from a folksy track he didn't like, and instead put on one of his favorite songs, called "Drink Alone" by a local Wasatch band. Music typically had a positive impact on his mood. He wasn't singing along—something was up.

"You need to help me. Could you go to your doctor to get the meds and give them to me?" he asked.

"Uhh. What would I even say in order to make sure I get that pill specifically?"

"It's easy. I promise. Say you have a racing mind. Can't sleep. Thoughts won't turn off." He waved his hand around his head.

"I don't know. My doctor knows me really well. I'm in there all the time for actual health problems. I feel like he might suspect something is off. I've never had any mental health issues or anything. Isn't that gonna seem suspicious?"

"You owe me!" The fuse had finished burning and now the explosion had arrived. "You need to go in to the doctor and get me my fucking pills!"

"Whoa, Dan. Calm down. I didn't say I wouldn't! I just have doubts."

"You entitled piece of shit! You know I need those. You're trying to keep them from me! You are so fucking selfish!" He gripped the steering wheel with white knuckles, squeezing.

"I'm just concerned that he would know something's up! I don't wanna get in trouble. C'mon, doesn't it seem unlikely? He's not a therapist, he's a general doctor."

"This is the least you can do for me! You promised you'd be there for me." His right fist rose and connected squarely with his temple.

He hit himself again and again. He whimpered like a beat puppy as he did it.

"Stop, Dan! Stop that! We can talk! I didn't say I wouldn't do it. I just said it seemed like it would be suspicious." I barricaded his fist from his own head. I hesitated from grabbing his arms since he was still driving. I watched the road with wide eyes, fearing how out of control he was becoming.

"No! We can't talk. I have to die! You put me through hell. You're the reason I went to the psych ward and you're the reason they took my pills away!" he screamed.

"Okay, I did call the police, but that was just to check on you when you wouldn't answer me. You said you were gonna kill yourself! I didn't have a choice. I didn't ask for you to be put in the psych ward. I didn't decide for your meds to be taken away! It's not my fucking fault!"

"You made that phone call, bitch! You're directly responsible!" he yelled. He started punching the driver's side window.

"Quit it! I'll go in and try to get the pills! It seems unlikely that I'll get prescribed the right stuff though, is all I'm trying to say. The doc already seems annoyed with me since I have so many problems and get hurt all the time."

I was trying to be honest with him, not drive him to suicide. He'd told me that honesty was the best option when I dealt with his outbursts, and that I should stick to that instead of lying and making empty promises. Whenever I'd lied to him in the past to calm him down, and then he'd found out about it later on, it pissed him off even more. He wanted neither truth nor lies; I was damned if I did and damned if I didn't.

I had to choose between danger now, or danger later.

"You clearly don't care about me. God. I can't believe I've wasted my time with such a bitch!" Window punch for emphasis. "You don't know all the terrible things they did to me at UNI! It was worse than rape—being stuck with needles and held down and everything!"

He kept bringing that up. How could he know it was worse than rape? My blood boiled. He acted as if that would make me remorseful for calling the cops on him.

His fist was bleeding now from impacting the window. His forehead was swollen from where he'd punched himself.

"Dan. Breathe. Can you please pull over till you calm down? I don't think you should be driving." I was nervous asking this, and I leaned as far to the right into my passenger side door as possible, assuming my typical protective position.

He started kicking the windshield. I was horrified as a giant crack propagated across the glass. I watched the Mojave unfold before my eyes from inside the cage of the truck. Joshua trees blurred by outside. White sand lazily blew across the vacant road. There was no one around on this desolate stretch of highway.

Dan screamed and grabbed the rearview mirror. He ripped it right off the windshield and threw it out his window. I quickly turned around, watching the hunk of plastic clunk to a stop on the road behind us. I cried and begged him to stop.

"You make me want to die, Fallon! I hate you! You"—*thud*— "fucking" —*thud*— "cunt!" Each word was drawn out to match the blows to his head.

He looked bewildered. Sweat rolled down his face. The torment he felt in his mind was escaping through his body.

I desperately scanned the highway in both directions, praying there would be a cop, or another car, or literally anyone to notice what was happening, and help me to stop it.

Dan banged his head on the driver's window repeatedly. I leaned over and tried to hold him back so he would stop. His strength far outweighed my own, and he threw me off.

His right elbow flew up and back, breaking the truck window behind the bench seat. I screamed as the glass shattered above me, sending shards flying across the cabin. I was covered in a blanket of glass. Pieces dug into my back and under my bare legs on the seat. I had been crying because of fear thus far, but now I was hurting physically, too.

"Pull over! I'm bleeding! I need to get up and shake the glass off me! It's all over the seat and my clothes!"

His elbow was bleeding from the impact. The drops fell, one, two, three, weaving their way through the labyrinth of glass pieces. He kept driving and writhing around in his seat.

"Dan! Fucking pull over!" I shrieked.

The truck darted around the highway, disregarding the painted lanes. I was thankful there were no other cars to hit, but I also wished someone else was there to witness this. I needed help. I begged him to stop the car.

He pulled over unexpectedly. I immediately jumped out and shook the glass off my clothes and skin. I poured water on a paper towel to wipe the seat off. I was sobbing and could barely see. I looked around for a place to run, but I was surrounded by miles of open desert with no towns for god-knows-how-long.

"Oh no! My rope! My shoes! Fuck!"

I realized that my rope and climbing gear were right below the shattered window. My brand new climbing rope was exposed, and had been covered in glass. My climbing shoes were filled with glass. Pieces were mixed into all my slings and other equipment. I was devastated at the thought of my gear being useless if the glass had cut into any of it. I had no money. My gear was everything.

I picked up my rope with the intention of saving it, to take care of it before any damage could be done. I shook it over the shoulder of the highway, trying to inspect it for shards of glass.

"You idiot! It won't hurt climbing gear! What would you know,

Fallon?" His voice was condescending. I was beyond livid, but mostly scared.

"You must value the rope more than my life. I'm suicidal! I should be the focus right now! Do you really care more about a rope than if I live or die? If you do, then you should die too! That's fucked up!" he screamed, literally foaming at the mouth, bleeding all over from his self-harm. I just wanted to clean up the glass and secure the gear before more damage was done. In my overwhelmed state, I was fixated on that mission for some reason. I didn't see what that had to do with his suicidal thoughts. I hyper-focused on my gear since it felt like all I had of value in my life, since it allowed me to pursue climbing.

I felt cornered. Glass spilled out across the hot pavement.

I started running.

It wasn't a conscious choice; it was my nervous system reacting. Fight wasn't working, so it was time for flight. My sandals hit the pavement as tears rolled down my face and I gasped for air. Dan lurched into motion, taking off at a sprint. I had no chance against him since he was a runner. I tripped on the uneven gravel of the highway shoulder as he caught up to me, with only ravens soaring above to witness the chaos. I sobbed on the ground.

He grabbed my arm and pulled me up. "Get up."

Left with no other choice and no one to help me, I reluctantly got back in the car, silently crying while he continued to scold me across the long stretch of barren desert.

"You don't get to just sit there all pathetic and cry. Jesus! I'm the one who's suffering here. It's your fault I do this to myself! I'm the one who needs comfort!" he yelled.

Dan continued to bang his head against the side window. He

clawed at his own skin, one moment full of fury and the next dragged down by anguish.

As the Las Vegas skyline filled the horizon, my head felt heavy. I was drained by the whole situation. I didn't know what to say, or how to get out of this, so I sat there, silent, my eyes dead, staring off into the distance, fixed on no point in particular, trying not to exist. I didn't know it at the time, but fight and flight had failed, so it was time for the freeze response. Full dissociation. Totally checked out. *I'm not here. This isn't happening.*

"You fucking zombie! How can you just sit there and not care when I'm suicidal? You never cared about me!" He looked over at me—my vacant stare, dead while alive. "What? Nothing to say?" My silence somehow made it worse. He wanted a reaction.

I decided to strategize and consider an alternative plan for dealing with him. *Maybe,* I thought, *I can pull him out of this behavior if I pretend to be sweet to him rather than giving him silence. Sometimes that works.* I hated that I had to think like him; I didn't want to be a manipulator, but survival meant employing his own tactics against him.

My feigned sweetness seemed to improve things. He whimpered. I patted him on the back, which was now even more drenched with sweat through his holey gray t-shirt, and I gently but firmly made him pull over to a gas station.

I felt the tension leave my shoulders as we rolled to a stop on the asphalt. I'd felt entirely unsafe flying down the highway during his breakdown.

"Let me go in and grab something for us to drink. We can chill out and calm down from this. But you have to promise you won't do anything"—I shot him a knowing look—"while I'm in the gas station."

He trembled and lightly hit himself in the head with a half-hearted punch. He wouldn't promise me anything. I felt defeated as the truck started moving again before I could get out. *How in the world can I make him calm down?*

Now that he knew I was trapped, he returned to his evil side.

"You fucking bitch. I need my meds! You owe me!"

I abandoned my new tactic. "You know what? I'm fucking done! I can't be sweet when you treat me like this. Fuck you!" I felt a rush of power. "Pull over at the next exit. I'm getting out of this. I'm gonna get all my stuff out of the truck, and you're going to drive away. Fuck you, Dan! I'm done! I'm sorry, but I can't help you. I'll figure out the rest. Just pull over, goddammit!" I'd reached my breaking point.

Suddenly, he seemed terrified, and the tables turned. Now he was pleading with me. "You can't leave me. I need you. We have to keep climbing together. I'll be better. I'll get help."

He nodded maniacally, head bobbing while he drove north. We bombed down the highway, and he still wasn't pulling over.

"I told you to pull off. Next exit. You always have said you'll change, and guess fucking what? You never do! You're worse. I hate you! You said it yourself, you do better when you're single. So drop me at the next exit, and we'll both be better off!"

I couldn't grab the wheel without endangering us both. With my luck, he'd probably let us wreck. He was still suicidal and wouldn't pull over despite my best efforts.

Las Vegas receded into the rearview mirror, and we kept talking. I was trying to employ his master manipulator tactics. He had stopped screaming for the time being and was ready to talk more rationally.

"I was testing you back there," he explained. "You were sweet, and then I got mean again. You always leave me when I get psychotic! And what just happened, case in point!"

No shit, I thought, *it's exhausting to put up with you when I'm the target.* I was hesitant and tired. I had to think fast to say the right thing for my safety.

Lying through my teeth, I told him, "If we're going to stay together, major changes have to happen, okay? No exceptions."

He rolled his eyes, but kept listening.

"First condition. You can *not* touch me in a mean way, under any circumstances. No throwing me on the bed. No grabbing me. No hitting me. No breaking shit on or near me."

I started to feel more power welling up within me. *Maybe I can stand up for myself a bit. Maybe he'll listen this time since I'm being firm, and since he was pleading with me to stay.*

I continued with a list of terms that were non-negotiable in order for me to feel justified in accepting his pleas to stay together. Not that I was planning on staying. It was just buying me time.

We entered the Virgin River Gorge near the southern border of Utah. I had only gotten through a small portion of my list when he finally interjected.

"You know, Fallon, I'm suicidal! This isn't fair. I can't handle you listing off fucking conditions for my behavior!" Dan shouted. He banged his head on the driver's side window. *Here we go again,* I thought. *I don't want to die on this road.*

"Alright, fine." I stopped talking altogether. I couldn't win, and I certainly couldn't help him, so I might as well not even try. The rough limestone canyon walls passed by above me, late afternoon light illuminating millions of years of geologic history. I breathed in and out, refusing to even look in his direction.

This isn't significant in the history of the world. You know that. Keep it together and get the hell out when you get back north, I told myself. I dissociated again and tuned him out for the rest of the drive.

Back at his parents' house in St. George, he had a panic attack, claiming that he was traumatized from his time in the psych ward. I brought him water and ibuprofen for his swollen head. We each took showers, a welcome relief after the sweat and glass. I felt itchy, and traumatized, and wanted to be able to sleep that night, so I took a few Benadryls. I asked him if there was anything I could do for him before it kicked in and put me to sleep. He was enraged that I hadn't planned on cooking him dinner and watching a movie with him after we'd had such a shitty day. I had eaten just a protein bar that morning and then nothing else because of our fight.

"I don't have the energy to cook or stay up for a movie. If you wanted that you should've told me earlier. I'm not a mind reader, Dan," I sighed. I was so tired.

"I can't believe you're putting your own problems above my needs!" He threw a chair across the dining room and screamed at me.

The Benadryl was kicking in fast; it was the most I'd ever taken. Normally just one pill would put me to sleep within an hour, so a few were knocking me out, and I couldn't resist the drowsiness. I laid down on the couch. This was a living nightmare. Sleep pulled me into its dark arms and my eyelids closed involuntarily. I was grateful for the sweet relief. I didn't want to be awake anymore; reality was too harsh.

Different arms pulled me up. Dan carried me to the bedroom and threw me on the bed. I felt his hot breath as he screamed in my ear. I didn't respond—a combination of the intense grogginess, exhaustion from the day's events, and choosing not to give him the satisfaction of upsetting me.

He licked my face from chin to cheekbone.

Picked me up again and chucked me back down on the bed.

The Benadryl tried to pull me under, and I didn't fight it. I played into it in the hopes that he would give up and let me rest in peace. I lay there unresponsive, disgusted by the horrifying way he'd licked my face, wishing I would pass out completely.

He checked my pulse. He screamed and asked me how many pills I'd taken. I mumbled to him, knowing it hadn't been enough to hurt me, but plenty to knock me out. He put his mouth next to my ear and said the most haunting thing I'd ever heard in my life.

"Sleep well, babe. You're gonna wake up next to a corpse."

I drifted off to sleep to the background noise of him destroying things around the house.

The next morning, his prophecy had not come true. He was apologetic, and played the piano between sips of coffee. Music filled the stillness of the giant house. Such a peaceful scene was nearly unbelievable after the violence of the previous night. We started the drive back north in silence. I put on mellow music to ease the tension; usually that would put him in a better headspace. His voice was almost gone from screaming, and he was reserved and quiet. We talked about the fight. He absolved himself of all guilt, as if he could ever say words with enough weight to excuse his unforgivable behavior.

Once he said we were good again, then we were good again, and that was that. It was a one-sided decision; I had no say in the matter. It was easier that way, to go along with him. Resistance only brought more suffering.

CHAPTER 20

SHATTERED

April – May 2017

I resolutely folded the check into the congratulatory letter, sealed the freshly stamped envelope, and sent it back to the Utah Geological Association. My internal monologue was scornful. *Holy shit, Fallon. You're fucking insane. What are you doing? Refusing scholarship money! Dropping the Geology Field Camp class this summer! You've gotta be kidding yourself. How will you ever be a professor if you can't even get through undergrad?!*

The terms in the letter were remarkably clear, and without doing Geology Field Camp this summer, I couldn't keep the money. I returned the $1000 check, just hours after watching a different $500 scholarship disappear from my online university financial account when I informed them of my decision to bail on Field Camp. Dan had told me that I couldn't go this summer. Six weeks away from him was not going to fly. He'd watched me as I submitted another Leave of Absence request and dropped the course from my online student account.

I had $24 in my bank account, and it wrecked me to not be able to accept the relatively enormous scholarships after years of hard work in college. *There's always next summer,* I told myself. I remembered playing Sims on our old desktop computer when I was a kid, and how my sisters and I had learned the cheat code for unlimited money in the game. I wished I had something like that now, but in the real world, it's not that easy.

I spent a few days in Logan recovering from the disaster of a trip to Joshua Tree. I ran errands and substitute taught. Life almost felt normal again for a moment, except for the fact that I was so alone. Thanks to Dan, I'd lost touch with most of my friends, and wasn't talking to family either. I withdrew from my roommates, too ashamed to explain what had been happening. When I wasn't working or climbing, I wasn't sure what to do with myself. I still wanted to climb all of the time, but I felt drained, and Dan wouldn't allow me to climb with anyone else.

Where was the ultra-motivated academic powerhouse I'd once been? I couldn't tap into that anymore; that part of me felt absent. All I had now, my sole purpose in life, was climbing with Dan. I didn't have the energy or motivation to bother with anything except those moments of pure joy and freedom while climbing. Soon enough, Dan convinced me to go back to St. George to climb, with promises that he'd be better this time. I don't know why I believed him. I probably didn't, but climbing in the desert was too tempting anyway.

The drive down I-15 used to inspire me because it meant good weather and climbing were waiting for me at the end. Now, I was worried about being far away from any semblance of a support system and my own car. When we went on trips, it was always in Dan's truck. It made it easier for him to keep me in his control since it meant I didn't have a way to leave. I wriggled nervously in my seat. Long gone were the days of me sitting in the middle of the bench to be close to him. The wind howled near our heads since he hadn't replaced the back window yet. We were in the recovery phase again after the last fight, so Dan was treating me well, but I was wary.

Prophesy Wall and Chuckawalla gave us a quick day of sport climbing, and then we found ourselves back in Zion, our sights set on 'Organasm,' a roof crack on the Organ below Angel's Landing. The Virgin River was swollen with spring snowmelt, turbulent hazy blue water roaring over the rocks in the streambed. It was the highest I'd ever seen it, and even the ever-popular Narrows were closed because of the dangerously high water levels. When Dan suggested we cross the river to get directly to the route, I refused.

We instead backtracked to the Angel's Landing trailhead, used the bridge there, and then quickly deviated from the trail and bushwhacked all the way around the point of the Organ. It was a longer approach, but avoided the river. I climbed the first pitch of the route, and as I got closer to the roof crack above, I marveled at how amazing it looked as I battled what should have been an easy offwidth.

Thunder rumbled as raindrops blew in on the breeze. Weather moved in quickly here, and the rain fell with increasing urgency. You can't climb sandstone when it's wet, so we bailed. Dan wanted to cross the river right there to get to the nearby shuttle stop. I argued with him, but he put his foot down—he didn't want to reverse the long approach in the rain. We were going to cross the river, end of discussion.

I skated down the sand and rocks to the bank of the river in my approach shoes. We walked up and down the shore, gazing across for what looked like the path of least resistance. I put my hands in my pockets and squinted in the rain. Nowhere looked suitable to cross and I was plagued by anxiety. The river was wide, deep, and moving fast. Eventually we settled on a spot. Dan pulled on logs and tried to rig makeshift planks to shorten the distance of the crossing by utilizing a sandbar partway in the channel. I figured if I was going to get wet, it didn't matter much if the crossing was lessened by ten feet, but I waited for him anyway.

He waded into the deep water, fighting against the current. The waves lapped at the bottom of his backpack, and his legs resisted the force of the water as he tiptoed on the invisible rocks below. After much effort and uncertainty, he made it across, and motioned for me to follow.

I waded in and grimaced from the cold water. I felt like I'd jumped into an ice bath, but I kept moving. The polished rocks were slick underfoot, and my heavy pack threw me off. I unbuckled it so it wouldn't drown me if I fell, and kept wading deeper and deeper. The rushing water was dizzying. I tried to make my foot placements purposeful and strong.

I was reaching the center of the channel now. Water pummeled my legs, creeping up to my hips. It was too deep for me to resist its force, and suddenly, I was cast off. I went for a swim, my feet kicking in the water, bobbing along under the weight of my pack. I thrashed around, gasping in the cold water, eventually getting my footing again downstream. I was soaked from head to toe. Adrenaline had carried me back to the original bank of the river. I plopped down in a wet pile, my pack made even heavier by its new water content, and yelled at Dan for making me do something I wasn't comfortable with.

He left his pack behind, and crossed the river back to me. He took my pack for me so I could cross unencumbered. I cursed him for making me do this, but was glad he at least helped with my pack. I shivered my way across, terrified of drowning, and was relieved when I arrived safely on the other bank.

I've always had a knack for getting in bad situations with water: nearly drowning in a swimming pool as a toddler, canoeing into a headwind across Payette Lake in fourth grade summer camp and eventually requiring a rescue, and flipping over in a raging rapid and losing my paddle while whitewater rafting in high school. I hate being in water. Ironic since my mom had been a springboard diver and lifeguard, and both my parents had been triathletes and strong swimmers.

It stopped raining, and we realized we hadn't even needed to bail. It had just been a brief storm, a desert trick, not enough rain to affect the rock. On the shuttle bus, tourists looked at me in confusion as water dripped into a pool around me and my teeth chattered on the way back to the visitor center. I clutched my soaked backpack and avoided their stares.

The next day dawned clear and cold. We climbed the 'Dark Tower,' a multi-pitch in a different area of Zion. Dan quested up the first pitch, a crack leading to a bolted traverse in a roof, and then I took over and led up patina face holds on the second pitch.

I yelled down to him, "Holy shit! This is amazing! You won't believe this!" and we hollered together over the rumble of a long snake of cars making their way through the nearby tunnel. It was some of my favorite climbing I'd ever done, and in a beautiful position above the park. *This is why I'm here. This makes it all worth it.*

At the belay, I zipped my puffy all the way up, and stomped my feet to force blood to my toes. Dan had given me this puffy on our first trip together, but now he hated that I wore it constantly—apparently, it had been a gift from his ex-girlfriend, and it reminded him of her. I didn't particularly care though; it was a nice coat, and I needed it in this weather. It was the end of April, but since we were in the shade, we were bitterly cold. I waved my arms around and danced to stay warm.

On the third pitch, Dan encountered a runout slab on sandy edges.

"Take!" he yelled. I took up the slack and felt his weight rest on the rope. "Dude! This is kinda fucked up. I just need a sec." He pulled out a cigarette and spent a few minutes smoking it while he gathered the courage to finish the pitch with numb fingers and toes.

Slacklining in Kolob Canyon made for an idyllic bluebird rest day, and we stuck our noses in the Zion guidebook, plotting. The next day was May 1, and the temperatures were much hotter than just a few days prior. We climbed the first half of 'Monkeyfinger,' one of the classic harder free climbs in the park.

Dan took the bullshit approach pitch, and then I led up the 'Pillar of Faith' pitch, which required a delicate traverse to establish into a crack only big enough for fingertips. I strained with my right arm to place a microcam and transitioned into the layback, a full commitment with my feet pasted on the blank wall. I made it a couple moves before whipping, shocked that my tiny Metolius cam held the fall, and then got back on. The crack slowly widened up through fingers and hands, culminating in an offwidth finish. The pitch challenged me, especially since I had a backpack on. I executed an ungraceful belly flop mantle onto the ledge, and peeled off my layers, baking in the sun.

Dan took the next pitch, the notorious 'Black Corner,' and fell a few times on the slick 5.12 tips and finger locks. The black rock radiated heat. We swung leads for the next couple pitches and then decided to retreat once the heat became unbearable and we were absurdly thirsty. Thoughts of a Nalgene full of cold water tortured me as we rappelled the pitches in the merciless heat.

In the span of a few days, we'd gone from numb white hands while climbing in the shade, to getting sunburned and nearly heat-exhausted while climbing in the sun. The desert spring in Zion was temperamental and we were just along for the ride.

Climbing together was mostly neutral ground—easy enough to ignore our dysfunction and avoid fights when we were united by a common goal and task. It reminded me of my highpointing days in high school with my mom. We butted heads constantly, but on those long road trips and endless days of hiking and peakbagging, our singular focus and teamwork brought us together. When you're that motivated and concentrated on a goal, your energy gets poured where it's required, and little is left for petty bickering or fights. We put our heads down and plodded through miles and miles of trails across the country, fighting our own battles, and only occasionally each other. I was used to being isolated in nature with someone close to me who I didn't get along with; I'd been primed for putting up with Dan for the sake of pursuing climbing.

Back in the Wasatch, I had my first photoshoot with my new climbing sponsor in Rock Canyon, near Provo. I met up with the athlete coordinator and photographer, and had a blast exploring a crag I'd never been to before while playing with brand new gear. I was thrilled when I got to keep all of the equipment we used in the shoot; my gear was getting super worn out from constant climbing, so anything new was helpful.

I was proud to be there, and grateful that I had this for myself. It was my first time climbing outside without Dan in months; being free of his judgment was a welcome change. I hadn't realized just how much his moods had been tarnishing some of my climbing experiences. His tendency to belittle me when I fell was hurtful and had made me shy away from trying hard.

This day of climbing and this sponsorship deal was for *me*, not for anyone else. I had lost so much to Dan, but at least I had this. I did this. I earned this. He couldn't take that away from me, and I grasped onto this assurance as I danced up vertical crimps on the steep canyon walls.

"Fuck. No! Why is this happening?" I stared down at the lit-up dash of my dusty 2001 Suzuki. In the middle of the Interstate, she'd decided to lose all power. I pressed down the gas pedal with no response. Panicked as coming vehicles nearly rear-ended me, I steered her to the shoulder and put on my hazards. The onslaught of southbound traffic arriving into Lehi zoomed by a couple feet away. Tow truck called, I sat there and waited in the heat. *Happy Cinco de Mayo.*

I'd spent that day substitute teaching up in Logan, and now was supposed to hop in with Dan in Lehi to travel down south to the desert. I roasted in the oven of my car for an hour on the side of the highway until the tow truck arrived.

"Ya know, I used to be pretty into that rap-pell-ing stuff myself," the heavyset driver said proudly upon learning I was a climber.

"Uh huh. Well, us climbers are more focused on going up than down, but that's nice." I tried to explain the difference to him, but quickly dropped it when I realized he didn't care.

Dan picked me up from the shop. It was a Friday night, so my car was unlikely to be seen immediately. The next day, we climbed in American Fork Canyon to kill time, and then a gruff mechanic called me and told me they were unsure why she'd broken down. They'd replaced the fuel filter; hopefully that would do the trick.

We left my car at Dan's parents' house in Lehi and started the monotonous drive down to the desert. As we passed Rock Canyon, I excitedly mentioned the recent photoshoot I'd done there.

"Ugh," he groaned, "Please don't talk about your sponsorship or the shoot. It's too hard for me . . . I know I said I'd try to be happy for you, but I just can't stand it."

"Sorry. I'm just psyched. You were the one who was so focused on me getting sponsored in the first place. I thought you'd be stoked since we're getting free gear. You're benefiting too," I reminded him.

"Well, I dunno," he said, thinking. "Don't remind me about it. I'm only going to be able to be mean about it."

"Sheesh, sorry I even brought it up. I didn't know you'd be so jealous. Not sure how I'm going to just pretend it doesn't exist, but okay." I put my hands in my lap, played with the hem of my shirt, and looked out the window.

"You don't even deserve it! *I* am the one who should be getting sponsors calling me up, okay? Fuck, dude!" he yelled, like a child throwing a tantrum for not winning a prize. He was so desperate for accolades and recognition.

He would always get upset when the YouTube videos of his free soloing got snarky comments about how he didn't look solid enough to be ropeless. This was not surprising; they were right. He was fucked up in all of the videos, soloing after a cocktail of wine, weed, and prescriptions, practically tripping shit while unroped on some cliff in the Wasatch. He thought he looked badass in the videos—and I admit that I had thought so too when I first met him—but everyone else knew he was actually just being dangerous and stupid.

I knew I wasn't that strong in the grand scheme of climbing, but it didn't matter. I was pushing myself, I was having fun, I was expanding my horizons, and most importantly, I had stories to share that other people connected with. Meanwhile, Dan was only interested in having people glorify him and feed into his narcissism. I kept this to myself as the miles rumbled by under the truck.

He'd worked himself up so much that after blowing up at me, he gave me the silent treatment and refused to say another word to me for the remainder of the drive. Hours passed by in stifled tension, broken only by the endless Spotify queue of music. When we arrived at the house in St. George, he yelled at me briefly, and then resumed his oath of silence, downed a bottle of wine, and went to bed. I wasn't sure if I hated his yelling or his silence more. Both were torture.

The morning brought a quick, silent trip to the grocery store to grab some breakfast food, followed by Dan unleashing his fury upon me.

"You're an ungrateful cunt! You make me sick," he fumed.

"What did I do wrong this time?" I said, exasperated.

"You don't deserve fucking sponsorship! You're just a sport climber wannabe. They're only giving you gear 'cause you're a girl. The funny thing is, you're not even that pretty. And you'd climb better if you weren't a girl."

I thought we were past this already. It was just like the time in Patagonia when he'd put me down over and over.

"Maybe you're just jealous! Remember, this is what you wanted! You took all those photos and videos of me and told me to network," I spat back.

"Yeah, you should be giving me *all* the gear you get from them. I earned that shit. Not you. You wouldn't have even done all that climbing if it weren't for me!"

He started hitting himself, the typical escalation. I was used to his routine at this point, and I was sick of it. I tried to intervene, but was unsuccessful since he easily resisted me. My begging for him to stop went nowhere.

Boom! Hole in the wall.

Thump! Fist contacted skull.

Crack! His mother's vanity mirror shattered on the back of his head, sending rivulets of blood down his head and neck, seeping into his cotton t-shirt.

He cornered me in a bathroom. As he yelled, I kept backing up to create distance between us. I was all the way in the back of the bathroom, my spine against the bathtub, arms wrapped around my legs, head buried in my knees, trying to tune him out as he screamed right in my face. The insults were shot at me like arrows to the heart. I sobbed and begged him to calm down.

He'd tire of the yelling, lock me in the bathroom alone, rampage around the house, and then return at his leisure to continue the attack.

I dissociated to a new level. I was gone while I was there. Like a fire-breathing dragon, his hot air carried humiliating provocations, his face as close to mine as he could manage for maximum effect. The cold tile of the bathroom grounded me. I meditated upon it, disappearing into myself. He shoved me and demanded responses, but I was nowhere to be found. Gone.

He had been pushing me for so long, breaking me, breaking me, breaking me. Now I had shattered into so many pieces that he couldn't break me anymore. He had to look around at the carnage and realize that the object of his torture could only withstand so much. He could go right on smashing and stomping and huffing and puffing. My trauma made me implode to the point where I was no longer human, no longer able to react.

My body was a hostage curled up on the bathroom floor. My eyes gazed through salty tears at the barricaded door when he decided to spare me for time periods of his choosing. My ears let in his affronts but my brain lacked the capacity to process them. My arms shook as they protected my legs, shielding my torso. Hours passed like this. Hours, and hours, and hours.

Finally, there was a period of calm long enough to allow my protective dissociation to lift, and I snapped back to the present. I thrust myself against the door to force it open, and confronted him.

"I'm leaving. Since you said I can't call the cops, that's my only option. I can't stand this, and I can't call, so I need to leave," I snapped.

I sat outside the garage with all of my belongings: a duffel bag of clothes and toiletries, a couple backpacks of climbing gear, and a school-type backpack with books and my laptop. The southwestern sun beat down upon me and my heap of stuff. In a moment of desperation, I posted on Facebook asking for someone to pick me up in St. George. No one offered. Not surprising since most of my network was up in Logan.

Dan came out into the heat. "Are you really leaving? I can give you a ride to the St. George Express office."

I raised my eyebrows at his offer. Since when did he switch from "you can't leave" to "let me give you a ride to the bus station"? I weighed my options. A taxi would be absurdly expensive. I was broke and shell shocked. Best to accept his offer and get the fuck out of here.

We drove south through town and parked outside the station in a gray concrete strip mall.

"Before you go, please just talk to me," he said with pleading eyes.

"What is there left to say? I want to go. You've put me through so much . . ." my voice broke and I trembled. I was afraid to sit next to him. I should've known it was a trap.

We sat in the truck for an hour. He convinced me to stay with him, making empty promises about our relationship and his mental illness and self-medication. Every time I defended my choice to leave, he had an excuse and a counterargument to make me feel like I was the crazy one, like I just needed to be more understanding and patient. I gazed over at the shuttle buses coming and going, tormented by the thought of stepping onto one and never looking back.

I finally caved and reached for the door handle. In this last-ditch effort to get out of the truck, he grabbed my arm and refused to let me leave. In my most vulnerable state, he took advantage of my weakness and made the decision for me. He started the truck and drove away from the station, not giving me a chance to get out. My heart sank. I was so traumatized and tired, I couldn't fight it.

He drove back to the house and his rage continued. I kicked myself for letting him manipulate me once again. I couldn't think straight. Couldn't escape. Couldn't do anything.

"You wasted my whole fucking day!" he screamed. "I just wanted to climb today and look at how we've spent it!"

"I wasted *your* whole day? You're the one raging around and screaming! This isn't my fault. This was your choice! I wanted to leave. You should have let me leave. You're making my life a living hell!" I countered.

"I fucking hate you!" He grabbed a knife and pressed it hard against his neck.

Talk about déjà vu.

I felt powerless once again, like every word I said carried the weight of a human life. I thought I loved him, in our special deranged way, but I felt a pang of something new. I wanted him to do it. I wanted him to end his own misery so that it would end mine, too. I felt guilty for even thinking about it.

"I just want to die! You make me want to die!" he said through tears, his face screwed up in pain. After a few tense minutes, he lowered the knife, but kept it in his hand.

"We're going climbing. That will help me feel better. We've wasted this whole day and I don't want to waste any more of it!" he exclaimed, preoccupied with the thought of climbing.

He threw our climbing shoes and crash pad into the truck, and made me get in with him. I didn't want to go; I was exhausted and upset. The knife stayed in his hand by his side.

"If I don't touch rock within thirty minutes, I'll be dead! I'm fucking serious!" he shouted as he sped down the road toward Moe's Valley. I sat there quietly in my human shell, trying to disappear again.

Apparently this response was not satisfactory.

"You should die with me! You're basically a zombie anyway! Look at you. You don't even talk now. It's like you're already dead!" he screamed at me. He had a point. I felt like a zombie and I wished I was dead. Anything would be better than this.

He put the knife in his lap and picked up a green metal canister of propane camping fuel off the floor. He struck himself in the head with it as he drove.

The truck revved up as it gained speed. We were on a random residential road now, with perfectly manicured lawns framing giant Mormon mansions.

"This is it, Fallon! Hope you're ready. We're both going to die! How does that feel? I'm gonna fucking crash!" he raved. *Holy shit, this lunatic is actually gonna kill us both*. I could do nothing but cry. I felt so stuck.

He held the knife up to his throat once again as he steered the truck recklessly.

"Dan! Put the knife down! You don't have to do this. Take a deep breath." I felt like a broken record. He didn't want to listen to reason, and didn't appreciate my input.

He reached his right arm over and swooped it around my neck, putting me in a chokehold. His arm constricted around me and he latched onto my left bicep, squeezing with all his might. I felt like he might rip the muscle clean off. I saw pedestrians on the sidewalk up ahead, and started screaming frantically to try to alert them. *Maybe they'll call the police!* I hoped foolishly.

He tightened his grip to gag me to try to muffle the screams.

Don't want to draw attention. As if a truck careening down a neighborhood street at double the speed limit was going to fly below the radar. The pedestrians paid us no mind. The knife was in his other hand now and sliced open part of the vinyl siding in the driver side door as he swerved around violently.

"How the fuck do I get to Moe's?" he demanded. The climbing area was hidden behind a convoluted neighborhood and network of dirt roads, and he couldn't find it in his blind rage.

I tried to give him driving directions, but he was far too distracted. I willed my body to melt and fall through the cracks in the seat. I scanned the road for police, but came up empty handed. *How the fuck do I get out of this?*

I shook uncontrollably. *I can't handle this. I can't do this. This can't be happening.*

He gave up on trying to go bouldering, and drove back to the house. He was worried the police would be looking for him after his erratic driving, or that someone might have heard my screams after all.

We were both exhausted from the ordeal. I wanted things to be happy and normal again more than anything in the world. I couldn't take any more of the fighting and the meltdowns.

He showered, and I offered to clean up his head wounds with my medical training, but he refused. I offered to make him dinner, but he said I was a horrible cook and he didn't want me to cook for him. He had asked me earlier to put on a movie, so I put one on, but he didn't want to watch it. I was itching to make amends and to put this behind us, yet nothing was working.

If I tried to leave him, I knew he'd just hunt me down, so it felt pointless. He'd convinced me that he was the best life had to offer;

if I left, there was nothing waiting for me at home anyway. I was broke and alone and sick. Since I felt forced to stay with him, I at least wanted us to be able to live in harmony and end the incessant fighting. I could never say or do the right thing. Now I understood why he'd evaded answering me months ago when I asked about how to best handle his breakdowns. He didn't have an answer because there was no solution. Anything I tried was completely useless. I'd never felt so powerless.

He slumped over the dining room table, melancholic, drinking beer. I watched the movie with vacant eyes, unable to focus, the scenes of the day overshadowing the scenes on the screen.

CHAPTER 21

MEMENTO MORI

May 2017

"Shit!" I shouted in mid-air, whipping off my climbing project in the Hurricave. I was having a high gravity day, eager to fall through air that pushed back, to *feel* something, to try hard. Immersing myself in difficult movement on the limestone freed my brain from torturous flashbacks for brief, glorious moments during my climbing. We spent a few days cragging in the desert before bailing north.

When we got back to Dan's apartment in Salt Lake City, he chatted in the cramped dining room with his roommate. They smoked weed, strummed guitars, and ignored me.

I scrolled my phone out of boredom. My climbing sponsor had posted a Q&A with me on their website along with the new photos from the recent shoot. I lit up as I read through my profile and admired the rad climbing shots. I'd never seen myself like that before, through the lens of a professional. It felt like a big milestone. I shared a link to the article on my social media and went to bed while Dan stayed up with his roommate.

Not long after I'd drifted off to sleep, Dan barged in, flipped the lights on, and jerked the blanket off of me. Alarmed and blinded, I asked, "What's wrong? What happened?"

"You bitch! I cannot fucking believe you! Leave. Now!" he shrieked.

Still groggy, I didn't understand what was happening.

"You misrepresented me. I can't date a lying bitch. You're so selfish, Fallon. Jesus Christ," he said self-righteously.

"What are you talking about?"

"Your Q&A! You hardly mentioned me."

"What the fuck are you on about? I literally wrote the whole thing so carefully. I made sure to mention you multiple times. Like, I made a conscious effort to make sure you'd be happy with it and paint you in a positive light. If I mentioned you any more, it might as well have been an article about you, not me! Are you joking right now?" I said in disbelief.

"No! You made it sound like I'm just your second-rate climbing partner. You need to email them right now. Make them update it. You need to thank me in your answers and talk about how I made you into the climber that you are now. Actually, just let me write it so I'm not misrepresented." He grabbed my phone and yanked the charger out of it as he opened up my email and left the bedroom.

I got dressed and grabbed all of my stuff, ready to call an Uber so I could leave. My car was still at his parents' house a half hour south in Lehi. I walked past him on my way out of the apartment. "Give me back my phone so I can go. I'll have them update the answers, don't worry." I looked at the clock. It was almost midnight. Not an ideal time to be getting kicked out.

"No, I don't want you to leave," he said, handing back my phone.

"What the hell? You just told me I needed to leave! What do you want?" I was bewildered by his constant flip-flopping.

"Just stay. But promise me you'll have them update it. It's embarrassing for me."

"I don't get how it's embarrassing. I literally only spoke highly of you in the article. But okay. I will." At this point, I just wanted to avoid a fight, so I conceded. Any shred of resilience left in me had long since evaporated. We slept on his bed together on opposite sides, as far apart as possible.

In the morning, his diatribe against me seemed never ending. He criticized my climbing, my appearance, my worthiness, my intelligence. He called me undeserving. A cunt. A bitch. I was hearing these words directed at me so often that I was almost starting to believe them.

"Please, give me a ride back to my car. I just want to go. I don't want to sit here while you bash on me. I don't want to be with someone who treats me like shit! I don't deserve this! You're so unsupportive. If you think I'm all those terrible things, then why do you stay with me? I want to break up with you," I admitted. "If you won't give me a ride to my car, at least let me get an Uber or something."

"Fallon, don't leave me. If you can't date me, I can understand that. But at least be my climbing partner. Without each other, we'll lose climbing. We both need to climb," he said persuasively. He sounded like he was in a job interview . . . except it was for a demotion from boyfriend to platonic climbing partner. He looked hopeful. After some arguing, I reluctantly agreed just to appease him.

"Fine, we can climb. But that's it. I'm fucking over this."

Dan acted nonchalant as we drove up to Little Cottonwood Canyon, playing Simon & Garfunkel while he smoked weed with a smile on his face. He seemed almost the same as the day we'd first gone climbing there. Same clothes, same truck, same cigarettes, same canyon. We even had the same status now—just climbing, not dating. *Could it really be this easy?* I wondered. I felt happy again for the first time in a while. *Maybe this will work.*

We romped up a granite multi-pitch climb called 'Stiffler's Mom,' enjoying the variety of sport protected sections mixed with engaging cracks, and then rappelled the seven pitches back to the ground. Now that we were "just climbing partners" and not dating, we were getting along well, and joking like old buddies. I was amazed that he was able to handle this transition so easily. It seemed too good to be true.

It was too good to be true.

Dan's facade faded when we got back in the car. He wanted to get back together, and drove us to Bombay House, our favorite Indian restaurant. We ate, talked until the restaurant closed, and then talked more in his truck in the parking lot until two in the morning. I had written a poem about him recently, and I showed it to him. He read it and his eyes welled up with tears as he took in the flattery, the references to our favorite musicians and authors, the imagery of his bipolar disorder and his competing sides.

He was extremely convincing, able to maneuver the conversation however he pleased, and managed to coax me into getting back together with him. It was a roller coaster that left me reeling from the up and down, back and forth. I'd lost track of how many times we'd broken up and gotten back together. I knew it was unhealthy and unsustainable, but he had all of the control, all of the power. Any time I tried to resist, he wore me down repeatedly until I was forced to take the passive option of going along with him.

A return to substitute teaching in Logan was short lived. Dan wanted to see me, and he needed help moving out of his apartment. He worried if I strayed too far for too long that he would lose his grip on me.

After school got out, I hopped in the car and drove down toward Salt Lake City, but didn't make it very far. Something was wrong. I pulled off at a random exit and closed my eyes. Was I just sleep deprived? Did I need water? Sugar? Salt? What was happening? I felt so lightheaded that I couldn't focus on the road. I bought some gas station snacks and started driving south again.

"What the fuck?" I said in frustration. I couldn't force myself to concentrate. I pulled off again, my hands shaking. It was as if I were asleep while conscious, like I could see what was happening but not take the reins. I was locked out of my brain and banging on the door to get in. I ate some candy and chugged water. I wasn't actually asleep, but I felt like my brain was shut down. I couldn't drive safely, but I didn't have much choice. I slowly made my way down the highway with frequent stops. While I drove, I kept hitting myself on the thigh to try to stay focused, desperate not to drift off into this new, severe brain fog.

In Salt Lake, I helped Dan pack up everything he owned. He was going to store his stuff at his parent's house in Lehi while he lived out of his truck for the summer to save money. We unloaded his belongings into the mansion, and slept in the basement guest room.

The next day was a Saturday, and we had a big climbing goal: a "Half Dome" day where we wanted to climb 23 pitches. We got up a couple hours later than intended. I felt sluggish, fatigued, and lightheaded, but I tried to rally. Dan was amped and ready to go. He charged up the approach, bushwhacking and boulder-hopping to the base of The Thumb.

"Dude," he called back to me, "Why are you dragging ass? Let's go!" He motioned for me to hurry up.

"I don't know. I feel like shit. I'm trying my best . . ." My words trailed off as I navigated the boulders.

While I belayed him up the first couple pitches of climbing, my body felt like someone had turned off the power button. I followed the first two pitches in a daze, pulling myself over bulges and up cracks. Every movement felt labored, like my limbs were moving through silly-putty and my heart was giving out. Overwhelmed by weakness and dizziness, I practically crumpled into my harness when I clipped myself into the anchor.

"You good, dude? Do you wanna lead?" he asked me.

I looked up at him with lifeless eyes. He got the message and continued up the third pitch. The belay became like the driving struggle—I couldn't focus. I could see him climbing up and up, but I was in a trance. *C'mon, Fallon, focus on the task at hand. Just belay.* But I couldn't do it.

I got the feeling again that I was locked out of my brain, screaming at it to wake up, but unable to take control. The odd sensation of passing out got worse, and I urged Dan to climb quickly to the next anchor so I could take him off belay.

My body sat hanging in my harness, frozen, drifting in and out of consciousness. No matter how hard I tried, I simply couldn't make myself concentrate. He was struggling on the pitch, having to take at most of the gear placements to rest and warm up his hands. Through my fog, I tried to communicate to him how bad I was feeling. Forming words felt impossible. After what felt like an eternity, he made it to the next bolted anchor.

I took him off belay and burst into tears. *What is happening to me? How do I make it go away?* I was terrified, shaking and crying. It felt like I was no longer the pilot of my own body, and that loss of control was deeply frightening. My head was floating around on its own accord.

Dan yelled down to me, annoyed that I wasn't following the pitch. He finally caught on to what was happening, rappelled and cleaned his gear, and made it back to me. I was panicking.

"Something is really wrong. I don't know what's happening. But something is seriously wrong with my head. Please help me," I choked out.

He lowered me down the first two pitches, and then carried my pack down the trail while helping guide me down. I was moving ridiculously slow, and he was irritated with me. My visual field narrowed within a black vignette, and I lost touch with my senses as my consciousness struggled to hold on. The base of my neck hurt, it felt like my head was exploding, and I was so sluggish I could barely move. I was extremely disoriented and disturbed by the changes I was experiencing.

Back in his truck, I felt unsettled and out of control. He drove me to the ER, where the doctors took down a list of my symptoms, ran tests, and did a CT scan of my brain. I lay on the hospital bed, wanting to sleep more than anything in the world. My fatigue was overwhelming. Dan wouldn't allow it. He started throwing a fit.

"Dude, this brings me right back to the psych ward. I hate being in hospitals"—he squirmed in his seat—"because it gives me flashbacks. This is your fault. I don't wanna be here."

I told him he could leave to go get food or smoke, whatever he needed, but at first, he refused. He was flipping his shit in the visitor's chair while I lay on the bed, worried about what was happening to me. Rather than taking action to help himself, he chose to sit there whimpering about it and seeking attention. He tried to make me feel bad again for calling the cops on him since that had led him to the psych ward.

"I'm the one in the ER right now. Not you. I don't have the energy to help you," I grumbled. Finally, he went outside to smoke in an attempt to calm down, and I was grateful to be left alone for a few quiet minutes. He had been stressing me out even more.

After a couple hours, the test results came back, and everything looked totally normal. It was a relief, but it left me with no answers. What was the explanation? I knew, deep down, that something was seriously wrong. It would be two more years before I learned the name for my neurological disorder: a form of dysautonomia called Postural Orthostatic Tachycardia Syndrome (POTS). At the time, I felt like I was going insane. The doctors told me to rest and follow up with my primary care physician. I left the hospital frustrated, in pain, and severely lightheaded.

On the drive back to Lehi with Dan, the car gave me motion sickness, so I was quiet and leaned forward in my seat.

"You're mad at me, huh? Why are you ignoring me like that?" he hounded me.

I tried to explain to him how I was feeling, and that I wasn't mad at him, but he wouldn't listen. His mind was made up. I felt too terrible to fight him since I was preoccupied with fighting my own body.

We were supposed to go camping that night after climbing, so I suggested we stick to our plan. He insisted that we go back to his parents' house since he thought I'd be a liability while camping. I didn't want to face his parents in my current condition or fight with him in front of them.

"Let's just camp. It'll be fine. I don't want to ruin your plans even more, hun. Your parents have done enough for us, letting us stay all the time," I explained. My brain protested forming thoughts and forcing them out through my mouth. It required tremendous effort.

"No, we're not camping. If you don't come stay with me in Lehi, then I'm gonna lose my shit, okay? I already lost all my climbing today and then had to suffer in that hospital because of you."

Anger surged inside of me. I didn't want to go with him. I was pissed at him for making everything about him when I was so sick. Whatever he was going through was always worse, always harder, always more important. *Fuck this.*

"No, let's just go camping. Sticking to the plan sounds good. It doesn't matter if I sleep in a tent or a bed. I'll be fine," I said.

"Fuck, no! I'm gonna kill myself if you don't stay with me in Lehi tonight! My parents and I can take care of you," he demanded. I started crying. The fatigue, pain, and fear of the unknown were piling up on me in addition to his verbal assaults. He always threatened suicide and then it left me with no choice. It was his *gotcha* card, and he played it often. I was too tired to keep resisting, so we went back to his parents' house, where I ate dinner and then fell asleep on the couch. Surrender. My body needed rest.

I awoke from my nap to Dan telling me to get in the car. He wanted to talk to me where his parents couldn't hear us. We went for a drive. It was dark, and the southern ridgelines of the Wasatch were a muted black against the hazy backdrop of the night sky, with only small patches of snow hanging on this late into May.

"You're a horrible girlfriend. You make me miserable. You must hate me." He bought some wine and took long pulls from the bottle as he drove. I sat there silent, too upset with my body to entertain his insults.

"Why won't you just accept my love? I try to be so caring and it's like you don't care about me or us or anything," he said.

"It's not that simple, Dan. I just wanted to camp. I don't like it when people look at me like a helpless, sick person. I didn't want to mope around the house with your parents asking me questions." Driving was making me feel worse. The lightheadedness intensified.

"It's fine! You're overthinking it."

"Please, can we go back? This is making me feel sick. I just want to sleep."

"No! You're a fucking zombie," he said, driving erratically around Lehi. "You are such a waste of time. You don't have anything to contribute! I mean, look at you!" He looked at me sternly to try to prove his point. I sat there cowering, leaning against the passenger door. "Yeah, lifeless."

"It's our six-month anniversary. Did you know that?" I'd suddenly remembered.

"Shit. I forgot." He chugged from the bottle, pondering for a moment. "I can't do this anymore."

"Yeah. Me neither." My voice was a whisper.

We sat in silence for a couple minutes as he drove through the neighborhood. He broke up with me. I felt glad. Usually I was the one who had to break up with him, and this time it was his turn to end things. There was nothing left here but manipulation and abuse.

"Aren't you going to try to save this? Seriously, you're not going to fight for us?" he asked, incredulous.

"You just broke up with me and now you're mad I'm not resisting it? What the fuck! Are you really that surprised? Look at how many times we've broken up before! Jesus Christ. This isn't healthy. We both know that. You said it yourself. Let's just end it," I said, resigned. *I'm too tired for this. I just want to sleep.*

"If you don't try to get back together with me, then that really shows you just don't care! You never cared! I fucking hate you!" he shouted, slamming the steering wheel, sweat collecting on his forehead. I was too drained to respond. Same argument, same truck, different day. Cycling through the same loop.

We got back to the house, and I went to bed. I could hardly sleep despite my fatigue, but the breakup gave me some peace. I heard him walking around all night, pacing.

In the morning, he woke me and said he was ready to take me back to my car. I quickly gathered my things and threw my bags in the truck. The drive was quiet at first. What was left to say? We were broken up. I looked out the window at the high ridgelines of the Wasatch so I could avoid eye contact with him.

Dan took a detour up Little Cottonwood. We were going to talk through our relationship and how to fix it whether I liked it or not. I sat there, hostage in the truck, as he dissected our personalities and analyzed the problems. Dan tried to take back the breakup, but I wasn't on board. My head was swimming and I felt too lightheaded to think straight. He drove back to where my car was parked, and then we sat there for a couple hours talking. I looked over at my car longingly and wished I could just leave, but he wouldn't let me.

"You need this macho climbing partner to keep up with you! I can't do that right now," I explained. "You want a girlfriend who is submissive and nurturing, but that's not me. I can't meet your needs! You want me to be what I'm not. That's why I've been trying to leave so many times." We talked ourselves in circles. Again and again. "I doubt you can find a girl who does all of the things you want simultaneously. You want a dirtbag girl, but she needs to have perfect hair and makeup and clothes? You want a badass climber who also happens to be a pushover to your controlling bullshit? That's so impossible! The traits don't add up."

"I don't know, Fallon. I'm an abuser. Most people can't admit that. I know. I'm dark and controlling and moody and no one wants to put up with me. I love you. You love me. We have to figure out how to make this work."

"Go back to therapy. Try mood stabilizers. Get your shit together. I don't want to be dragged along anymore. You insult me so much, and I'm so tired, and I'm so sick, I just can't fucking do this anymore," I said, aggravated and out of patience. I rubbed my temples.

"You're just a hypochondriac. You're pretending to be sick to sabotage our relationship!"

"Shut the fuck up," I said aggressively, almost surprised by my own force. "You have no idea how awful I feel. I just want to feel good so I can keep climbing. This sucks and it's really scary. I can't believe you would say that." I shut down and put my head in my hands.

"You fucking zombie. I can't stand you, but I don't want to lose you. I am so fucked up about all of this," he rambled. *No shit.*

I probably did look like a zombie. I responded only when required. I stared blankly ahead. I didn't want to look at him. I didn't move at all, except when my chest shook when I burst into tears. I was a hopeless mess, broken beyond repair physically, mentally, emotionally.

"If you don't want to lose me, maybe you should've thought of that before breaking up with me. And treating me like shit," I added.

He tried to convince me to get back together, or to go to couples counseling with him, or that he'd get back on mood stabilizers. He talked through options for how our relationship could move forward, but none of them sounded promising to me.

"Let's just stay broken up. I guess we can climb sometimes though. But just as friends," I compromised. I wanted to leave more than anything, so I was trying to figure out what would be my golden ticket out.

"Fuck, dude! I thought I was reeling you back in after casting you out last night. I thought this was in the bag. I don't want to break up!"

"Jesus. I hate your games, Dan. I have *some* self respect left. I need some time." I shrugged and refused to make eye contact as he wept on my shoulder.

"I took such good care of you yesterday! How could you do this?" he cried. I raised my eyebrows.

"You insulted me and yelled at me yesterday," I reminded him. "I'm gonna go." I finally worked up the courage to get in my car and drive away. I kept checking my rearview mirror to make sure he wasn't following me.

The drive to Logan passed in a murky haze between my lightheaded brain fog and my muddled feelings. I recognized Dan's hurtful behaviors, but I also prioritized climbing to a point where I was letting it destroy me. Our relationship served a purpose so we could accomplish our common goals. But I felt incredibly hurt and unwanted, and less motivated to push myself in climbing since it led to Dan putting me down. *It can't be worth it. I'm only 20. Fuck this. Fuck Dan.*

Cache Valley opened up before me as I exited the final canyon,

Logan's abundant green fields cut by the Bear River's broad meanders below the gentle snow-capped peaks rising on its west and east flanks. This felt like coming home. Pastoral. Quiet. A safe place.

A pack of light blue American Spirits slid over the gas station counter into my hand. I wanted to see what Dan was so addicted to. Maybe I could understand him better this way.

My Suzuki rumbled up the gravel road to the mouth of Green Canyon, and I put her in park with the bumper pointed toward the Wellsville Mountains, facing right into the sunset. I loved this spot: the threshold between society and wilderness. Right on the East Cache Fault. Right on the Bonneville Shoreline. Right where I belonged. I'd hoped for a spectacular sunset, but instead the orb hid behind thick clouds. I rolled down the window and turned up Bob Dylan.

I peeled the plastic off the pack and removed a cigarette. I spaced out and held the lighter to the end of it for too long. I was lost in thought and admiring the limestone outcrops above me on the mountainside. It burned black, and a centimeter on the end was completely charred. I couldn't salvage it. The stench made me gag. I pulled out another. This time, I paid closer attention and got it right. I decided I couldn't die without at least seeing what it was like. Part of the human experience. An experiment in human sensations. *Memento mori.*

At first, I let the smoke into my mouth but not my lungs. I kind of liked the taste, which tracked since I enjoyed the smell of tobacco smoke. I risked a hearty inhale, letting the toxins into my lungs. I felt like I was burning my insides, as if I'd inhaled the flame itself, and coughed in pain. I puffed on it half-heartedly a couple more times. My curiosity had been satisfied. I still felt empty, and no closer to understanding Dan.

I didn't like it. There's a first time for everything.

CHAPTER 22

SLOW CRAWL

May 2017

"I took the time I needed. I can't do this anymore. It's not healthy for either of us to break up and get back together all the time. This is it. I'm sorry, and I hope things get better for you." I hit send on the message and felt nothing.

It was early in the morning, when the birds weren't even up yet, and the first shades of dawn hadn't broken through the trees in the valley. I curled my hair before work and saw a response light up my phone. *Already? I thought he'd still be asleep.*

Dan ripped me apart over text, clearly upset by the finality in my message. Grasping at straws to save our relationship, he fired off text after text. I responded when I could while substitute teaching that day. He continued to insult me and call me names. I don't know why I didn't just block him.

"At first I told you we could still be climbing partners sometimes. But I don't think that's going to be possible since you keep insulting me. I don't want to even climb with you. You're so mean!" I messaged him back. I felt braver than usual thanks to the distance between us.

I found comfort in the fact that I was taking the high road. His texts were impulsive and rude as he realized his control had lapsed. I had given him too many chances. This was better for both of us.

Later that night, he texted me that he was suicidal. I tried to comfort him, but also reminded him that we weren't dating anymore, and it seemed like we were ruining a boundary. He called me. He'd clearly been crying and having a psychotic breakdown.

"I hate you! I can't believe you want to end things permanently! I want to die! I'm gonna kill myself!" He was so loud I had to hold the phone away from my ear.

"If you keep up the suicidal talk, I'm gonna have to call the cops. We aren't doing this again. Tell me you'll be okay so I don't have to call them." I put my foot down.

"No! You bitch! You don't even care," he moaned.

"You're right. I *don't* care. I'm not responsible for you. My friend is coming over and I don't want to keep talking to my ex-boyfriend." I hung up on him. Texts streamed in constantly, but I ignored them. I had no sympathy left for him after what he'd done and said to me.

I spent the evening hanging out with my friend Sarah for the first time in what felt like ages. I didn't tell her everything that had happened, but I mentioned that Dan and I had broken up. I'd been so isolated from everyone for months, hiding the difficulties of the relationship. It was refreshing to hang out with her, but in the back of my head I was wondering if Dan had made it through the night.

I worked for a couple days, happy for the stability of teaching and reassurance that I'd have a paycheck coming soon. I took a day off to go to the doctor because my symptoms were getting worse: headaches, head pressure, lightheadedness, severe tendon pain, neck pain and stiffness, tight jaw muscles, inability to concentrate or focus on anything, fatigue, etc. They tested my urine and blood, and asked me about Mono, Lyme, my thyroid, and more, unsure of the culprit. I caught a cold, on top of everything else. My body couldn't fight off bugs while it was fighting itself.

On Facebook, I posted a list of all of the insults Dan had said to me during our relationship. I hid the post from him, unfriended him, and updated my relationship status to single. Friends and acquaintances reached out, some of whom I had hardly spoken with before, all offering their help and making sure I was safe. I was touched by the kindness of these people, the concern in their messages. The burden of his abuse was no longer my secret to carry. I had people who cared about me. People who wanted to help. People who were also appalled by his venomous words and actions. As I lay in bed sick with my mystery illnesses, this community provided me with a level of love and consolation I couldn't have anticipated.

The fatigue, headaches, brain fog, pain, and lightheadedness became so severe that I could hardly function. I missed work. I slept longer than normal. I couldn't drive safely. My roommates Ashleigh and Taylor were gone on an extended geology research trip to the Grand Canyon, and I wasted away alone in my apartment in Logan.

Dan called me after a few days, and in my sorry state, I picked up the phone. He told me he'd done a "death camp" in Moab, which is when an inexperienced person does a BASE jump off a cliff. The video popped up on my phone and I stared in shock. Dan's limbs flailed as he plummeted off the sandstone cliff, followed by the billowy parachute that saved him from certain death. He'd been obsessed with BASE jumping since we'd met, and we often watched videos of it, but I figured he'd go through the typical process of skydiving and proper instruction before he actually did a jump. This was reckless and manic, but he was stoked. He'd gotten a new credit card to buy a used BASE rig online for almost $2000.

When he asked how I was doing, I told him about my illness and how much I was suffering. My body was confusing and my symptoms were devastating. This was a point of weakness, and he used it to attack: this was his way back in. He insisted on coming up to help me since I was so unwell and alone. I was hesitant, but he was persuasive, and assured me that he was just going to assist me with tasks that I was finding too difficult. He sounded gentle and caring, like he genuinely just wanted to help. In my desperation and exhaustion, I reluctantly agreed. I was so afraid of being alone while experiencing such alarming symptoms that I figured having him around was better than no one. He'd conditioned me for this and knew exactly how to manipulate me.

He drove through the night, let himself into my apartment, and crawled into bed with me.

"No! What are you doing? We're not dating anymore. You can't sleep here," I protested. "Go down to the couch or bring in a sleeping pad."

"C'mon, Fallon. Where else am I going to sleep?" He sleepily smiled and started touching me. I resisted, and it only made him grab me harder.

"Stop! I don't want this. I'm so tired and sick. I'm not in the mood. And we broke up for a reason!" I objected. He didn't listen. I struggled against him, but he easily overpowered me and yanked down my pajamas.

I cried and wriggled, trying to break free. "Stop! Listen to me!" It was useless.

"Relax." He turned me over onto my stomach and got behind me.

I gasped in pain. This was something we'd never done before. It felt like I was going to tear in two. I silently cried and tried to dissociate while I endured it.

When he finished, I ran to the bathroom and locked the door. I winced whenever I moved. When I went to clean myself off, I saw blood. I slept on the far edge of the bed, trying not to touch him.

In the morning, he chastised me. "This feels so complicated. Fuck!" he yelled, turning his lighter over in his hand nervously.

"You promised you were coming here as a friend, to help me! That's clearly not what you wanted. This isn't complicated at all. You really hurt me. I didn't want that. You've made it so much worse . . ." I said, hating myself for letting him come here, for thinking he could just be there for me as a friend. Regret gnawed at me.

He went outside to smoke, and I thought he was going to leave since he was mad at me, so I locked the front door behind him. A minute later, he was banging on the door and demanding I open it up. I sat there, contemplating if I should let him back in. He called my phone and kept knocking loudly. I didn't want to make a scene with my neighbors, and I was scared of what he'd do if I kept it locked. I let him back in.

"Fallon, you're so sick. You can't be alone. You need someone to help you. Let me help you," he said, more gently now. "We can make things better."

I didn't feel like a person. I felt like I was dying, drowning, suffocating. I felt so weak and violated. He decided we were back together, and I didn't agree, but I also didn't fight him about it. I had no energy left to argue; if I did argue, I knew how it would end for me, and for him. He left my apartment. The rest of the day passed in a blur.

The next day, the bleeding continued. I researched my symptoms and wondered if I should go to the doctor since he clearly tore something in me. No matter what position I was in, the pain was ever present, so excruciating that having a bowel movement made me sob. Dizziness and fatigue confined me to my bed. I felt like I was getting a fever, and the bleeding started to get worse.

I got a message from Dan. "Hey. I'm over the games. You're smart enough to figure out how to say SINGLE on your profile, but somehow telling me you can't update it to reflect that we're in a relationship."

It was true—I had never updated it since he'd decided we were back together. I updated it back to 'in a relationship' now to appease him. I was too sick to deal with this pettiness. *Who cares? I have bigger things to worry about.*

"Dan, that's not really my main concern right now. I'm bleeding. I think I might need to go to the hospital," I messaged back.

"Anything to get out of a conversation with me, right. If you're too good to be in a relationship with me online, then you're too good for me in real life. I won't tolerate being humiliated by you, and then tolerate you lying to me, telling me you're incapable of having it show up," he messaged.

"I just updated it! I don't know why it won't update on your end."

"Take your fucking fingers and put them on the fucking mouse and do your social media shit. So that I can actually want to take care of you."

"Please. I updated it! I feel so sick. Something is wrong. I might need to go to the hospital because of you." He didn't seem to care about that at all.

"I want to fucking die every single time I pull open Facebook. Fucking display it on your profile! How stupid do you think I am?"

His messages started arriving with increasing frequency, and in all caps. He accused me of lying over the course of hundreds of messages. My phone could hardly handle the incoming onslaught as he melted down about the relationship status not updating. My eyes glazed over. I couldn't type fast enough to keep up. Finally, it showed up on his end, and I could breathe again.

I was sick for days, and time passed in the way it always does when your body is failing you and you're confined by four walls: a slow crawl. I was so beaten down and checked out that I couldn't muster the courage to see a doctor. What would I say? *Hey, my ex-boyfriend raped me, decided we're back together, and then left me here to suffer from whatever mystery illness I've developed.* The thought of explaining what had happened mortified me. Shame and fear ruled me. I didn't want to relive it all over again, so I dissociated and did nothing. One hour softened into the next, the time fading from memory as soon as it passed, unremarkable.

Since Dan didn't have an apartment anymore, he often camped in the mountains above his parent's house, dropping in to visit when he needed food and supplies. He tired of it quickly, and decided he wanted to go climb with me. We rolled into City of Rocks, a climbing area nearby in southern Idaho, and I could hardly stay awake as the familiar granite monoliths towered above the truck.

Ropeless, we scaled a crack and giant chickenhead holds up the east side of Bath Rock, covering the 200 feet of 5.5 climbing in a few minutes. Free soloing while dizzy was particularly exciting. We drove down to Elephant Rock, and I followed him up 'Wheat Thin,' a classic 5.7 crack. Continuing our irregular tour, we stopped at the Breadloaves next. I found myself at the base of 'Bloody Fingers,' a long, arcing crack, almost vertical, with a notoriously tricky start.

Growing up in Boise, all of the "trad dads" at my gym had talked up this route. As an Idaho climber, it was a rite of passage to climb it, and I looked at it with reverence. I hadn't been back to City of Rocks in a few years, not since I'd learned how to trad climb.

I thought back to my first visit to City of Rocks. I was 13 years old and 90% of my climbing experience had been in the gym. My dad had let me go on the trip alone with my climbing coach, her husband, and their church group. I didn't realize it was a church group until a couple days in, when they asked me something about the Bible and Jesus Christ, and I had no idea how to answer. I'd been atheist my entire life.

We'd rumbled in on the washboarded dirt road in their big church van, with "The Distance" by Cake blasting through the speakers. I was the only child, and felt lucky I got to join adults on a trip like this—some sort of special exception. It was pitch black outside, so I could only see as far as the headlights of the van. When we got to our campsite, I set up my tent, excited and nervous for my first night ever camping alone.

In the morning, I unzipped the door and emerged to a scene I will never forget. It felt like someone had knocked all of the air out of my chest. I tripped on a boulder in my rush to get a better view. It must have been no later than six in the morning, the first light of day selflessly brightening the wide, sweeping bowl of the City. The giant fins and domes of granite rose out of the broad sagebrush valley and surrounding hillsides, a magical labyrinth of rock unfolding before me in the brilliant glow of sunrise under a strikingly clear blue sky. I breathed in the high desert. I wiped the tears from my eyes, and felt love surging within me. I'd never loved a *place* before.

That day marked the beginning of a long love affair with the City. From my first kiss in high school on the top of Jackson's Thumb with a boy on my climbing team after junk-showing on our first multi-pitch, to rager day trips in college where we'd run around trying to get in as many pitches as possible, the City felt like home.

This was my first time sharing it with Dan, and I felt uneasy. I wasn't sure if I was ready for 'Bloody Fingers' with how sick I was feeling. There were other climbers at the base, and he wanted me to pony up. I racked up and tried my best, but found myself taking often and complaining about how much pain I was in. My muscles protested and buckled, my tendons felt like they were on fire, and my body was too weak and exhausted to cooperate. Moves that should have been cruiser felt impossible. I made it to the top and lowered off in defeat, knowing I'd blown my onsight and butchered the route. Dan made fun of me with the other climbers.

"Jesus, Fallon. We didn't need a whole play by play," he laughed. "I mean, it's only 10a. How hard can it be?" I packed my gear with my head down, ashamed. *He's right. I should be able to climb a route of that grade. What's wrong with me?* I didn't know yet about any of my health conditions—POTS, hEDS, MCAS, lupus, and more. At the time, I just felt broken, confused, and overwhelmed by all of my symptoms, and frustrated with their impact on my climbing ability. Like so many other routes from this era, I returned years later and sent the climb in an easy, enjoyable fashion, making a positive new memory on it.

That night, we camped on public land, and I could barely respond when Dan talked to me. Checked out. It was all too much. I felt like shit in every possible way. The sunset put on a show through the aspen branches above, with gray-cerulean fading down into a gradient of yellow, coral, and salmon above the blue rolling mountains of southern Idaho in the distance.

Morning Glory Spire dominated the next day, with runs up 'Skyline' and 'Fall Line' before we hid from the inevitable afternoon rainstorm. In the evening, Dan battled 'Crack of Doom' and had little success—the bouldery start thwarted his send, but he managed to thrash his way to the top before the sun went down. I opted not to follow it because I had no energy or strength remaining. I didn't want to subject myself to more bullying.

Back in Utah the following day, Dan and I climbed limestone in Logan Canyon. We got into an argument and only managed to climb one route, which was called 'Illusions.' It was fitting: I could see nothing clearly anymore. In our relationship of ups and downs, gaslighting and violence, love and hate, it was impossible to know what was real and what was merely an illusion.

I was in a dream state. The dysfunction of our relationship combined with my mysterious symptoms obscured reality. I yearned for a fresh start, for wellness, for freedom, for the truth.

A vertical splitter crack of sandstone shot out of the ground and into the sky above me in a perfect line. I hardly remembered how I got here, but it didn't matter much.

Here I was.

Here was the desert.

Here was a climb.

Simple.

The heat of summer had descended upon Bears Ears, and was radiating up from the baked red earth, land of pinyon and juniper, coyote and rattlesnake, dirtbag and rancher. Buff-colored cliffs tinged with crimson and rich brown lined the hills of Indian Creek, guarded only by brief approaches up the sandstone talus. We were at Optimator Wall, a popular area.

After warming up, I racked up for the crown jewel of the crag: 'Annunaki,' a sinuous, jagged crack perfectly splitting a gently overhanging face. I cruised through the hand crack portion, but was shut down by the upper finger locks at the chains. My joints and muscles refused to comply, the sinister fatigue and achiness defeating me. Still, I enjoyed the movement, thrilled by the position and quality of the climb.

After climbing the next day, Dan told me my recent weakness was disappointing—embarrassing even. I struggled on routes I should have been able to send, mentally failing while his bullying swirled around in my head. In tandem, my body and mind gave out. Dan ran out of weed, so we mobbed across the desert to Colorado, where a dispensary filled his need for the good stuff. To make the drive worthwhile, we stuck around and bouldered at Turtle Lake, got burgers at a local hipster joint in Durango, and crashed at a motel (a rare luxury).

We had to head back north for work, and made a pit stop at the Crackhouse on our way home. His truck crept along the slickrock sections of the dirt road, yawing on the rough boulders until we were deposited at the cave. It was almost June, and as I snuck off into the desert to pee, careful not to step on the cryptobiotic soil, the sun seared my bare skin. The orange fins of Arches National

Park were visible in the distance in a glorious panorama with the La Sal Mountains. I went back into the Crackhouse and projected it with Dan.

So much had happened since our last visit here. This time, I was much more capable. In one motion, I could jam my hands above me, engage my core, and kick my legs up into the roof to get established. My hair was getting long, swinging below me in a brown curtain, as I swam along the roof crack, climbing horizontally. Left, right, left, right, sink the hand deeper, twist the foot harder. There was comfort in the security of the jams, the abrasion on my forearms where the tape gloves ended, the weightless moment of slipping out of the crack. This was sacred ground to fall upon.

CHAPTER 23

"I'LL KILL YOU"

June 2017

The MRI whirred around my head, clanging and thrumming in bizarre rhythms. I closed my eyes and tried to focus on the music coming through the headphones. When it was over, I went to the climbing gym, where I'd recently gotten my job back as a routesetter. The next day, I found out the MRI was normal—my brain looked fine and dandy. That didn't help my situation as I drove south toward Salt Lake City to meet up with Dan. The lightheadedness was overwhelming and I struggled to stay focused as I drove. I was forced to take frequent breaks.

I got a text from my roommates, Ashleigh and Taylor, telling me they needed to talk to me. They happened to be driving north on the interstate on their way back from the Grand Canyon, so we chose a gas station to meet at in Ogden. I pulled off, and gave them hugs. They cut to the chase: I needed to move out. My unstable finances and Dan's scary behavior concerned them, and Taylor's boyfriend was going to move in. I agreed, pretending to be totally chill about moving out to avoid any drama. I didn't want to lose my friends over this, so I smiled and told them I understood. It felt like a punch in the gut, but I had seen it coming. I told them I'd be gone for a bit, but promised to sort it out when I returned to Logan. I needed friends now more than ever.

I finished the drive to Lehi, left my car at Dan's family home, and hopped in with him. We drove down to Provo to meet up with his friend who was an experienced BASE jumper. He inspected Dan's new rig and taught him how to pack it properly. It was well after midnight, and his parachute was splayed out in a random parking lot under bright lights from a campus soccer field. I sat criss-cross on the asphalt, observing them as they carefully folded the black and white fabric into the pack.

I thought Dan was completely nuts. Who just buys a BASE rig and skips all the training steps? I'd recently finished reading *Learning to Fly* by Steph Davis, so I was intimately familiar with the typical process people use to learn BASE jumping. Dan's method seemed like a suicide mission. That was on brand for him though—couldn't be too surprised.

After a quick couple hours of sleep, our destination was the Perrine Bridge in Twin Falls, Idaho. There was no better place in the region for beginner BASE jumping. As we drove I-84 through southern Idaho, his leg bounced up and down at the same cadence his head bobbed to the music. He sang along to "When My Time Comes" by Dawes at full volume. He was ecstatic. The nervous energy of knowing he was going to throw himself off a bridge soon fueled his mania. He sucked down American Spirits and Red Bulls and drove far over the speed limit.

Hopping out of the truck in Twin Falls, Dan felt the wind and looked at the clouds—unsafe conditions to jump. He needed to wait for the wind to die down. We ate Mexican food and waited around for the weather to change. He scrambled partway down the basalt hillside to scope out the landing zone next to the Snake River. It was hard to believe this was the same river I'd grown up on, hiking for days at a time through sagebrush wasteland along its banks in the

Owyhee Mountains near Boise.

Finally, he saw other people BASE jumping, and figured that meant the winds were safe now. In a frenzy, he placed me on the canyon rim adjacent to the bridge, set up his big DSLR camera on a tripod, and reminded me how to use his drone. I was still shaky on operating both devices, but told him I'd try my best.

"Oh, and don't let any cops see the drone. I'm not super clear on the rules here."

With his rig on, he ran off to the center of the bridge where the other jumpers were perched. I lost track of him in the group—it was too far away to tell who was who, so I wasn't sure when it would be his turn to jump. I recorded everyone just in case. I got the DSLR and drone into position to capture the entire scene: the dark brown metal bridge, the flight down between the steep black hillsides, and the landing in a clearing of trees on the bank of the river.

Dan was up. Time slowed to a halt, and I left the cameras recording in their current positions, almost forgetting to man the controls. He stood on the railing, and then plummeted off the bridge, limbs flailing with the pilot chute trailing behind. *Whoosh*! His parachute filled with air. His arm got tangled in the lines, but he freed it and grabbed the toggles to steer. It was an extremely easy jump for someone who knew what they were doing. But Dan did not know what he was doing, and that became immediately evident as he struggled to aim for the landing zone.

He was losing altitude fast. I tracked him with the camera, but the drone was getting buffeted by the wind. I thought he might clear the water, but within seconds he was in the river, just a few feet shy of landing on solid ground. Waterlogged, he swam and emerged from the river onto land with his soaked parachute, apparently unharmed.

I flew the drone back to where I stood, but forgot how to turn it off for landing. A nearby spectator came over to me and snatched the wayward drone out of the air while I struggled with the controls, trying to figure out how to turn off the propellers so they wouldn't slice this kind bystander. I eventually solved the problem, packed up the camera equipment, and booked it back to the truck. I texted Dan the footage so he could watch the video of his jump on the hike out. The sun was setting, and he returned at dusk.

"Dude! What the fuck? That footage sucked! You didn't zoom in to get a close up of the jump!" he criticized.

"I was trying my best! I thought you'd be stoked on it. I'm sorry . . . How was it to jump? Is the rig okay from the water?" I was expecting him to be psyched on the jump, not pissed about the video.

"Yeah, yeah. Whatever. I'm just bummed I didn't get better footage. It's seriously so shitty! You fucked it up," he said, irritated.

In my head, I was thinking about how it was a good thing I hadn't zoomed in—people would've been able to see him flailing and fucking it up, and would surely make fun of him for his incompetence. Instead, I just apologized and explained why it had been difficult for me to get a good shot.

Recently, he'd started a social media page for his videos that he dreamt of making into a production company. He aimed to have badass climbing, free soloing, and BASE jumping videos on it, and he wanted my help. Now, he retracted his offer and told me I couldn't be a part of it anymore. Internally, I laughed. *So what? It's not like he's making any money off of it or like he's some master filmmaker. What a joke.*

"Look, I tried. I'm not super familiar with your DSLR or the drone, okay? I mean, to be fair, I got everything in the frame. It was windy up here. The footage wasn't shaky. You can see everything. And you didn't really tell me how you wanted it to be shot. Like, you didn't give me much guidance."

"Whatever. Your video is fucking unusable," he spat. "Let's go to Salt Lake so I can pick up some bud from my dealer, and then we can go climb in Lander." He stopped at a gas station to change into dry clothes, and then reversed the same stretch of interstate back toward Utah. It was getting late, and I fell asleep in the passenger seat.

"Whose pipe is that?" I awoke to the police officer shining a light onto the seat of the truck. *Oh, fuck.* Dan had left his multicolored glass pipe full of weed sitting in plain sight on the driver's seat. He couldn't sweet talk his way out of this one.

"Um," I offered groggily. Dan walked back over from where he'd been peeing in the bushes off the side of the road. I got out of the truck and looked around. We were in the countryside near the exit for Willard, getting pretty close to Salt Lake.

"Where's the dope?" the cop demanded before radioing in for backup. Dan reluctantly told him since he knew the officer would find it anyway. It was better to just cooperate. There was hardly any weed left in the plastic bag since we were en route to resupply.

Another officer showed up. The four of us stood in a sphere of light created by the headlights facing opposing directions, with mosquitos attacking us due to our proximity to the water of Willard Bay. They told me to lean against the cop car off to the side and stay out of the way. I followed their directions. My dad was a cop; I knew how to handle these guys.

They interrogated me.

"Have you had anything to drink?"

"No."

"Any drugs?"

"No."

"Anything else we should know about in the truck?"

I told them about the bottle of fernet in the cooler.

"What's fernet?" They looked at each other in confusion.

I explained that it was a type of alcohol—Dan had fallen in love with fernet in Argentina, and bought it often now. The cops tore apart the bed of the truck, dumping out our backpacks, searching our duffel bags, peeking inside the guitar, ripping open anything and everything. When they got to my personal bag, they opened up my toiletries and found an unmarked bottle with a mixture of pills. One of the officers brought it over to me.

"What's in here?"

"Benadryl, ibuprofen, Tylenol, and vitamin C."

"You really shouldn't have pills mixed up in an unmarked container. Could get ya into trouble," he explained.

"Yes, sir." I stayed polite. They were far more concerned about Dan's controlled substances as they examined all of his prescription bottles: Adderall, Seroquel, Xanax, Ambien. Dan hadn't been drinking that night. He blew zeros in the breathalyzer and passed their sobriety test.

When their search was finally complete, the officers chucked all of our stuff back into the bed of the truck haphazardly in a giant jumble. I shifted my weight side to side nervously. I knew Dan was going to be pissed about the charges and I worried what he'd do to me. I prayed that they would book him so I wouldn't have to find out.

White privilege saved his ass. They confiscated his miniscule amount of weed and his pipe. He got two misdemeanors: possession and paraphernalia.

"Oh, and one more thing. We coulda got ya for indecency, what with peeing outside and all, but we'll overlook that one tonight, alright?" one of the officers explained.

Dan nodded. He had been surprisingly calm and obliging throughout the interaction. He knew how to play his cards to lessen the blow. They let him go, and my heart sank. I was hoping they'd cuff him and save me the trouble.

It was well after midnight when we got back on the interstate. At first, Dan was calm, processing what had just occurred. Then, he blew up.

"Why the fuck didn't you hide my pipe? You were trying to get me in trouble, huh?" he accused.

"No! I was asleep, I swear. I woke up to him asking whose pipe it was. I swear to god. By that point it was too late to try to hide it."

"You should've tried anyway! You could've grabbed it real quick!"

"Oh, and that wouldn't have been obvious? Not suspicious behavior at all to just lunge for something? He had already seen it," I emphasized. "It's your fault that you left it out in the open, not mine."

"I can't fucking believe you. First, you get me locked up in the fucking UNI, and now I have two fucking misdemeanors because of you! My life is over, dude." He shook his head. "Damn, I wish I had my weed to help deal with this. Fuckers took it from me."

"I'm sorry, okay? It's never enough." I didn't feel sorry at all, but I didn't want to contribute to the rage that was welling up inside him.

"You've ruined my life! I'll never be able to get a job or an apartment now! It's over. Fuck me! My life is gonna be impossible now! I hate you. Dumb bitch!" he screamed.

The accusations and blame continued as he projected his life problems onto me. I sat there, exhausted, taking all of it. I knew not to fight back. It would only make it worse.

He swerved around the highway near Ogden. There were no cars around to witness the scene that was unfolding as his screaming escalated.

"Did you or did you not fuck up my life, Fallon?" He turned the wheel toward the concrete divider splitting the interstate. The truck crept across the lanes closer to collision with the median barrier until I answered him correctly.

"Holy shit, stop!" That wasn't what he was looking for. The truck continued on its collision course. "Okay, yeah!" I blurted out. He straightened out the wheel for a moment.

"Not good enough, cunt! Tell me word for motherfucking word!" he screamed, pointing the truck back at the barrier.

"Oh my god! Please stop turning toward the concrete wall!" This wasn't satisfactory. "Okay! I fucked everything up in your life!" I said urgently.

He kept asking me similar questions. The game was that I had to answer correctly the first time. If my answer was wrong, then I had a very narrow time frame to choose my words more wisely before certain death. He barrelled down I-15 helter-skelter at over 100 mph, threatening suicide and homicide with every turn of the wheel. His questions were meant to target me, to make me take the blame for all of his problems. To fuck with my head as I feared for my life.

Bang! His skull impacted the driver side window, over and over until he bled. When the window wouldn't break from his head, he used his elbow. That did the trick. The glass shattered, and small shards rained down within the car and onto the highway. I cried and pressed myself against the passenger door. At high speeds without a window, the air rushed in, making everything louder.

His foot flung up toward the windshield, trying to kick the glass out. I gaped, horrified. It was just like the time we were coming home from Joshua Tree. I prayed for a cop to be following us, or waiting in a speed trap, for someone to notice this atrocity. He used his left foot on the gas pedal while his right kicked the windshield. The awkward angle wasn't ideal for generating force, but he did manage to add another crack to it.

His leg resumed its regular position. He'd replaced his rearview mirror after throwing the last one out into the Mojave. This replacement faced the same fate; he tore it off and threw it out the hole where the driver side window used to be.

"Please, Dan. Just bring me back to my car! This is so scary!" I didn't say anything about the future of our relationship, or about our plans to climb in Lander. I just wanted out of the situation, away from his violence and destruction.

He didn't listen. *Bang.* Fist to skull. We were in Salt Lake City now. He exited and went into a neighborhood I hadn't seen before.

"This is where my dealer lives," he explained, pulling up next to some modest houses. Everything was dead quiet now. The silence was almost shocking after all of the screaming and destruction on the highway.

"The guy put my weed in a thermos in the garage," he whispered. Since he lacked a window, we had to keep our voices down. Anyone on the street could've heard us. "I texted him earlier and he confirmed it should be there. I'll just leave my money in the thermos before I go."

He ran across the street, ducked into the garage, and came back empty handed.

"Fuck! It wasn't there." Dan called the guy, but it went to voicemail. It was almost 3:00 a.m. He texted him, but got no response. He ran over to the house and peeked inside a window before returning to the truck.

"I can see him and his junkie friends passed out in the living room. Fuck!" We sat in the truck. The glass from the window was all over the seat and floor, and Dan was bleeding and bruised from his self-inflicted chaos. Now he was panicked at the prospect of not having weed.

A young man approached the car. "Hey, buddy, you look pretty drunk. You shouldn't be driving. You guys should get out of here."

Dan snapped back to being fine. "I'm not drunk, just having a rough night. Sorry. Don't worry about us, okay?" The man went back to his porch where he'd been listening. I got the creeps and told Dan we should leave, but he was fixated on finding a way to get his drugs. I asked him what we should do, and he got pissed that I was asking questions. He took off down the road, and started circling random deserted streets in the city.

I felt helpless. I had no way to get him weed, and that was apparently his only option for calming down. He spiraled and spewed manic nonsense. Fear and exhaustion overwhelmed me. Finally, he returned to the dealer's house. Armed with his phone flashlight, he circumnavigated the house, trying to find a way to wake up the dealer. He came back unsuccessful.

A girl came up to the truck now. She was friends with the guy who'd approached us earlier.

"Hey, you don't look so good. You guys should go." She sounded concerned. I admired her boldness—coming up to a stranger that was tweaking out at three in the morning in the middle of a city. Dan dismissed her and off she went.

"You should go over there and try. It probably won't work, but one last ditch effort," Dan requested.

I crunched across the dry lawn, phone in hand, and peered in the windows. Sure enough, the junkies were passed out all over couches and the floor. I knocked on the glass, but no one budged. I banged on the front door and looked for movement inside. I scowled in frustration as I went back to the truck. I wanted to help Dan so I could protect myself.

"I told you so! I told you they wouldn't help! And your effort didn't do anything extra to help since they didn't answer!" he yelled while running his hands through his hair aggressively.

"Okay, I'm sorry. I tried." I couldn't remedy the situation. My heart raced with fear.

He drove off toward Lehi in the hopes that he had some weed stashed there. Rather than anger and accusations, his words shifted to suicide. He resigned himself to death.

"I'm really gonna do it this time! Fuck! It's gonna happen! It's tonight! It's over! There's nothing you can do!" His neck muscles strained as he scratched himself and contorted in the driver's seat.

I tried to calm him down, and he became quieter. He acted as if the suicide was a done deal. His serenity was creepy now, an unwelcome contrast to his deafening rage. He was set on killing himself, and eerily calm about it. He put his foot to the floor in a mad dash to get back to the Lehi house. Upon arrival, he shoved the truck into park and beelined it for the front door.

The neighborhood was dark and quiet. The night would be over soon. It was completely silent and still. His parents' mansion stood proudly above the long driveway and steps cutting up the flawless lawn.

I bounded up after him, fighting off sleep. The all-nighter was making the symptoms of my illness worse, but I had to set that aside.

"This is it. This is fucking *it*. I'm done. I'm gonna do it." He'd surrendered to his unquiet mind. "I'm gonna take the drill in the garage, put it right in my head. I'm doing it, Fallon."

I pleaded with him to stop. I grabbed his arm as he tried to go into the garage. He pulled away, but I maneuvered around him to block the door.

"No! You're not doing this. Stop it."

"Let me through!"

"You've felt this way before, and you got through it. You'll get through it again. This will pass," I reminded him. At that moment, I hated him more than anything. For putting me in this position. For putting me through hell. But I still didn't want him to give up.

"I don't know . . . I want to die. This is it. Move!" His voice was hoarse and unsteady.

"No. You still have climbing left to do. Things left to write. Places to visit. You can't die yet. Please, Dan," I begged.

He gave me an exasperated look. "It's too late for that."

He forcefully moved me from the doorway. I tried to grab the door and hinder him from entering the garage, but had no luck.

"If you call the cops, I'll kill all of them. I'll kill you. And then I'll kill myself. I will do anything not to get locked up again." He locked himself in the garage and I heard sobbing. I ran through the house, out the front door, back down to the truck.

Fuck. Where's my phone? Everything was a mess from the police search and the erratic driving. I searched frantically and found it.

I poised my thumb to dial 911, but had second thoughts. He said he'd kill me. He'd threatened it countless times. But he seemed so sincere in his intentions to kill himself. He was really gonna do it this time. I made a split second decision and connected to the operator.

"911. What is your emergency?"

I held the phone between my shoulder and ear as I tore my belongings from the truck. Climbing gear and clothing spilled out everywhere.

"He has access to weapons. He's gonna kill himself. He said if I called that he'd kill me and the cops too. I'm trying to leave."

I tossed my stuff into a chaotic pile on the sidewalk while answering questions and giving her my location. Dan was all the way up in the garage, so I didn't bother to talk quietly. It was almost 4:00 a.m. now, the very first dim hints of light illuminating the sky just before the blue hour.

I went around the truck to move the seat and grab more of my stuff. I wanted to get out of there quickly, but I needed to grab everything first. If I left my gear now, I'd never get it back. I glanced up at the house. Because of the slope of the hill, I could only see the top half of the front door.

The door swung open.

Fuck. In an instant, I realized Dan had left the garage and had been listening behind the front door.

He knew I'd called the cops.

He was going to kill me.

I dropped what I was grabbing, and took off at a sprint. I only took my phone with me, abandoning my pile of belongings on the sidewalk.

I ran for my life in my sandals. Down the hill, heart thumping, feet pounding the concrete, arms pumping. The 911 operator was concerned. All she could hear was my heavy breathing.

"What's happening? Stay with me! What's going on?"

"He's chasing me! He said he's going to kill me! Where are the cops?"

"They're coming. Keep running. They'll be there soon. Stay with me!"

"He said he's gonna kill the cops too!"

I turned the corner, legs flying wildly with disregard for my bad hip and improper footwear. I stopped talking so he wouldn't be able to hear me. I ran up the next street, satisfied he was far enough behind to not be able to see me for a moment, and dove into the bushes in someone's yard.

Everything was still and silent. I calmed my breathing the best I could while my heart tried to escape my chest. I whispered into the phone to the operator, explaining what was happening. I'd never been so afraid. He had been abundantly clear about the consequences for me if I called the cops on him. An eerie quiet settled over the suburb and my heartbeats felt like eternities while I waited for him to find me.

I saw lights in my peripheral vision, and looked down to the intersection. Cop cars with red and blue lights swirling. I breathed a heavy sigh of relief and realized my entire body was violently shaking.

The cops flooded from their cars toward the house, guns out. I ran back toward the house, rounding the corner with my hands up to show them it was me. I ended the 911 call, and the cops rushed me over to a safe car. Some of them stayed with me to reassure and protect me while the rest swarmed the house. Dan had made it back inside, and they asked if I could call him and then give them the phone so they could talk him out of the house.

Dan materialized calmly. He pretended to be totally sane, like nothing was wrong and it was just a regular night. The only problem was that his appearance was a dead giveaway—there was blood all over him, his hands were swollen from hitting the windows and his head, and his face was puffy and covered in bruises. I cried and hyperventilated in the car, not wanting to look at him.

The officers told me that Dan wanted to talk to me. I refused. At this point, Dan's parents had woken up and were talking with some of the officers. The cops told me that they'd calmed him down. He'd requested to not go back to the psych ward.

I seethed. I couldn't believe how calm he was acting as he cooperated with them. He was sneaky. He could so easily flip that switch and pretend to be totally normal when it was warranted. *What a fucking psychopath.*

One of the cops explained to me how to get a protective order from the court if I didn't want him to have contact with me again. I wasn't thinking straight, but told him I'd consider it.

Dan requested again to speak with me, and I wanted no part of it. He'd crossed every line possible, and I was done. Finally, permanently done.

The cops helped me carry my stuff from the sidewalk to my car. I meticulously checked through the truck one last time to make sure I had everything since our gear had been mixed together. I knew this was my final chance to grab my belongings. The cops protected me while I looked, and they told me Dan's mom wanted to talk to me. I hesitantly agreed. She apologized and hugged me, and told me how sorry she was that all this had happened. She offered to get me a hotel somewhere since I hadn't really slept, but I politely declined. I knew that if I accepted her offer, Dan would find out where I was staying and come kill me.

I thanked the cops for helping me, and got in my car. The sun was rising.

Shaking, exhausted, and with my nerves shot to hell, I drove away and never looked back. I cried tears of relief. It was over.

It was finally over. This time, leaving felt different.

When I ran from him, it was the most fear I'd ever felt in my life. The bravery it took to leave could not have existed without the fear; it was a solution born of necessity. My body and mind were dying to get out—and I would have died had I not left when I did.

On auto-pilot, I drove north. I entered survival mode. I curled up on the floor in the back of my car in a random parking lot in Salt Lake City, and granted my body the sleep it needed.

When I awoke, my joints were stiff. I kept driving north. I stopped at my apartment briefly to grab a few things, but knew I couldn't stay. He'd find me there, and I was supposed to move out anyway. I needed to go somewhere he wouldn't find me. I hit the road in a daze, lightheaded and numb to the world around me.

I found myself in City of Rocks and put on my climbing shoes.

The smell of sagebrush reached me, carried on the high desert wind that tangled my hair. I welcomed it.

The Idaho sunshine burned my exposed shoulders and warmed my aching muscles. I welcomed it.

Immersed in upward motion, I lost myself in order to find myself again. I climbed and climbed, ropeless, hands and feet moving of their own accord, melting into the wall, allowing it to melt into me. I welcomed it.

Scraped knees and elbows and hands, like a child playing rough. Still, I climbed. Tears streamed down my cheeks. The sides of Bath Rock took me in like a mother. Enveloped, alone, together with the rock. My blood drip-dropped onto the granite. I welcomed it.

I was able to breathe again between involuntary sobs. Sweet oxygen.

I was free. I had chosen freedom.

I welcomed it.

(iv)
death doesn't kiss me anymore
now he just creeps in
through the back door
hovers in the frame
peeks slowly into my room
whispers my name.
i can't hear through this gloom—
i sob into trembling hands
slumped alone on the bed—
over me, he stands
pats me on the shoulder
i feel betrayed
my body grows colder
"death wherehaveyoubeen
i have been shaking
and fainting
and waiting
for you"
shuffles his weary feet
those soles have trampled souls
today i must accept defeat
death doesn't kiss me anymore
he leaves again
and i collapse on the floor

heartbeat drums in my ears
i feel my pulse skip
like it has for all these years
gurgling atrium with a broken electricity
thirsty for air, i'm awoken
to death above me, humming
a melancholic tune
to match my heart's thrumming
i sweat through my sheets
eyes thrown open, surveying—
dark as the night
he brushes my hair to the side
depresses my chest
CPR for the living
gasping
"death, you've interrupted
my nightmare"
he laughs
"don't you remember?"
death doesn't kiss me anymore
he tucks me back in
slips out through the door

EPILOGUE

Two years after I escaped Dan, I told my story to strangers for the first time in a domestic violence support group. My entire body shook violently as I told my story, the words sounding worse as they left my mouth than they ever had in my head or my journal. It felt like an exorcism to speak these horrors back into existence, to admit out loud what had happened.

My relationship with Dan had lasted seven months, but it took years to work up the courage to choke out the details. I trembled uncontrollably through involuntary sobs and broke out in a cold sweat. I knew I wasn't in real danger anymore, but reliving the experience made my body feel like it was. The nervous system struggles to tell the difference.

The other women sitting silently around me had a range of responses: eyebrows up, mouths agape, vacant stares, or knowing nods. I'd listened to all of their stories, and the similarities floored me. Each of our abusers followed a similar script, used the same tactics, and trapped us in impossible cycles. Though the severity and the specifics varied, we'd all dealt with different versions of the same toxic character.

One week, the counselors handed out fancy planners someone had donated to the organization. Black leather cover, brilliant white pages. The planner contained sections dedicated to setting goals for different time periods: six months, a year, five years. You were supposed to map out goals and steps to achieve them.

I remember staring at those pages and realizing that in the two years since I'd escaped Dan, I hadn't let myself dream of the future. I was 22 years old, planted in survival mode, just trying to get through each day, struggling to pay even my basic bills, and battling undiagnosed chronic illnesses. Navigating relentless PTSD—with flashbacks, nightmares, depression, and hypervigilance—exhausted me as I stumbled through my shifted reality. How was I supposed to think of what my life could look like in five years when I didn't know if I could get through the next five days? 2019 was my low point, and I was drowning.

By isolating me and making me financially dependent on him, Dan decimated my support system and removed some of my options to leave. By threatening suicide every time I tried to escape, he made me feel like my hands were tied and like I was obligated to save him. By displaying physical violence towards himself, me, and random objects, he flexed his power through intimidation. By belittling and insulting me, and making me think I could never do better than him, he convinced me that I was worthless—and therefore staying with him was my best option. By striking in my most vulnerable moments, like when I was ill and alone, he was able to strategically regain power over me. By the end, I felt like a brainwashed zombie. No wonder so many people lack the capacity to leave situations like this; they need a tremendous amount of help.

It took time, but I'd finally been able to find some help, in therapy and in the support group. With that essential support, I let myself expand beyond the immediate demands of survival to reach for what I wanted in the bigger picture. Hesitantly, I was able to scribble some goals on the page. Pay off debt. Figure out my health problems. Climb 5.13. Finish college. These all felt totally out of reach. I was alone, hypervigilant, afraid, exhausted, sick, broke, and lost. I worried constantly about Dan hunting me down, about financial security, about my medical issues, about the one class I had remaining to finish my degree . . . But a flicker of hope ignited within me when I wrote down the goals, like the first tiny reclamation of my power.

I had a life beyond what had happened. A better future beckoned to me, if only I could get my shit together. I wouldn't let this experience define me. I read somewhere that living well is the best revenge, and I took that seriously. I couldn't let Dan win. I didn't know how long it would take, but I looked at that goal page like a north star.

(v)

death kissed my window
left the condensation
briefly puckered on the pane
but i couldn't see for the rain.
a giant boom woke me
death yanked me up
squirmed out of sleeping bag
threw open the car door
slammed by the downpour—
feet into sandals
a cocoon of displaced leaves
squinted through the night:
cottonwood lost the fight
brought down to earth
its heavy trunk finally at rest
feet from where i slept
thunder clapped, lightning struck—
illuminated death, fleeing,
decided to spare my being

i remember when death finally
kissed me again
bats swirled overhead:
sunset on the Green River
chill in the air made me shiver.
he'd been on my mind
with legs hanging in cool water
fire dancing in the sky
submission made me cry.
i gave up and laid down
sunk into the soil of my sorrow
longed for death to borrow
my soul, as before—
life felt like a chore.
he mustered the courtesy
to pay me a solemn visit
sprawled next to me on the shore
"death, i can't do this anymore"
turned his face to mine
said, "not this time"
a kiss on the cheek
pressed into my tears
gentle, like the breeze
and he floated off—
death down the river
that feels like my home
that feels like hope

AFTERWORD

If you haven't survived the cycle of abuse, it can be hard to wrap your head around why victims don't leave sooner. If you felt exhausted and frustrated reading this book, know you're in good company. That was the point. I want readers to understand what it feels like to get spun round and round in an endless cycle, each phase faithfully following the last: tension building, violent episode, reconciliation. Rinse and repeat. Familiarize yourself with one of the many diagrams of it, and avoid it at all costs.

There are many types of abuse—emotional, mental, physical, sexual, financial—and they often occur simultaneously, like they did for me. Ultimately, abuse is all about control and power. The abuser is never willingly going to give up either of these; the victim must have the courage to reclaim enough power and control in order to leave. Easier said than done when under the threat of death or other consequences. You have to play their game, steal their tactics, and sometimes even adopt their aggression in order to survive or escape.

People tend to have strong feelings and connotations for words like "victim" or "survivor"—honestly, it doesn't matter what specific word you do or do not identify with. Assigning blame or determining culpability are not helpful, and neither is floundering in weakness or playing the victim. No matter what you call it, we're all people trying our best to move beyond shitty situations, regardless of what part we played.

Writing this book helped me own my story. If even one person reads this and is able to avoid a similar situation, or feel less alone, then it was worth writing. I wanted to show the climbing and adventure sports communities that abuse is often happening right under our noses. Of all people, I never expected myself to end up in an abusive relationship. I come from an educated family, my dad was a cop, I'd learned about domestic violence, I'm tall and physically strong, and I'd thought I was smart enough to see through manipulation and gaslighting. I didn't fit any classic "victim" stereotype. Still, I was young and susceptible and got dragged into Dan's web. His addicting energy and charisma captured me initially, and his threats and manipulation trapped me after that.

I screamed at my younger self the entire time I wrote, willing her to get out sooner. It's maddening to look back on. So many times I tried to escape, and failed. It took the most dramatic incident for me to finally get out for good. The timing must be right—immediately after the explosive incident, but before any reconciliation. Unfortunately, countless people never make it out of the vicious cycle.

In hindsight, I know logically that I could have tried to run off to one of my family members in another state. But at the time, in my exhausted zombie mode, I felt like it wasn't an option since he'd isolated me so effectively. He made me think that my family hated me and that they would never help or understand. I know now that this is false, along with so many other lies and ridiculous narratives he told me.

In a recent conversation with one of my sisters, I realized that my inability to lean on family was probably rooted in shame and the stubbornness of youth. Back then, I was ashamed that I'd let the relationship become so toxic, that I'd willingly gone back to Dan so many times, that I couldn't seem to wrest myself from his grip. Survivors often carry shame and guilt for thinking they "allowed" these things to happen to them. Unfortunately, that shame can prevent us from being open and honest about what we've endured, and make us feel like we don't deserve help. Our trauma shrinks our world to a fiercely independent bubble where we can't trust others and we're too ashamed to admit what has happened, so we shut everyone out.

Of course, I was complicit in letting the toxic codependency continue for months. It takes two, and I enabled him. Upon reflection, I wanted to stay and keep trying to make things work with Dan partly because there was a real sense of love buried underneath the dysfunction. I wanted to believe he could get better: get on mood stabilizers, succeed in therapy, escape his addiction, and change his behavior so we could live happily ever after. I gave him so many chances because I saw the good in him—few people are evil all the way through. Abusers often use the promise of improvement as a tactic to convince their partner to stay. "I'll get better this time" is a lie they desperately want to believe.

Someone as out of control as Dan is fully at the mercy of their mental illness, addiction, and aggressive impulses. He lacked the capacity to make rational choices; he moved at the whim of his wild patterns, never in full control of himself or his mind. I doubt his behavior was intentionally malicious toward me. He loved me, but was so unwell that he couldn't express it in healthy ways, and he was unable to shield me from the fallout of his turbulence. If it hadn't been me suffering beside him, the target of his chaos just as easily would've been someone else. I saw the red flags early on, but my laissez-faire attitude, naive belief in his ability to change, and fear of his threats led me to stay for far too long, which enabled the escalation.

I give grace to my younger self for doing the best I could given my age, health, and other circumstances. I choose self-compassion since it's far more productive than kicking myself for the choices I made and the ways I was responsible for what happened. I used to be tormented by memories and flashbacks, and wracked by guilt for not pressing charges against Dan. Thankfully I've moved past all of that.

Dan burned brightly and set fire to my life. At first, I basked in its warmth, luminance, and energy, but eventually, it burned so hot it reduced my life to ashes. No one was going to help me rebuild and recover. I had to do it on my own. I couldn't sit around feeling sorry for myself and waiting for things to get better. Moving forward required work, not passivity.

I fully leaned into Stoic philosophy, embracing its wisdom and taking comfort in its principles. During a few long years of undiagnosed illness, as I grew increasingly disabled, I had ample time to read and study Stoic texts—Marcus Aurelius, Seneca, and Epictetus. I accepted that my life was my responsibility. No one else could disturb my mental clarity and safety, or prevent me from reaching my goals. I had the power to focus on what was in my control, to not let the past rule me, to make the present moment the best possible, to live in alignment with my values, and to follow my true nature.

I got the word "autonomy" tattooed on my right wrist to remind me to never let anyone else control me. Freedom cannot be given or received; you must reach out, grab it, and hold on like hell. On my left wrist, I got the word "autarkeia," a Stoic concept of self-reliance and contentment with what you have. And on my right forearm, a portrait of Marcus Aurelius to guide me and keep me company. He's always watching, always there for me, and I try to behave in a way that would make him proud.

In 2019, despite fighting severe undiagnosed dysautonomia and healing from multiple surgeries to reconstruct my foot and ankle after a climbing accident, I managed to finish my last field camp course and graduate with my geology degree. Since then, I've worked as a high school science teacher, a cartographer, a fine art model, a climbing coach and guide, a geoscience researcher, a photographer, and a writer. Life has thrown me new challenges, but it's also been varied and full of possibilities.

Looking back at my relationship with Dan, my attitude has shifted from resentment to compassion. No one wants to be tortured by their own thoughts, to live in a constant state of chaos, or to struggle with substance abuse. His mental illness in no way excuses the way he treated me, but it certainly explains much of his behavior.

In the years following our relationship, I never saw Dan again, but I watched his deterioration over his public social media accounts. His mental illness spiraled into schizophrenia, and his posts grew increasingly nonsensical, paranoid, and alarming. He constantly got himself into legal trouble. When he found out I was writing this book, he threatened me, and I backed off sharing about it for years out of fear of retaliation. I saw his posts about reckless BASE jumping and drug use, and waited for the day I'd hear of his fate—prison or death seemed like inevitable outcomes.

Years dragged on. After I wrote the first complete draft of *Pay No Mind* in 2022, I told my story on a popular climbing podcast called the *Enormocast*, and I never revealed Dan's identity. When Dan listened to the interview, he foolishly outed himself online, and his other victims reached out to me. This was a pattern of behavior; I'm sad to say he did this to many other women, not just me.

Eerily enough, I found out about Dan's death a few hours before getting the publishing offer for this book. The timing felt like mysterious forces needed to shift to allow me to move forward. Receiving these two pieces of life-changing news on the same day felt connected, though rationally I know it was a coincidence. Dan was running from legal trouble, crossed the border illegally, was chased by law enforcement, and opted to end his own life rather than face the consequences of his actions. It's a tragic ending for someone who once had so much potential and passion. I've chosen to give him anonymity out of respect for his family, and because his true identity is not essential for me to tell my story. Finally, his suffering is over.

As I write this in 2025, eight years after I escaped, my life has improved dramatically. Along with Stoic philosophy, years of therapy (particularly EMDR) were essential to working through my PTSD. The flashbacks, nightmares, and hypervigilance have all but disappeared. For a long time, I was too wary to get into cars with men, even if they were friends or climbing partners, but I've slowly rebuilt trust. The only remnants of the trauma I still notice are claustrophobia and hating the feeling of being trapped.

Through most of my twenties, my chronic illnesses became a living hell, but I advocated for myself and never gave up on my quest for answers. At my most disabled and desperate, I clung to a shred of hope that I could figure out what was wrong with me, that there would be a chance for a better life. Eventually, I got my health sorted out, and picked up diagnoses along the way: dysautonomia (POTS), hEDS, MCAS, and lupus. Now, I manage my health well and I'm committed to advocating for climbers who deal with these conditions. I could fill another book with just that journey alone.

What I'm most proud of is getting my life back after surviving abuse, poverty, and illness. I clawed my way back to climbing hard, and ended up with more sponsorships from brands that have allowed me to live out my dreams—free gear and trips, and the support I need to push myself as an athlete. Little me drooling over climbing magazines and dreaming of the future would be shocked and psyched if she found out I actually made it happen. I'm so lucky that climbing still brings me more joy than anything else in the world.

This is merely one story about seven months of my life. Much has happened before and since—I'm eager to tell my other stories next.

ACKNOWLEDGMENTS

Thank you to the team at Di Angelo Publications for believing in me and giving me the opportunity to publish this story.

To John, for your patience, guidance, and support. You saw the potential in my rough manuscript and helped me polish it in ways I never expected. I couldn't have asked for a better mentor—your skill as a writer, your knowledge about climbing, your familiarity with addiction and mental illness, your wisdom about abuse and toxic relationships, and your compassion for my story and struggles were all invaluable during this process. I'm eternally grateful, and will carry your lessons with me in every future writing project.

To my family, for taking me back after this experience that tore us apart. I'm so glad we came out the other side. I love all of you, and I'm grateful our relationships have grown stronger ever since. Thanks for putting up with me.

To Jen, for stepping in to be the mother I always needed. Your steadfast friendship, selfless support, and incredible tolerance have blessed me. The love I feel for you and from you is one of the greatest gifts of my life. Thank you for welcoming me into your home for the summer when I wrote this book so I could finally complete it.

To Sarah, for being the friend that stuck with me through it all without judgment or shame. When I escaped, I vividly remember you as my main supporter and safe person. Growing with you the past decade has been a pleasure. Thank you for believing in me.

To Mikaela and Erin, for seeing me through a sometimes painful evolution, and for encouraging me to keep going, to be brave, to stay curious, and to own my story.

To Landon, for dragging me out of hell, and back into the beautiful light of climbing. You made me feel like anything is possible, like limitations are meaningless. Your support when I wrote this manuscript was essential.

To Chris, for never doubting me, for reminding me of my capabilities, for your friendship through some of the darkest times, for listening to me ramble for hours on end.

To Levi, for showing me a kindred spirit, and dismantling my imposter syndrome. You've made me feel seen in ways I could never put into words.

To Sam, for your encouragement and insightful feedback on the early manuscript.

To CAPSA, for the counseling and support at the lowest point of my life. The community of Logan is so lucky to have your critical resources available.

To Anna Daley, Naomi Kerns, Savannah Fritz, and Sally Mitchell, for being an incredible lineup of high school English teachers. Thank you for giving me my entire foundation as a writer, and for expanding my mind and worldview through literature. You are amazing educators and people.

To Marcus Aurelius, for being my guiding light and hope in every situation. I wouldn't be here today without *Meditations*.

To all of the brands that have supported my climbing, for making my dreams come true.

And to everyone else who has encouraged me and cheered me on, for helping me become the person I am today, for making this book possible. Thank you.

ABOUT THE AUTHOR

Fallon Rowe grew up in Idaho, and then earned her geology degree at Utah State University. She thrives with multiple identities: dirtbag climber, high school science teacher, writer, geoscience researcher, photographer, climbing coach and guide. As a writer, her true loves are non-fiction and poetry. Since 2017, she's been a sponsored rock climber with support from multiple brands, allowing her to live out her adventure dreams. Rock climbing has been the central focus of her life since 2003, but on her Instagram @fallonclimbs, she also shares her passion for nature, science, literature, and Stoic philosophy. She lives in St George, Utah, where she enjoys wandering the desert.

ABOUT THE PUBLISHER

Di Angelo Publications was founded in 2008 by Sequoia Schmidt—at the age of seventeen. The modernized publishing firm's creative headquarters is in Los Angeles, California, with its distribution center located in Twin Falls, Idaho. In 2020, Di Angelo Publications made a conscious decision to move all printing and production for domestic distribution of its books to the United States. The firm is comprised of eleven imprints, and the featured imprint, Catharsis, was inspired by Schmidt's love of extreme sports, travel, and adventure stories.

www.ingramcontent.com/pod-product-compliance
Lightning Source LLC
Chambersburg PA
CBHW031613160426
43196CB00006B/116